CRESCENT CITY SCHOOLS

PUBLIC EDUCATION IN NEW ORLEANS   1841 - 1991

CRESCENT CITY SCHOOLS

PUBLIC EDUCATION IN NEW ORLEANS
1841-1991

By

DONALD E. DEVORE AND JOSEPH LOGSDON

With an Epilogue *by*
EVERETT J. WILLIAMS
and an Essay on New Orleans School Architecture by
JOHN C. FERGUSON

Publication of this book was made possible
by grants from the

Louisiana Endowment for the Humanities
and
CNG Producing Company

Additional assistance was provided by the

Junior League of New Orleans
The Metropolitan Area Committee Education Fund
and
Drison, Inc.

First Softcover Printing, 2011
ISBN: 978-1-935754-15-2

Published by
The Center for Louisiana Studies
University of Southwestern Louisiana

Dedicated to the children of New Orleans
and their teachers

Contents

Acknowledgements

This history of public education in New Orleans represents much more than the work of two historians. To tell our story, we relied upon a large number of people. They made our project a community effort.

Without the preservation of the Orleans Parish School records, our task would have been almost impossible. From the beginning of our research, we learned how deeply indebted we were to Freda DePolitte, the veteran secretary of the School Board, who had jealously guarded the system's records through several moves of the central office during her fifty-year tenure. To Al Kennedy of the Public Information Office, we owe thanks for his efforts to create the New Orleans Public School District's Historical Collection and to persuade the Orleans Parish School Board to designate the University of New Orleans as the depository for those records. To Al Kennedy and Rose Drill-Peterson, also of the Public Information Office, we are grateful for having suggested several years ago that we accelerate our research, already well underway, in order to complete a comprehensive history of the public schools in time for the one hundred and fiftieth anniversary of the New Orleans school system. At each step of our work, we drew heavily upon the boundless energy and sound judgment of Rose Drill-Peterson. She always made things happen.

We want to express our thanks to the Orleans Parish School Board and its superintendent, Everett Williams, for depositing their records at the University of New Orleans where we had full access to a well-arranged collection. Even more, we wish to thank the officials of the Orleans Parish Schools for requesting a thorough evaluation of the development of the public schools and then stepping aside to give us full control over the content of this work. At the same time, we accept full responsibility for any of its errors or shortcomings.

Without the skilled arrangement of the Orleans Parish School Board Collection by D. Clive Hardy and Beatrice Owsley at the Archives of the University of New Orleans, we could never have completed this work in time for the anniversary year. Over a three-year period, they also added to the large core collection by attracting additional material from individual schools and former teachers. Beatrice Owsley's encyclopedic recall of material in the large collection saved us countless hours of work, and Clive Hardy's knowledge of resources in other depositories uncovered important documents and photographs. Special thanks are due to Samuel I. Rosenberg, attorney for the Orleans Parish School Board, whose donation of his vast collection of legal files opened important sources for our research.

New Orleans has been blessed with local depositories and archivists dedicated to the rich history of the city. We are especially grateful to Bert Harder of the Louisiana Museum; Wayne Everard, Tito Brin, Judy Martin, and Collin Hamer of the New Orleans Public Library; Dode Platou, John Magill, John Lawrence, Jessica Travis, and John Mahé of the Historic New Orleans Collection; Clifton Johnson and Kenneth Coleman of the Amistad Research Center; Wilbur E. Meneray and Joan Caldwell of the library at Tulane University; and Lester Sullivan and Robert E. Skinner at Xavier University.

Outside the city, especially in the Northeast, where records concerning the early history of New Orleans schools have survived, we depended heavily upon the staffs of the Massachusetts Historical Society in Boston, the American Antiquarian Society in Worcester, Massachusetts, the McDonogh School in McDonogh, Maryland, the manuscripts division of the library at New York University, and the unexcelled depositories and libraries of Harvard University. We especially wish to thank Abby and Steve Thernstorm at Harvard for their assistance and hospitality.

Both of us want to confess how much we relied on the critical reading given to the final manuscript by Jerah Johnson at the University of New Orleans. He deserves to be accorded partial authorship of this book. At earlier stages of various chapters, our work also benefited from the suggestions of Gaines Foster and Robert Becker at Louisiana State University, of Clarence Mohr at Tulane University, and of Rick Ginsberg at the University of South Carolina. Both Mohr and Ginsberg generously shared some of their own work on the history of public education in New Orleans and Louisiana. Throughout the project, the guidance and suggestions of our editor, Glenn R. Conrad, director of the Center for

Louisiana Studies, improved the design and concept of our work. His unending patience and good humor helped us over many hurdles.

Finally we want to acknowledge and laud the public and private groups that gave needed support for this project. Their help enabled a host of persons to organize the records, to conduct research, translate documents, and publish this work. From the beginning, the Louisiana Endowment for the Humanities recognized the need for the community to recapture the history of public education in New Orleans. At various points, the board, its chairman, James Olney, and particularly Michael Sartisky and Kay Mettelka, who both believed in the importance of a published history, helped make the project possible.

The intellectual and financial support of the LEH encouraged others to provide additional support not only for this project but also for other activities connected to the anniversary celebration planned by the Orleans Parish Public Schools. We especially want to thank Rodney Ackerman and CNG Producing Company through the CNG Foundation for the generous donation of matching funds that turned a proposal into this published history. To Ann Hanemann and Sandy Shilstone, who were instrumental in obtaining support from the Junior League and the Metropolitan Area Committee Education Fund, we express our thanks for their consistent support. Frank Peterson of Drison, Inc., we remember fondly for the very first donation, which secured the translation of French records.

For many of the rare photographic glimpses into the past, we want to thank Warren Gravois, Robert Brantley, Rick Olivier, John Clif Roland, Frank Lotz Miller, Frank H. Methe, Villard Paddio, A. Bedou, Keith Calhoun, Chandra McCormick, Al Kennedy, Bryan Hithe, Don Vavasseur, Del Clare, Barbara Gasdaglis, and the many photographers who took pictures of the public schools over the years. We thank Girard Mouton for his excellent research assistance and his willingness to share, Henry Williams for his treasure trove of memorabilia, Pamela Nicholson for securing a likeness of James Dillard, and Gloria Boyd for her discovery of key data when we needed them. Finally, we thank the entire staff of the Department of Information and Community Services, Henry Joubert, Tina Perrin, Jerrilyn Carmouche, Carmel Trouard, Myrna Bright, and Renate May, who assisted us throughout this project.

All of the marvelous support and cooperation that helped us produce this historical review of public education in New Orleans will, we hope, serve as a prelude for greater community interest and involvement in the far more important task of educating the children of our city.

CRESCENT CITY SCHOOLS

PUBLIC EDUCATION IN NEW ORLEANS 1841 - 1991

Introduction

Ideals and Institutions

Why look back now at the difficult travail of public education in New Orleans? First, because it is an appropriate time to recall the one hundred and fifty years of public schools in New Orleans. In 1841 New Orleans started its public schools with the personal assistance of Horace Mann, the champion of modern public education in the United States. Those first schools inaugurated public schools not only in the city but also throughout Louisiana and much of the Deep South. Many of the leaders who founded the New Orleans system shared Mann's idea that free public schools lay at the foundation of democratic order and decency in the United States. One of the early school directors in New Orleans captured the spirit of the new movement when he declared that the public schools would offer "republican education." He and his fellow school directors, he declared, had a duty to educate the "children of the people" who were going to take "our place and support the happiness and dignity of this republic, in times to come."

During the many decades since the evocation of those fond hopes, countless citizens, teachers, and administrators have contributed to the maintenance of the ideals embodied in our public schools. This book has been written, in part, to remember their contributions. Whatever may be the shortcomings of the present school system, the challenge of educating the "children of the people" would be even more difficult today without the skills and devotion that so many men and women brought to their tasks during past decades.

At the juncture of the hundred and fiftieth anniversary of the Orleans Parish Schools, a sense of urgency has combined with the spirit of commemoration. In New Orleans, as in so many large American cities, the public schools are facing a major crisis. As most privileged citizens of the nation have abandoned our central cities, they have left urban schools underfunded and filled with the society's poorest children. The Orleans Parish Schools now face an awesome challenge.

Fortunately the sense of crisis has also produced a widening sense of responsibility. Public and private leaders have come forward with renewed commitment to the faith that inspired those who so boldly founded the public schools a century and a half ago. The current sense of crisis rests upon an awareness of both past failures and future opportunities, and it has evoked the same spirit of responsibility that has so often emerged in America's democracy when the country has encountered its gravest dangers.

If a look backward at the public schools can contribute to a public school crusade, it must focus on more than celebration. The look backward must also elucidate lost opportunities as well as the obstacles that have so often stymied earlier reformers. The recollection of achievements and triumphs may well inspire change, but the recall of failures can also guide the architects of institutional reform.

Several years ago a similar sense of crisis compelled scholars and community leaders in New York City to recover the history of public education there. Despite the almost unrivaled concentration of universities in that metropolis, only a few scholars had studied the evolution of its public school system. Indeed, even the system's records remained almost totally neglected in a damp, dirty basement in Manhattan until leaders felt the need to understand the roots of their educational crisis and the awesome nature of their challenge. The studies which resulted from their efforts, particularly those of Diane Ravitch, helped produce the current national efforts to improve all American public schools.

The problem of recovering the history of the public schools in New Orleans almost duplicated the New York experience. Local university scholars had likewise made little effort to look hard and long at the development of education in the Crescent City. Except for a small series of unpublished masters' theses directed at Tulane University more than four decades ago, historians have done little to recover the memory of the city's attempt to educate its children. Fortunately, however, the Orleans Parish School Board had carefully preserved its records and turned them over to the University of New Orleans in order to make possible the present exploration of the past.

Existing studies of other large cities such as New York may help New Orleanians face the challenges of their public schools. But, despite some obvious similarities found in all large urban school systems, no American city can serve fully as a model for another, particularly when a city's development in the United States has been so clearly unusual as that of New Orleans. Those peculiarities go well beyond the city's unique physical appearance or the exotic remnants of its Afro-French and Latin heritage that show up in its music, cuisine, and public festivals.

Perhaps nowhere did public education face greater obstacles than in New Orleans. Its colonial past left it with none of the common town schools that dotted the landscape of New England. Nor did the early New Orleans past engender such democratic visions as those of Thomas Jefferson in Virginia. Without such historical foundation, New Orleans educational leaders had to import an educational plan from the outside and then put it into place, often in the face of opposition from local citizens who were deeply attached to the city's feudal and elitist colonial traditions. Indeed, New Orleans was the young republic's first experiment with trying to impose its institutions, not only of education but also of language and democratic government, upon an essentially foreign society. The tension between the host population of New Orleans natives and the American newcomers plagued the public schools well into the nineteenth century.

One hundred and fifty years ago, New Orleans was also the only large city of the slave South in a majority black state. The problems of race are, as a result, deeply rooted in the public schools of New Orleans. Racial oppression rested at the center of all of the city's institutions. Public authorities not only excluded all black New Orleanians—free or slave— from public education, but they deliberately tried to shackle them with ignorance. By its very nature, New World slavery enveloped African-Americans with tyrannical oppression. Less than a mere century ago—just five generations from the present—slavery helped to assure that almost half of Louisiana's population remained illiterate.

As it shaped its legacy of slavery and racial discrimination, New Orleans also drew into its midst more European immigrants than any Southern city. In fact, up until the Civil War, New Orleans attracted over a half million immigrants through its port, more than any other American city, except New York. The poverty and unusual ways of these immigrants placed burdensome strains on the early New Orleans public schools even without the enrollment of any of the city's black population.

Social change did more than simply buffet the public schools. Hardly had the city begun to solve some of the problems of mass immigration, when it was suddenly engulfed in the Civil War. Union generals seized control of the public schools and ran them by martial law. When the war ended, Reconstruction visionaries framed a government that brought even more revolutionary change to the city's public schools. Alone among Southern schools, the New Orleans system experienced extensive integration. But, as a result, it also faced more violent disruption when the so-called Redeemers purged the schools in order to restore segregation. The severe reaction almost destroyed the entire system of public education. And, after the schools slowly emerged, fully segregated, the city responded with another round of violence and neglect in the middle of the twentieth century, as federal courts forced it once again to desegregate its classrooms.

The painful racial struggle in the city's public schools needs to be remembered not only by concerned citizens in New Orleans and Louisiana but also by educational leaders in other cities of the United States who have only recently been forced to face the massive dilemma of racial justice. Indeed, the scholars who launched the study of the New York public school system recognized that black Southern migrants were not just another wave of immigrants to Northern cities, for black Southerners encountered and brought with them far greater problems. The scholars understood the admonition of Richard Wade that "the proper analogy for Northern cities was not the immigrant experience, but rather the black experience in Southern cities in the decades following the Civil War."[1]

It would be hard to find an urban public school system anywhere in the Western world which has faced a level of turmoil and travail comparable to that of New Orleans. That the founders' original ideals came down to the present era flawed and unfulfilled should not be surprising. It is more amazing that the public schools have survived at all, and that they have often prospered.

Understanding that survival and achievement should evoke admiration for those educators and civic leaders who remained committed to the ideals of public education. Their dedication rested not only on an abiding faith that public schools could help shape a better society but also on a tested conviction that the schools could enrich the lives of individual pupils. Their faith and conviction form the basis for celebration and commemoration. They overcame conflicts in the city to improve the future for many of the city's children. They believed in the mandate that was given to them by the founders of the city's public schools that such an institution should help "the rising generation." It was an outlook that others have called the American dream. It deserves exploration and reaffirmation.

I

Launching the System

In the spring of 1841, Horace Mann learned that favorable reports of his reforms of public education had reached even New Orleans, then the most distant point from his office in Boston—far off in the southwest corner of the United States. News of his success had caught the attention of a powerful leader in that southern city, Joshua Baldwin, who requested "reports & lectures" from the Massachusetts secretary of education "to assist in the establishment & organization of public schools here."[1]

As a transplanted Yankee from Pennsylvania, Baldwin knew well that Horace Mann had not invented the notion of public schools; in fact, some version of publicly supported schools had existed in all of the Puritan commonwealths since the early seventeenth century. But Mann had expanded upon that celebrated tradition in New England. After becoming his state's first secretary of education in 1837, he put together a uniform system of "common schools" supported for the first time by state taxation.

Mann's tireless efforts gave shape to the formerly disparate town-schools by coordinating their efforts and supplying them with a cadre of well-trained teachers produced by a network of normal schools that he had set up across Massachusetts. His skillful promotion of the program through his annual reports and his first-rate *Common School Journal* captured the imagination of the nation. He had finally shown a practical way to invigorate and extend public education. By transforming many of the popular theories of reformers into a statewide operation, Mann also gave public school activists more than hope. He heralded a working model that could be replicated in other states and communities.[2]

Joshua Baldwin had been looking for such a model. Public education had never taken hold in New Orleans or anywhere else in Louisiana. As a French and then a Spanish colony, the state's early history had evolved outside the boundaries of the Anglo-American experience. It lacked both the complex of excellent town-schools that dominated the New England landscape and even the "patchwork quilt of public, quasi-public, religious, and pauper schools" in Virginia and other states of the Old South. True, a few Catholic religious orders, particularly the Ursuline and Carmelite

5

6

1   Horace Mann, Massachusetts Secretary of Education, 1837-1850.

nuns, had steadfastly maintained several primary schools in New Orleans, and some individual schoolmasters had recruited small groups of students in private academies. But these efforts had managed to raise the educational level of only a tiny segment of New Orleanians.[3]

After Jefferson purchased French Louisiana for the United States in 1803, American officials failed to transfer American schemes of schooling to New Orleans. The first territorial governor, William C. C. Claiborne, saw in Louisiana the possibility of instituting some rather ambitious plans for public education. He and his associates conceived an elaborate system based, it seems, on New York and French models. The comprehensive scheme envisioned the College of Orleans at its top, with a network of local academies, libraries, and primary schools below, all governed by a board of regents. Despite Claiborne's ability to win legislative approval of this ambitious proposal as well as major appropriations of public funds, all his efforts to establish public schools failed abysmally. Imposing American institutions on Louisiana's foreign culture, Claiborne quickly learned, was no simple undertaking.

Claiborne envisioned his public school system as a key agent in the Americanization of the polyglot population of Louisiana. He wanted the schools to enroll "the children of native Louisianians and the native Americans, of the native Frenchmen and the native Spaniards" and to

2   College of Orleans.

3   W. C. C. Claiborne.

encourage some early association and friendship that might "induce the rising generation to consider themselves one people."[4]

Claiborne may have been the first governmental leader to articulate this assimilative ideal, one that would later reverberate throughout America as other cities came to host equally diverse foreign populations. Despite his elaborate designs and noble ambitions, Claiborne, as well as subsequent leaders in Louisiana, failed to create a workable system of public education, even in the compact settlement of New Orleans. Their efforts floundered because a deep rivalry over power led to a paralyzing conflict about the goals of public education.

The creoles, as Louisiana's French-speaking natives were called, had their own ideas about the future of their society and the kind of education it required. The way they saw it, they were not immigrants coming into some new society in need of "Americanization." From their point of view, the Americans were the newcomers who should adapt to the well-rooted culture. The creoles set themselves to defend their society against the interlopers. With fresh allies among the "foreign" French who continued to emigrate from Europe and the West Indies, the creoles early seized control of the state government and appointed French speakers as the teachers and directors of the College of Orleans. The depressed level of literacy in the city, however, made it impossible for them to run the college as a institution of higher learning. During its first two decades of existence, it remained a secondary school with only a small number of students. Frustrated at seeing the college fall into creole control, American leaders began to oppose it. In March, 1826, the board of regents appointed a famous French educator, Joseph Lakanal, as head of the college. But when it became rumored that the revolutionary exile was a defrocked priest as well as a regicide, he lost support among the largely Catholic creoles, who joined Americans in calling for the closure of the controversial college.

The creole and American rivals tried to heal their ethnic quarrel by replacing the College of Orleans with two primary schools—the Upper School in the American-controlled uptown neighborhood, and the Lower School, housed in a former convent in the downtown creole sector. Attached to the latter was the city's only secondary school called *L'Ecole Central*. Both the uptown and downtown schools offered bilingual programs to give their graduates fluency in French as well as English. Before long, however, even this elaborate compromise failed. Enrollment in the schools seldom exceeded a combined total of 250 students, and rivalry over control of the secondary school continued to pit creoles and Americans against each other.[5]

In 1836, in order to solve the ethnic dilemma that had paralyzed not only the schools but also much of the city's governmental and business activity as well, key American leaders in New Orleans engineered legislative approval to restructure the city's government in a fashion untried elsewhere in the United States before or since. They divided New Orleans into three separate municipalities: the First Municipality covered what was essentially the old colonial city, the area between Esplanade and Canal; the Second Municipality, largely American in makeup, included everything above Canal Street; and the Third extended below (or downriver) from Esplanade. Each municipality had its own council as well

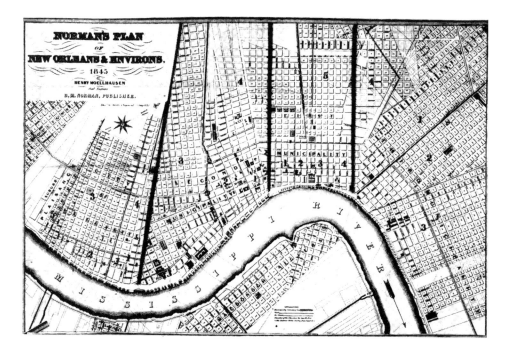

4 The municipalities of New Orleans and the suburb of Lafayette are shown on this map. In 1852, after the city was consolidated, the boundary lines of the school districts remained the same but the numbering changed. The First Municipality became District 2, the Second Municipality became District 1, the Third Municipality became District 3, and Lafayette became District 4. The numerals on this map refer to wards, not to the municipalities.

as a powerful executive and judicial officer called a recorder, and each enclave conducted its own affairs, virtually as an independent city. This unique arrangement finally allowed the Americans to adopt their own school system.

Joshua Baldwin, the recorder for the Second Municipality, took the lead. As the economy began to boom in the American sector after the Panic of 1837, Baldwin and his circle of associates in business and politics turned quite naturally to New England for ideas. Most of them, like Baldwin, had migrated not from the Old South but from the northeastern states, and also like Baldwin, these newcomers frequently returned to their homes not only to carry out mercantile operations but also to escape the intense heat and yellow-fever epidemics that usually afflicted migrants from the temperate zones of the United States.[6]

During such trips, Baldwin talked with several educators in the North before he wrote to Horace Mann. He developed a particularly close friendship with Henry Barnard, superintendent of education in Connecticut, who apparently sent a design for a school system to Baldwin in 1839, which the recorder used to shape the enactments that established a public school district in his municipality.[7]

Baldwin began by convincing the state legislature to pass a law on February 16, 1841, which allowed each of the three municipalities of New Orleans and the new uptown suburb of Lafayette to set up a school system managed by its own board of directors. The law also apportioned to the councils of the municipalities shares of the existing state appropriations for public education, on the condition that they match those funds with their own appropriations.

Very quickly, on March 26, the council of the Second Municipality endorsed the rest of the Baldwin blueprint. Led by Samuel J. Peters, council members passed an ordinance which called for a board of directors made up of sixteen members which assembled for its first deliberations on May 15, 1841. At that meeting, they agreed to seek further information "from other parts of the United States."[8]

Joshua Baldwin, the driving force for schools in New Orleans, had already been accumulating that information and had even decided that Massachusetts had just developed the system that he wanted to use as a model. After his initial correspondence with Horace Mann, he pushed ahead to get someone from that state to "launch" the schools of his municipality. Well before he got the new school board to come to a similar

5   Samuel J. Peters.   During the 1840s, as president of the Second
Municipality's Chamber of Commerce and a member of its Council, Peters played a
key role in the founding of the public schools in New Orleans.

conclusion, Baldwin had reopened his own communications with Mann. He told the Massachusetts educator that the new system was already "dependent on the north" for school teachers, but now he wanted to go further:

> I now address you, and ask your friendly aid, in ascertaining, whether a person suitable to organize and superintend these public schools, can be found there willing to come here to organize and superintend them . . . . We would require no more, but would not be satisfied with any less, than is required in Boston. Yet you are aware of our peculiar Institutions, and with what tenacity southerners cling to them, and of the impropriety of engaging any one entertaining objections to slavery.[9]

When Baldwin received no reply from Mann, he wrote again, not knowing that Mann had been too busy and then too ill to reply. Baldwin may have worried that he had offended Mann with his request for someone safe on the slavery question. Actually the request had caused no problem. Mann had ignored such racial questions in his own state and even warned his subordinates to avoid any promotion of abolitionism or of integrated education in Massachusetts schools. True, he personally disapproved of slavery and eventually became an outspoken, antislavery congressman. But in 1841 he still held to a naive faith that public education could root out such social evils in the long run.[10]

Mann had actually been flattered by the news of his fame in far-off New Orleans, and before Baldwin's second appeal arrived, he had already brought the offer to the attention of John Angier Shaw, an able educator and Mann's close friend. Shaw had been a chief architect of the new Massachusetts development—first as a state senator and then as chairman of the education committee in the lower house of the Massachusetts legislature.[11]

During the past year, Shaw had led successful counterattacks against two frontal assaults in the legislature that tried to close down the state department of education that Horace Mann was directing.[12] Mann was always ready to do favors for his friends and supporters, and just before Baldwin sent his first request for a superintendent, Shaw had written to Mann indicating that he was ready to move beyond the confines of his job as the director of a private academy in his hometown of Bridgewater. "I cannot but feel," he confided, "that I ought to be doing better for my family and for the public too." He was ready to move from the "home of my fathers."[13]

John Angier Shaw had deep roots in the Puritan commonwealth of Massachusetts. Both of his grandfathers were Congregational ministers. His paternal grandfather pastored the town church in Bridgewater, and his father became a medical doctor in the same town, which was just south of Boston. Initially John Shaw followed in the footsteps of his father. He dutifully went off to Harvard College in 1807 and, after his graduation four years later, continued his studies until he too became a minister. For a while he served as the registrar at Harvard and a teacher at Andover Academy. But then his career took an unusual turn.

In the early nineteenth century, the rooted ways of his Puritan ancestors must have lost some appeal for him. First, he became a Unitarian, and then, in 1818, he went off to the new frontier of Mississippi where he tried to set up a congregation and school in Woodville. After a few years, however, he gave up the ministry—in part, his friends later recalled, because he could not adapt to the style of sermons relished by his new Southern parishioners. He left the ministry but not the state. He continued to teach and also took up the life of a slaveholding planter. But by 1825 the new life had lost its appeal for the restless New Englander, and he returned to Bridgewater.

For the next sixteen years, he continued his teaching career as the principal of the town's private academy. But he remained restless and flirted with various reform movements, particularly temperance, which were then sweeping Massachusetts and other northeastern states. At the same time, as a descendant of Puritans, he remained nervous about the darker impulses of human nature. He felt that law and morality had to work hand in hand with the expansion of democratic rights so that ordinary citizens could meet their responsibilities in a democratic republic. His move from temperance reform to educational reform proceeded quite naturally. If intemperance with alcohol invited "ruinous excess," education promised to remold human character so that both the home and the ballot box would be secure. He insisted that "the friends of man" had to save "our brethren of the human family" from "bondage" to the twin demons of rum and ignorance.[14]

What made Shaw different from his Puritan forefathers was that he was ready to move beyond the confines of the institutional church and work in secular campaigns in order to help humanity find a better lot on earth as they prepared for heaven. In 1835, the Whig party allowed him to continue his reform efforts by electing him to the state legislature for the next six years—twice to the Senate and four times to the lower house where he chaired the education committee.

By 1838 Shaw's reputation as an educator and reformer had admitted him into the inner circle of New England schoolmen—the American Institute of Instruction. Formed in 1830, the group admitted not only teachers but also businessmen, clergy, and any other professionals who shared their faith in public education. Despite the group's embracing name, almost all of its members came from New England. They chose the name because they sensed the new excitement running through the nation in favor of public school systems. The American Lyceum of New York City, which also began in 1830, likewise reflected the popularity of the new idea. When they observed the success of Horace Mann in Massachusetts and read a report written in 1838 by Calvin Stowe about the program of universal public education in Prussia, the New York group scheduled "a National Convention" at Independence Hall in Philadelphia and invited every state government to send a delegation.[15]

It is easy to see what led to the flurry of activity among the transplanted New Englanders who were running the Second Municipality of New Orleans. Joshua Baldwin's closeknit circle of associates on the sixteen-member board of directors quickly came to share his overall vision. They endorsed his call to hire someone to direct their new schools who was conversant with the systems of New England and optimistically looked beyond their own municipality. They expected that their local initiatives would soon be "the foundation and model for those throughout Louisiana." Enthusiastically, they approved Horace Mann's recommendation of John A. Shaw as the man to come to Louisiana and "launch the system."[16]

Shaw responded in the same spirit when Mann presented the offer to him. He wanted the job as much as the New Orleans directors wanted him. Since Baldwin's letter had left the question of salary open to Mann's advice Shaw told his friend to suggest the handsome sum of $3,000 per year— fifty percent higher than the salary that Boston paid the superintendent who ran their venerable urban system. Even before he received confirmation of his appointment at $2,500, Shaw urged Mann to let him know as soon as possible about a response from New Orleans, to relieve his "suspense." He was so anxious that he was willing to hide his misgivings about slavery and hoped that Mann had not mentioned them to Baldwin:

> I cannot say that I "have no objections to slavery," but having formerly been myself a slaveholder in Mississippi, I am too well acquainted with the state

6   John Angier Shaw.

of things in that part of the world, to have any wish to interfere with the institutions or disturb the tranquillity [*sic*] of the south.[17]

The Yankee slaveholder-turned-reformer was made for New Orleans. Few others had the skill and doggedness to create a school system in the Deep South and wean it into stable existence. He articulated his strong sense of mission in one of his last letters to Horace Mann just before he set off for New Orleans: "So much is depending on this first attempt to establish a school system in Louisiana," he wrote, "that I must have your aid. In view of its importance I almost shrink from the attempt, but I cannot fail to derive a cheering hope from the prospect of rendering such a service to my fellow-men, should I succeed."[18]

During his journey southward, Shaw ignored the request of the New Orleans directors to survey the urban school systems of Philadelphia and New York City so that he could reach New Orleans in mid-December before the new schools officially opened. Indeed, such a detour would have made little difference, for Shaw had already decided to set up the lower level schools of New Orleans on the basis of the Boston grammar schools and to cap the system with high schools like the Boston Latin School—the proudest achievement of that city's public system. Because he knew that the first teachers had already been recruited from his state, he confidently ordered textbooks, furniture, and equipment from Boston to stock the first two primary schools—one for boys and one for girls. New Orleans' first schools literally came from Boston lock, stock, and barrel. And the school board never wavered; they wanted something that would work; and Shaw gave them just that.[19]

On January 3, 1842, the Second Municipality's first schools opened in rented quarters in two adjoining buildings on Julia Street, between Magazine and Tchoupitoulas.[20] Only twenty-six students initially enrolled in each school, but the favorable response of the citizenry was almost instantaneous. The problem in New Orleans had never been the lack of demand for public education; the long history of failure rested with the inability of inept and jealous leaders to supply schools in suitable numbers and of suitable quality.[21]

Within a year, more than a thousand students swamped the new school system. Shaw was up to the challenge. He recruited a fine corps of additional teachers from New England and won support from municipal leaders as he sought to make physical improvements. For larger and more suitable facilities, he turned to the local Protestant churches, many of which

7   Franklin School. Founded in 1844, this school for girls in the Second Municipality stood on St. Charles between Girod and Julia.

had recently built large new structures in New Orleans. As a former minister, he was able to persuade the major Presbyterian, Methodist, and German Protestant churches to let him rent portions of their facilities during weekdays. By the beginning of the school term in 1844, Shaw had opened nine elementary schools and enrolled over 1,500 students, almost two thirds of the white children in the municipality between six and sixteen.

It was a triumph. In 1843, while on a tour of schools in the West, the former superintendent of the Connecticut schools, Henry Barnard, stopped in New Orleans, surveyed the progress, and reported to Horace Mann. "They have done wonders in the second municipality—and much, or rather most of it is to be attributed to the prudence and perseverance—the honesty and faithfulness of Mr. Shaw. There is a perfect control in the schools—both in their external organization, and internal management, condition and results." Mann quickly let the readers of his *Common School Journal* know of New England's success in New Orleans: "Not only was the Principal taken from Massachusetts, but also all the text books and apparatus

8   Henry Barnard, Connecticut Secretary of Education, 1838-1844.
He claimed to have helped New Orleans officials craft the 1840
designs for public education in New Orleans. He was twice offered a
position of superintendent in New Orleans.

for the schools, and all the school furniture, even to the chairs for seating
the scholars."[22]

Success nurtured success. The merchant-activists on the school board
knew how to sell Shaw's handiwork. They proclaimed that the schools
were raising the value of real estate in the Second Municipality where
families were relocating "solely with a view to educate their children."
Such promotion of the schools' impact on the "pecuniary prosperity of the
municipality" allowed Shaw to extend his innovations.[23]

In January 1843 he recommended that the board begin a high school,
and within a year set up the curriculum, hired the staff, and on December 4

opened the city's first modern high school for boys, with himself as the
headmaster. By the beginning of the 1845-46 school year, he opened a
similar high school for girls. Both became the pride of the school system
and quickly drew the wealthiest families of the municipality into the public
schools, since enrollment in the high schools required prior attendance in
the public elementary schools. Only later did the board drop that rule and
admit graduates of private schools, but only after a rigorous examination.
Each high school had the classical curriculum of the Boston Latin School.

Shaw had special reasons for wanting the high schools, particularly a
rigorous one for girls. Seeing a growing demand for teachers and
experiencing some difficulties with recruiting them from the North, he
wanted to train his own corps in New Orleans. From the beginning he had
held special training sessions for his teaching staff on Saturday mornings,
what he called his normal school, but his teachers frequently quit after they
experienced a wretched summer or an outbreak of yellow fever. At best
they refused to return from their six-week summer break until an epidemic
had passed. Such behavior angered board members and began to arouse
public resentments against outside teachers.

To train a native staff, Shaw recognized that he had to establish a sound
secondary system and open it to girls as well as boys. Besides, a supply of
talented, educated local women enabled him to save money. By hiring
primarily women (almost 80% by 1850), he was able to expand education
at a faster rate than governmental appropriations would otherwise have
allowed. Although salaries in the Second Municipality were higher than
those in Boston, women were still paid significantly less than men. In
New Orleans, as in almost all of the nation's urban school systems, cheap
and talented women teachers made possible the new revolution in public
education.[24]

During Shaw's many years as a teacher, he had stored up a fund of ideas
for improvements, and he augmented that fund during annual summer trips
back to the Northeast. When he took the job, he had negotiated an
arrangement that allowed him to leave the city at the end of each school
year in early July and not return until the end of October. He was thus able
to keep in touch with his New England colleagues and regularly attend the
August sessions of the American Institute of Instruction. He served as one
of the vice-presidents of the group along with such leading schoolmen as
Horace Mann, Henry Barnard, Calvin Stowe, and Cyrus Pierce.[25] On
occasion, he took some of the New Orleans school board members with
him in order to keep them abreast of educational developments.[26]

9 Lucretia Wilder. A native of Massachusetts, she entered the public schools of the Second Municipality in 1844 and graduated from the girls' high school in 1853. She began teaching in 1856 and retired in 1907.

Shaw was more than a mere transmitter of New England trends. He inaugurated in New Orleans several innovations that came to have national significance. He convinced the school board to distribute free school books before the idea took hold in Boston; he set up evening schools for working youngsters and adults, both male and female; and he created a free public library for his teachers and students that generated such local public pride that the municipal council provided it with handsome facilities in the new City Hall on Lafayette Square. The library eventually became the basis of the whole public library system of New Orleans.

New England educators who normally scoffed at the educational backwardness of the South took notice of the New Orleans achievement. Nate Allen, who was considered one of the "best Massachusetts teachers," stopped to visit the New Orleans schools near the end of Shaw's service in early 1851. It was "the first place in all the South" where he found "good

10 Gallier Hall. The city hall of the Second Municipality. It contained the school board office and the public school library which was founded in 1844 by an ordinance of Samuel J. Peters. John McDonogh made an anonymous contribution of one thousand dollars for the library.

Public Schools." Visiting "nearly all the schools," he found them well organized into three divisions—primary, intermediate and high—and "better ordered and disciplined" than any schools he knew in Massachusetts. He was especially struck by the "friendly feeling between the teacher and the taught." And he perceived the reason: "Mr. Shaw moves among the schools like a father, giving advice like a father to the teachers and pupils. They all welcome him to the school-room with countenances beaming with pleasure when he is near."

Allen noted that most of the New Orleans teachers were New Englanders and that one, Professor F. F. Mueller, formerly of the Boston Academy of Music, played the unusual role of a full-time music instructor in the schools. Allen's report led William Fowle, Horace Mann's successor as the editor of the *Common School Journal*, to highlight Shaw's innovations, particularly the use of a music specialist and the distribution of free textbooks. He remarked that New Orleans had started "things that it will not injure our New England schools to imitate."[27]

It is not clear how much Shaw's achievements in New Orleans influenced New England educators, but his work certainly shaped the development of public education in Louisiana and other areas of the South. In fact, Shaw's public school model may well be considered the mother of public education in much of the Deep South. The reputation of the Second Municipality schools led authorities in other cities of the region such as Galveston and Natchez to recruit key teachers who had worked under Shaw to start their urban schools. In Alabama, educators likewise turned to New Orleans for lessons when they set up schools in Mobile.[28]

In Louisiana, Shaw's success laid the foundation for a reorganization of public education in the entire state just as Joshua Baldwin had predicted in 1841. When American leaders took control of the Louisiana legislature away from creoles in 1845, they responded to the popularity of Shaw's schools by extending the provisions of the 1841 legislation for New Orleans to the state's other parishes. During the same year, a constitutional convention also called for free public education for white children in Louisiana. In 1847 the legislature complied with the new constitutional mandate by creating the office of state superintendent of education to oversee the operation of the nascent school system and by appropriating considerable funds for its implementation. Alexander Dimitry, who as superintendent of the Third Municipality of New Orleans had closely watched and copied Shaw's model, became the first state superintendent, from 1847 to 1852. National educators took notice of the reforms but soon

11 Alexander Dimitry. After serving as superintendent of the public schools
in the Third Municipality in 1846, he became the first state superintendent of
education (1847-1852).

wondered why such planning and such funding produced so few results.
Had they better understood the rural isolation of most Louisiana parishes,
the state's endemic corruption, inexperience, and elitism, they would have
known why no significant reforms succeeded outside of the New Orleans
area before the Civil War.[29]

The most immediate and lasting emulation of Shaw's work took place in
the other municipalities of New Orleans. Noting the success of the
American leaders, the creole-dominated councils of the First and Third
municipalities tried to match those innovations.[30] If nothing else, ethnic

pride and competition prompted them to keep pace with their uptown rivals. On May 10, 1841, the First Municipality Council passed an ordinance creating a new school board which met on July 3, 1841—about six months after their rivals across Canal Street had assembled. The results, however, were a study in contrasts.

The creoles moved slowly. It took a committee almost four months to draw up rules for the new operation and to summon a second meeting. The board made few fundamental changes: they kept the instructors from their old *Ecole Central* and made the English teacher, James W. Murrays, the acting superintendent. For the next two years, almost no further development took place. The board failed to gather a quorum in its January and February meetings of 1842 and met irregularly thereafter. By the fall of 1843, they had just 115 boys in their single, rented schoolhouse on Orleans Street near Rampart.

While predominantly French, the First Municipality had a substantial English-speaking minority who did not want French-language schools. To meet this challenge, the First Municipality school board began one of the nation's first experiments in bilingual education.[31] True, some teachers in cities such as Cincinnati had tried to accommodate German immigrants in schools that taught in both German and English. But the New Orleans innovators faced a far greater challenge, for they had no available pool of well-trained bilingual teachers and no easy access to textbooks in both languages. In addition, teaching in two languages added significantly to the cost of their operations, since they had to hire dual staffs of English and French teachers for each school.

Many other difficulties also plagued them. First, deeply rooted Catholic traditions made it impossible for them to teach boys and girls in the same classrooms. True, the Americans also retained sexual segregation during the antebellum period, but Shaw frequently set it aside temporarily when he began a new school and never drew any remonstrance from his board or the public for housing single sex classrooms of both genders in the same school building. In the creole districts, however, such innovation brought immediate condemnation from the board and threats from parents. To maintain community confidence, administrators even had to agree to expel any boys caught speaking to girls at a neighboring school during recess periods. Sexual segregation also extended to the teachers, especially to men teaching post-puberty girls or to women teaching boys beyond the primary grades.[32] The cost and scarcity of male teachers added severe difficulties.

The chief problem, however, was the still fierce ethnic struggle for control of the system. By the 1840s, new Irish and German immigrants not only added to the demand for schooling but also to the ethnic complexity. Frequently their leaders could not understand the proud language loyalty of the French. The new immigrants were ready to become Americans, and the Irish, of course, already spoke English. Despite their common Catholic heritage with most of the creoles, the Irish and Germans sided with the Americans on the language issue.

By the fall of 1843, Americans with the help of immigrant Irish and German voters gained a majority in the First Municipal Council, which in turn recast its local school board. Under the leadership of a German immigrant, Christian Roselius, the new board fired Murrays and began conducting their meetings in English.[33] They also explicitly acknowledged the success of the Second Municipality by requesting help from them.

12 Christian Roselius. An independent-minded German immigrant, he took an active interest in bringing the New English school design to the French Quarter schools. He also served as John McDonogh's executor and remained a Unionist during the Civil War.

13 Charles Gayarré. A prominent creole school board member, who was determined to maintain the First Municipality's innovative bilingual teaching program.

Joshua Baldwin was immensely pleased. His board responded with a message of congratulations and set up a three-member committee to provide assistance. They even lent their superintendent, James Shaw, to put the creole sector on the right track. He instituted teacher examinations, and when some of the understandably proud incumbent teachers, such as Murrays and Toussaint Bigot, refused to submit to a test of their teaching competence, the new Americanizers fired them without hesitation. Under Shaw's leadership, the First Municipality kept the use of French in the schools but only for French-language classes. With the money saved, they threw out the remnants of a monitorial system which used advanced students to teach younger students. In its place, they adopted Shaw's graded system of primary and intermediate schools taught by an expanded English-speaking and well-trained teacher corps. The new board also laid plans for high schools to train their own teachers but postponed implementation for several years.

The board started the reorganized system with four schools, two for boys and two for girls, each with a primary and intermediate department. One of the schools began in a Masonic lodge; another in a Protestant church, both to the horror of many of the creole Catholics. To cap off all this radical change, the board decided to hire a northern expert as their new superintendent. With Joshua Baldwin's assistance, they almost bagged the famous Henry Barnard but failed. Instead, they hired Franklin Sawyer, a Yankee resident of the city and a former graduate of West Point.[34]

It was too much humiliation for the creoles. The next year, in 1844, they regained control of the school board and promptly undid almost everything. They returned to meetings held in French, chased Sawyer away, and hired a prominent French exile, General Charles Cuvellier to take command. It seemed that a military officer was appropriate for the level of conflict on the board. Christian Roselius recognized defeat and spitefully resigned his position in favor of Charles Gayarré, a famous creole and former student of the embittered, dismissed teacher, Monsieur Bigot. The new board restored full bilingual training at all levels and rehired the old teachers.

However sweet for the creoles, their victory was only brief. In October 1845, the celebrated general died. Shortly afterwards the board replaced him with Thomas Théard, another French immigrant. But Roselius and his cohorts regained control before the next school year could begin. That restoration, in turn, lasted only for a year. The political pendulum seemed to shift without end during the 1840s: seven different superintendents spent more time undoing the work of their predecessors than establishing any order in the school system.[35]

The political instability resulted from the declining numbers of French-speakers in their own bastions of the city, especially in the First Municipality. Still, until the 1850s, the French-speakers remained the dominant plurality in downtown New Orleans. Although frequently challenged, they were able to summon enough support to retain their bilingual school system until after the Civil War.

TABLE I:

Nationality and Linguistic Survey of Students School District Two: 1852 and 1853
[Former First Municipality]

Birthplace	1852	1853	Mother Tongue	1852	1853
Louisiana	1408	1712	French	1288	1122
Other U. S.	307	236	English	968	1109
France	232	255	German	141	446
Germany	184	246	Spanish	42	44
Ireland	162	173	Italian	40	27
Spain	49	16			
Italy	44	19			
Great Britain	11	60			
Mexico	7	6			
West Indies	4	21			
Others	9	4			
Totals	2417	2748			

Source: Minutes, School District 2, May 17, 1852, December 19, 1852.

Throughout the ethnic turmoil, the school system of the First Municipality slowly adapted to the model that Shaw had created in 1842. Despite creole comebacks, the boards kept the graded system, bought English texts from the North, even conducted their meetings in English, and set up the proposed high schools, first for boys in 1846 and then for girls in 1847. The creoles learned quickly that the high schools helped solve their desperate need for competent bilingual teachers. By 1853, more than twenty-five teachers able to handle both languages had graduated from the girls high school.

The directors copied other ideas. In 1848, they set up a free library for teachers and students and, in 1851, began offering free education at night for those who could not attend classes during the day. Within this framework, public education finally took root in downtown New Orleans.[36]

To be sure, the hybrid construct was often less vigorous than the pure Yankee system of the Second Municipality, but the downtown schools had to face greater challenges of cultural and ethnic diversity. Because their districts were far less prosperous than the booming American sector, they also received far less financial support from their municipal councils. Nonetheless they drew a heavy percentage of the white student-age population into their schools, despite the objections of hostile Catholic prelates who wanted their flocks to build and attend parochial schools.

In obvious contrast, stability marked the school operations of the Second Municipality. Joshua Baldwin took over the presidency of the board there in 1842 and ran it until 1850. During that time, he kept John Shaw as superintendent and gave him a free hand to run the daily operations of the schools. As a result, the system became firmly rooted.

When Shaw finally left in 1851, he resigned voluntarily. By that time, he had completed his mission and looked forward to returning to his family and friends in Massachusetts. From the beginning, he must have anticipated only a temporary assignment, for he never brought his family to the city. They remained in Bridgewater, Massachusetts, to which Shaw returned after leaving New Orleans. There he continued to teach almost until his death in 1873.

Stormy politics had made Shaw's last years in New Orleans increasingly unpleasant. More than most cities, even those in the Northeast, New Orleans received a massive influx of immigrants during the late 1840s and early 1850s. Indeed, before the Civil War, only New York witnessed a greater flow of immigrants into its port than New Orleans.[37] The new arrivals, largely Irish and Germans, placed a heavy strain on the educational facilities of New Orleans. With its prosperity, the Second Municipality kept up with the financial demands better than the other municipalities of the city. It avoided any significant political conflict until 1850, when Catholic pupils became a large proportion of the enrollment in the Second District's schools. Shaw dutifully expanded the system by opening new schools and recruiting new teachers to accommodate the more than 3000 students who attended the schools by the early 1850s.

In the midst of the expansion, Shaw even managed to convince his board to seek major new appropriations from the municipal council to build well-designed, modern schools. When the council threatened cutbacks during the economic recessions, Joshua Baldwin managed, in his dual position as recorder and board president, to marshal enough political power and community support to block the threatened cutbacks and, usually, to win some increased appropriations. The old hands on the board constantly reminded new members that public schools were "too important and the consequences too great, for the rising generation, to be merged in the wranglings of politicians or the fanaticism of sects."[38]

The most difficult crisis for Shaw proved to be a religious and ideological dispute, which resulted in large part from his own fanatic beliefs. Although a Unitarian who shared the nonsectarian faith of Horace Mann and other New England educational reformers, Shaw found it difficult to expand his tolerance beyond the limits of Protestant ecumenicity. He remained, at heart, an Anglo-Protestant. When Catholic and Jewish immigrants began to demand that his school system tolerate their convictions, Shaw refused to budge. He opposed all moves to end either Christian prayers, which offended Jews, or daily readings from the King James Bible, which infuriated Irish Catholics. He had his teachers force children to stand on stools for refusing to participate in either exercise and insisted to the end that moral growth could never take place without the daily recitations of prayer and holy scriptures. He may not have sought sectarian teaching or conversion, but he would not accept the secular compromises that skilled politicians offered to accommodate the growing diversity of the population in New Orleans.[39]

When, in 1850, a new board (without Baldwin on it any longer) abandoned the religious rituals over Shaw's objections, the Massachusetts superintendent offered his resignation. Only the pleas of his old supporters on the board convinced him to stay for another year and to see them past another set of proposed financial cutbacks by the council. He even had to endure unsuccessful but humiliating moves on the part of other board members to oust him. Finally, at the end of the 1850-51 school year, after the municipal council itself resolved that "no religious service shall hereafter be introduced in the public schools," Shaw decided to bid farewell to the city.[40]

He chose an appropriate audience for his farewell remarks, his grand corps of seventy-seven teachers whom he had recruited and trained for their New Orleans mission. He made no maudlin appeal for their sympathy but apologized for repeating what most had heard before: some advice on how to improve their teaching. He remained, as always, a fellow teacher. He urged them to concentrate on instilling a mastery and a love of reading, and concluded with a fatherly admonition to be ever loving and gentle:

> You will find it is far easier to lead your pupils, by a kind and mild, yet decided and uniform course of action, than to drive them forward by rough words or rougher actions. . . . One who feels no interest in the happiness of his pupils, and who takes no pleasure in leading them by pleasant paths . . . will, hereafter, reflect on his heartless conduct, with pain. Everyone who reflects useful knowledge and habits of virtuous conduct . . . knows that no profession can have precedence over his.[41]

Shaw left New Orleans with no apparent bitterness. Before he departed, he even tried to help the school board recruit Henry Barnard to take his place. Shaw wrote to Barnard that he would consider himself "repaid a hundred fold for the petty troubles of the past year, by learning that you were my successor."[42]

Barnard edged out his chief competitor for the job, George Harby, a former board member who had been associated with the group that backed Catholic and Jewish parents in seeking a secularization of the school system. Apparently another group—recent migrants from the old South—had joined that coalition of dissidents by introducing their own resentments of the Yankee influence which Baldwin and Shaw had brought to the Second Municipality school system. Both Shaw and J. S. Copes, who headed the board's search committee, had referred to this sentiment in their letters to Barnard. Shaw described the faction as those "who contend that it is degrading to New Orleans to go abroad for a Superintendent." Copes was probably more to the point: "Some are more stringent than others regarding the expediency of confining ourselves to our Southern resources."[43]

Before Barnard responded to the board's offer, he apparently waited until he could talk with Shaw after he returned to Massachusetts. When, for whatever reasons, Barnard declined the offer several weeks later, he placed his supporters on the board in an embarrassing position. But they still managed to select Robert H. McNair, another candidate favorable to their interests. McNair was an early Shaw appointee, who had left New Orleans to start the Galveston schools and later returned to serve as principal of the boys high school. He served as superintendent until 1855 when a board member, William O. Rogers, took over the superintendency and ran the schools until the Civil War. During the latter 1850s, Rogers and the board responded to the growing sentiment of sectionalism which considered Northern teachers a subversive force, dangerous to the security of slavery. Several newspapers and periodicals in the city regularly played on the issue. The *Picayune* joined the *Delta* in condemning the habit of sending children to Northern universities or of hiring Northern teachers because "they can be had cheap." Similarly, *De Bow's Review* insisted that the New England system of public education was not "adapted to Louisiana and the South" or in tune with the "spirit of our public institutions." To train more local teachers, the board opened a post-secondary normal school for teachers in 1855, and in 1858, they secured a promise of state funds for a new building for the school and its designation as a state school that would prepare teachers for all of Louisiana.[44]

About the same time, from a private source, city officials obtained an even larger financial boost for their schools—the impressive bequest of John McDonogh. On December 29, 1838, several years before Joshua Baldwin and his associates inaugurated the New Orleans public school system, this eccentric, millionaire slaveholder had signed a will that promised half of his hugh estate for the education of white and free black youth in New Orleans. The rest was to go to Baltimore for similar purposes.

Although McDonogh died on October 26, 1850, none of his massive legacy reached city coffers until 1858, after seven years of litigation finally reached a resolution in the courts. At that time, New Orleans received $704,440. To manage what came to be known as the McDonogh Fund, the city council set up under its jurisdiction a special commission in 1858 and reorganized it in 1860. On the eve of the Civil War, in March 1861, city officials provided its first disbursements to help build four new schools.

From the interest and rents of investments made by the managers of the fund, the city council gave each of the four school boards $10,000 toward the cost of constructing a new school. When opened, the new, modern buildings provided a symbolic high point for the antebellum schools of New Orleans.[45]

But a growing conservative mood in the Louisiana legislature stymied any further development of public education at the state level. Though the state suffered as a result, the legislative conservatism had little effect on the

34

EXCERPTS ON EDUCATION
FROM THE WILL OF JOHN McDONOGH

*I give . . . all the rest . . . (subject to the payment of . . .
several annuities . . .) unto the Mayor, Aldermen and
inhabitants of New Orleans . . . and . . . of Baltimore and
their successors, (. . . one half to each, of said cities . . .)
. . . for the establishment and support of Free Schools . . .
wherein the poor, (and the poor only) of both sexes and all
classes and castes of color, shall have admittance, free of
expense . . . provided . . . that the Holy Bible . . . shall be
. . . forever made use of . . . as one, (and the principal one)
of the reading or class books.*

*The first, principal and chief object I have at heart (the
object of which has actuated and filled my soul from early
boyhood with a desire to acquire fortune) is the education of
the poor (without the cost of a cent to them) . . . in such a
manner that every poor child and youth of every color in
those places may receive a common English education
(based, however, be it particularly understood, on a moral
and religious one, that is, the pupils shall on particular days
be instructed in morality and religion, and school shall be
opened and closed daily with prayer).*

*And (I was near forgetting that) I have still one small
request to make, one little favor still to ask, and it shall be
the last—it is that it may be permitted, annually, to the
children of the free schools situated the nearest to the place
of my internment, to plant and water a few flowers around
my grave.*

14 John McDonogh. Although a slaveholder, McDonogh showed a rare interest among white Louisianians for the education of his slaves and the general education of free black New Orleanians. His bequest for black education was not met by public officials until Reconstruction. Despite the frequent appeals of Protestant ministers, all the school boards, except for District 4, ignored his instructions about religious instruction. The portrait at left shows McDonogh about the time he migrated from Maryland to Louisiana; the portrait, right, recalls him at the end of his life.

well-established school systems in New Orleans, save that they felt required to lock up copies of *Uncle Tom's Cabin*.[46]   Public education had taken firm root in New Orleans.

By the 1850s, even the creole leaders in the city had begun to speak in glowing terms of Northern systems of public education. Already in 1846, Charles Gayarré had urged the Louisiana legislature to apply "the system of Education now prevailing in Massachusetts" to the whole state of Louisiana. Alexander Dimitry, the first state superintendent and a creole from New Orleans, thought that everything that came from Horace Mann's pen "bears the impress of a master mind." Indeed, it was a superintendent of the French Quarter schools who issued what may have been the most elo-quent defense of public education made in New Orleans before the Civil War. Speaking before his board in 1852, the First Municipality's superintendent, Alexandre Fabre, proclaimed a justification for public education that almost

15 McDonogh No. 1. One of three schools built with McDonogh funds before the Civil War, it was the only antebellum school named after the benefactor. Numbering of the McDonogh schools did not begin until Reconstruction during the 1870s when Republicans rediscovered McDonogh's interest in educating black as well as white New Orleanians.

surpassed those evoked by Horace Mann and the most enthusiastic New England schoolmen:

> Now that illiberal and antiquated prejudices, which were formerly arrayed against the public school system in our city and state, have disappeared before the onward march of enlightened public opinion . . . the day cannot be far distant when to withhold the invaluable blessing thus brought within the reach of all, shall be looked upon as a violation of every social and political duty. Nor can I here protest too strongly against an idea which unhappily lingers in the minds of a certain number of our fellow citizens, by whom the public schools are looked upon merely in light of *asylums for the Poor*. In the emphatic language of the founders of that System—the wisest and best that was ever devised for the improvement of our race, and the perpetuity of our free institutions—"The schools are essentially Public, not intended for any particular *class, but for the whole rising generation*" . . . . In the empire of *mind*, at least, let there be no *Monopoly*, no *Caste*, no privilege.[47]

When Fabre gave his speech, ethnic rivalry still continued between the school boards of New Orleans despite their shared commitment to public education. Indeed, even after the city's political and business leaders decided in 1852 to reconsolidate the city and end the separate municipal governments, state legislators permitted the tripartite school system to continue. In fact, leaders extended the division by allowing the neighboring city of Lafayette, which was annexed to consolidated New Orleans in 1852, to keep its own school board. Thus the old demarcations stayed intact. Only a new numbering system confused their earlier identities. The Second Municipality school board became the First District School Board of Directors; the First Municipality board the new Second District board. The Third Municipality board retained its old identity as the Third District board, and Lafayette's old board became the Fourth District board in the consolidated city. Under the new arrangement, the new Common Council appointed all of the district board's directors and allocated funds on a single formula based on the number of white children in each district aged from six to sixteen.

Despite some criticisms of the continued division of the school system after 1852, the local autonomy probably helped sustain local support for public schools in New Orleans. The Anglo-American Protestants who dominated the Fourth District may have abandoned public schools if their board had not been able to keep its daily bible readings and prayers. Catholic creoles, on the other hand, in the downtown districts would have retreated from such strictures. Indeed, the downtowners never imposed any religious ceremonies in their schools and, unlike their uptown counterparts, totally banned corporal punishment in their schools.

Most importantly, the districts' autonomy muted the still rancorous language conflict that lasted until the Civil War. Only at that late period did some key creole spokesmen begin to join Americans in calling for an end to the complicated bilingual program. They felt it stymied the educational progress of both French and English speakers.

It was clear, as late as 1856, when the creoles successfully resisted another attempt to consolidate the school districts that they were not yet ready to educate their children solely in English. On the one hand, they insisted that they were as loyal to the United States as anybody. They declared that they had "always been aware of inculcating into the minds of the rising generation, the idea that we are one people, entirely separated from other nationalities, and bound together by a community of feelings and interests." They had, moreover, believed "that a truly American education should form the basis of the system" and challenged comparison between their schools and their "rival institutions."

TABLE II:
Attendance, District 1 [Formerly Second Municipality]

Year	Daily Average	Total Registered	Evening School
1842	1008	1397	
1843	1260	2443	
1844	1888	3069	
1845	1769	2840	70
1846	1945	3520	40
1847	2125	3775	45
1848	2644	4157	49
1849	2811	4800	156
1850	2831	5290	162
1851	3138	5978	245
1852	3314	5557	227
1853	2886	5627	241
1854	2865	5019	363
1855	3083	5197	442
1856	3080	5406	522
1857	3603	6062	726
1858	3562	6066	849
1859	3415	6083	753

Source: An 1860 report cited in *Annual Report of the Superintendent* (1920), p. 21.

TABLE III:
Daily Average Attendance, Districts 2-4

Year	District 2	District 3	District 4
1857	2375	1945	1689
1858	2687	2009	2070
1859	2757	2326	2164

Source: New Orleans Council Ordinances, Numbers 3497, 4100, 4754.

But the creoles had their own way of defining the American identity which they had come to prize. Although they felt "justly proud" that their schools were established "on a similar basis with those of their neighbors," they could not ignore that "in the 2nd and 3rd Districts there are thousands of families whose only language is the French." In some ways, it is too bad that their view did not carry greater weight with the Anglo-Americans: "We hope that this language will never be suffered to die amongst us; that, from the two main elements of our population, in the crucible of American institutions, there will spring a people with original characteristics. . . ."[48]

However much this ethnic conflict among white New Orleanians had troubled the cause of public eduction for over a half century, it was never the primary cause for the denial of educational opportunity for "the whole rising generation" in the city. Almost nowhere in the records had anyone dared to protest that almost a quarter of the population of New Orleans and over half the population of the state who were black Louisianians had been totally excluded from the benefits of public schooling. Before the Civil War, no public official seriously considered John McDonogh's request that poor black New Orleanians share in his legacy for the city's schools. A slave order made such policy, even if contemplated, virtually impossible. Still the regular sweeps of the schools in the creole districts of all those with any trace of African ancestry hinted that aspirations had already been awakened among some black New Orleanians for free public education.

Even if belatedly, Horace Mann had joined other Americans in recognizing that slavery and the color line had thwarted the highest ideals of American educational reformers. Once more, the man whose concepts and personal assistance had helped to found public education in New Orleans moved into the vanguard not only for the nation but also for New Orleans and other areas of the slave South. Before he resigned from the editorship of his *Common School Journal* to become a full-time antislavery congressman, he spelled out his new priorities. His words were probably read by a good number of his followers in New Orleans, because Joshua Baldwin had personally ordered a subscription of the magazine for every teacher in the schools of his district:

> Our motto used to be, "The cause of education, the first of the causes."
> Recent events, however, of a national character, have forced upon the public
> attention the great truth, that before a man can be educated, he must be a free
> man. . . . the Editor . . . now leaves . . . to assist in securing the *Freedom of
> Man*, in regions yet unoccupied by civilized races.[49]

II

Revolution and Integration, 1862-1876

The Civil War opened an era of revolutionary change in the New Orleans school system. For fifteen years, from the appearance of Union warships in 1862 to the withdrawal of federal troops in 1877, the schools of New Orleans stood at the center of the social and political turmoil of the Reconstruction era. Nowhere did Reconstruction begin earlier or last longer. True, the overhaul of the public schools was only one part of the momentous upheavals that ended slavery, enfranchised black citizens, and reshaped federal-state relations. But the schools of New Orleans often stood at the center of those tumultuous events. They not only absorbed the first black urban educational system in the South but also participated in a far more dramatic experiment. Alone in the South and almost singularly in the nation, the public schools of New Orleans reached for the most difficult objective embodied in the American common school ideal: fundamental racial integration—with black and white students, black and white teachers, and black and white administrators.

Such an achievement required a virtual revolution in New Orleans. Before the occupation army of General Benjamin F. Butler left their Union warships to patrol and garrison New Orleans, no single black child had ever been allowed to enter a free, public schoolroom in New Orleans. Louisiana authorities had pointedly established their public schools for white students only. What is more, they made it a serious crime to teach any slave to read, and that official policy mandated a terrible legacy of illiteracy for virtually the entire half of the state's population who were enslaved.

Perhaps nowhere in the United States had the racial contrast been so striking. In other areas of the South, many white children had no more opportunity for a public education than black children, while in most free states of the North, black children, by the 1850s, had gained access to public schools. In New Orleans, however, city authorities had created a school system that reached out to all white children—rich and poor, native and immigrant, Christian and non-Christian. At the same time, state laws and city ordinances forbade formal education for all of the 14,484 slaves who lived in the city in 1860 and denied free, public education to the largest free black community in the Deep South made up of almost 11,000 people. The disparity of effort produced a striking contrast of results. After the Civil War, only 6.5 percent of whites were illiterate, while over 61 percent of blacks could not read or write.

Despite the stark legal prohibitions, many black New Orleanians had managed to gain educations before the Civil War. Their rate of literacy in the 1860s was actually higher than comparable rates of most eastern and southern European nations at the time.[1] Indeed, by 1860, the free black community of the city probably had a literacy level which exceeded that of the white population of the state as a whole. How was that possible in such a hostile environment, without access to public schools? First, a tiny group with very light skin color managed to evade the law and attend the city's public schools, particularly in the downtown districts. The school boards tried to enforce the color bars but often had to be very careful not to embarrass prominent creole families who were considered white. Indeed, accusations of racial mixture proved very disturbing to the first state superintendent of education, Alexander Dimitry, whose son-in-law, a former public school teacher, had to resign from the city council in the mid-1850s because he was deemed to have African ancestry. Any rigid black-white color line proved quite difficult to draw in New Orleans, where many so-called "black" New Orleanians often had lighter complexions than many so-called "whites."

Such examples of "passing" in the public schools were probably not widespread. Most free black children went to private and parochial schools. The Catholic church offered some solace from the severity of racial discrimination. Although the church had only a handful of parochial schools before the 1850s and evolved its own policies of racial exclusion and segregation, its nuns, who were usually foreign-born, reached out to the free black community, which had always been predominantly Catholic. French orders, especially Ursulines and Carmelites, began to teach free black children in small, separate classes. In 1841, a few clerical leaders went even further and helped establish an order of black nuns known as the Sisters of the Holy Family, who took charge of a small parochial school on Bayou Road in Faubourg Tremé. Some white fathers, usually also foreign French, exerted their influence to place their racially mixed children in private schools of the city or, more often, to send them outside the state to Northern or European institutions.[2]

The free black community also organized its own schools. At first small classes met secretly in private homes. It was not until 1848 that a regularly organized school of high caliber opened for free black boys and girls of modest means—the children of the large group of black artisans who had traditionally dominated such crafts as plasterers, masons, cigar makers, and carpenters in the French-speaking areas of the city. As early as 1837, a free African woman named Marie Couvent left a bequest with Catholic church officials to begin such a school; but, because of negligence, and probably fear, another decade passed before the Couvent school opened. It eventually enrolled over 250 girls and boys and assembled a teaching staff of five to seven teachers.[3] In 1852, the school's directors constructed a new building which stood at what is today Dauphine and Touro streets in Faubourg Marigny. Boys and girls were taught separately, each group occupying different floors of the two-story structure. The school operated with the cooperation of Catholic clergy and, in order to meet the requests of the founder's bequest, called itself an orphans' school. That rubric also helped to disguise its larger role and to deflect potential opposition. In reality, it was operated completely by black lay personnel and also took in non-orphaned children, irrespective of their religious identity.[4]

From time to time, the directors of the Couvent school managed to convince white officials in the state legislature and the city council to grant appropriations for the care of its indigent and orphaned pupils. The directors based their requests on the injustice of black property owners having to pay taxes for public schools without having access to them. These grants may well have constituted the first governmental subsidy for black education in the South. Indeed, the legislature's action was so remarkable that Horace Mann's *Common School Journal* took note of the unusual departure in 1849.[5]

Eventually the Couvent school had a great impact on public education, for, after the war, its former students and teachers were among the chief leaders in the movement to create an integrated, public-school system open to every child in New Orleans. Madame Couvent's school was the nursery for revolution in Louisiana. Like most of the free black community, its founders said little openly before the Civil War. A few dared to teach slaves to read and even to advocate racial equality. Most, however, tried simply to survive and to nurture their own families in a city that, during the decade before the Civil War, became increasingly hostile to black people. For some, fear, and for others, protection of caste-like privileges, had kept them from directly challenging the unjust racial order of Louisiana. But, whatever their shortcomings, the Couvent school leaders, along with other black and white teachers in the city, had effectively challenged the racist assumptions about the potential of black children by producing graduates of unusual accomplishment.

Even before the Civil War, a number of black writers published literary works including *Les Cenelles*, the first anthology of Negro poetry in the United States. Some free black students and professionals also went abroad, usually to France, where they achieved rare distinction both in science and in the arts. Among the most notable were Edmond Dédé, who conducted a classical orchestra in Bordeaux; Louis Roudanez, who graduated with honors in medicine from the University of Paris; and Victor Séjour, who became a playwright and personal aide to Napoleon III.[6]

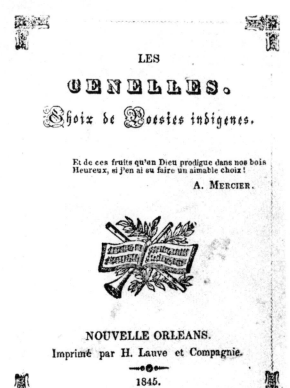

LES

CENELLES.

Choix de Poesies indigenes.

Et de ces fruits qu'un Dieu prodigue dans nos bois
Heureux, si j'en ai su faire un aimable choix!

A. MERCIER.

NOUVELLE ORLEANS.
Imprimé par H. Lauve et Compagnie.
1845.

16 *Les Cenelles* (1845) was the first anthology of poetry published in the United States by a group of African-American writers. It contains eighty-two poems written by seventeen New Orleanians.

17 Edmond Dédé. This gifted musician, after training in New Orleans, was sent to Europe by friends for further education at the Paris Conservatory, which he entered in 1857. He became a celebrated composer and the conductor of the clasical orchestra of L'Acazar in Bordeaux.

18 Norbert Rillieux. This bronze plaque was presented to the Louisiana Museum by the World Sugar Producers Association of Amsterdam, Netherlands, to commemorate Rillieux's technological inventions for refining sugar.

46

19 Dr. Louis Charles Roudanez. He received medical degrees from both the University of Paris and Dartmouth College. During Reconstruction, he founded the *New Orleans Tribune*, the first daily black newspaper in the United States.

However remarkable the accomplishments of the free black community, their achievement was still dwarfed by the enforced ignorance of the overwhelming majority of black Louisianians who remained enslaved. To be sure, some slaves had learned to read, but not many. Occasionally "in so large a city as New Orleans," one Civil War educator noted, "where great numbers of free blacks and slaves were crowded together," free black men and women ran "the greatest risks in teaching the slaves." But he guessed that among the vast ranks of the state's 331,726 slaves in 1860 not "one slave in a thousand learned to read, and a still less number learned to write."[7]

When Benjamin Butler came from Massachusetts with his Yankee troops, they had no intention of changing the social and educational order of New Orleans. True, Massachusetts was the first state to open its famed public-school system to black residents on a desegregated basis, but Benjamin Butler was no abolitionist. Indeed, as a Democratic politician he had denounced such policies in his native state. Abraham Lincoln, the president and commander-in-chief, had come from Illinois, which had refused to admit any black children to its public-school system before the Civil War. During his years in Illinois, Lincoln had shown no sign of resisting such measures. For both men, however, original intentions were soon altered by their experience in dealing with events in New Orleans, the first place where they had to take responsibility for managing a Southern city.

At first, Butler naively thought that he could run the city through its existing governmental system, but after a few months of facing total resistance by local officials, he resorted to direct military rule. He gave the system something of the appearance of civil administration by appointing an acting mayor and a military governor. But in reality, he made almost all of the key decisions himself.

Once Butler took over municipal operations, he found himself with the responsibility of running the local school system. And he did not like what he found. He could not comprehend the need for the city's complicated four-district system nor see any reasons for teaching classes in French. He insisted that all classes be taught in English after the close of the regular school session in June and, on July 31, 1862, issued military order No. 6082, which abolished the four old boards and replaced them with the Bureau of Education. It comprised five men: Lieutenant General Godfrey Weitzel, the assistant military commandant, who as acting mayor chaired the Bureau; Edward H. Durell, head of the Bureau of Finance; Julian Neville, head of the Bureau of Streets and Landings; Benjamin Flanders, treasurer of New Orleans; and Stoddard Howell, city comptroller. They all

held their seats on the new education board by virtue of their offices in the
military government, and as the offices changed hands, old members left
and new members appeared on the Bureau of Education. Several who
served were quite knowledgeable about the city's prewar educational system
or were themselves men of considerable education. Flanders had been a
principal in the old Second District; Durell was a Harvard graduate; and,
among later appointees, D. S. Dewees had been president of the Fourth
District School Board and John S. Walton, the manager of the McDonogh
Educational Fund. Almost all were of Anglo-American ancestry, and
several key figures, like Durell and Flanders, were New Englanders. Most
seemed bent upon accelerating the process of Americanization of the school
system.

Even without the Union army takeover, many of Butler's innovations
may eventually have occurred in New Orleans. Before the war, the state
legislature and the city council had tried to consolidate the city's school
boards because of the expenses involved in such a complicated
arrangement. In the French Quarter, or Second District, even some creole
members of the board had spoken out forcefully against the maintenance of
their complicated bilingual system, not only because it added to the cost of
the schools but also because it seemed to hinder the progress of many
children in the primary schools who were constantly held back until they
mastered reading and writing in both languages. But, without Butler's
intervention, change would certainly have come much later.

In handling the old linguistic and ethnic differences in the city's school
system, the new board moved more cautiously than Butler had. When they
met for the first time on September 5, 1862, they restored a semblance of
the old system by creating four subordinate "boards of visitors," one for
each of the old districts, to help them operate the varied school system. The
Bureau allowed the Second District visitors' board, for example, to work
out a compromise on the use of French. Schools in their district used their
French-speaking teachers to teach French-language courses after pupils had
mastered English skills in the primary schools.[8]

But the members of the new Bureau also made some important changes
that truly centralized the operations of the old system. First, they
administered the schools through a single superintendent, James Butler
Carter, the former principal of the Marshall boys school in the First
District. He ran the system until the end of the war. The Bureau also
demanded that the superintendent prepare and enforce rules that were
"uniform through out the City."[9]   In addition, they ordered standard

20 General Benjamin F. Butler and staff officers.

textbooks, mandated a single-salary schedule for all teachers, and set underway a process that ultimately consolidated the eight high schools of the city into three larger ones.

Under the new arrangement, the exact role of the subordinate visitor boards was never clear. The Bureau tried to get these boards to run the schools on a day-to-day basis by examining students, hiring teachers, and keeping the schools supplied and repaired. But the Bureau itself kept ultimate control and forced the local boards to send every decision to them for final approval. Behind such insistence was the reality of military power. The commanding generals may have known little about the operations of a school system, but they understood the nature of authority. They modeled the operation in New Orleans on the army chain of command and made sure that the military never lost control of the city or of the schools.

When, in mid-December 1863, a new commanding general, Nathaniel Banks, took over, he did not alter Butler's arrangements. By always appointing one of his officers mayor, which office made the incumbent chairman of the Bureau of Education, both generals kept the school system directly under their control. Whenever the subordinate civilian boards tried to assume unwarranted powers, the Bureau stood firm, even in the face of the mass resignation of the Fourth District Visitors Board. The Bureau made it clear that it had *"full charge and control of the Public Schools."*[10]

Although Banks was more willing than Butler to conciliate the former white power structure of the city, he did not halt the move toward consolidation. Under his administration, the Bureau of Education combined all four of the former district school libraries into the old First District library at Gallier Hall and insisted that only women be used as teachers in all of the elementary schools. Disregarding the secularization that had taken place in all but the Fourth District before the war, the new Bureau also demanded that every school open with prayer.[11]

Most of the new policies were economy measures; but some stemmed from renewed emulation of Northern models, since the Bureau sent the new superintendent in 1863 to visit "the northern cities and their public schools."[12] There Carter undoubtedly picked up on the new determination among Northern educators, particularly those in the National Education Association, to reshape Southern society by reforming and expanding systems of public education in the areas recovered from the Confederacy.

21 General Nathaniel P. Banks.

At the heart of the reconstruction effort in New Orleans was a determination to enforce Unionism and national loyalty in the school system. Unionist teachers were given preference in hiring, and the Bureau also tried to inculcate loyalty to the Union among both teachers and students by enforcing displays of the nation's flag and regular singing of "national airs." When students balked, school officials summarily suspended them for disobedience.[13]

Recasting the teaching force caused the greatest controversy within the local boards of visitors. When the schools had closed in the spring of 1862 as Union gunboats appeared at the mouth of the Mississippi River, the city had thirty-nine grammar schools and eight high schools in the four-district system, which employed about two hundred teachers and enrolled 12,000 students. The student total represented almost half of the city's white children between six and sixteen. When about a fourth of the students did not return after the schools reopened, the military authorities closed seven schools. As a result, the Bureau had to lay off teachers.

The new set of political qualifications placed some teachers in a severe dilemma. In the war ravaged economy of the city, teaching offered some measure of economic support, particularly to women who had no other choice of employment. They found themselves having to compete with outsiders who came to the city in the wake of the army to apply for the available teaching slots. Accusations of incompetency, favoritism, and disloyalty filled the deliberations of the boards, and the struggle left a lasting measure of bitterness in the ranks of local educators.

Despite the controversy and confusion involved in the terrible civil conflict, the public schools of the city not only survived but even grew during the war. Before the schools reopened for the fall term of 1864, their third year under military control, Unionist voters in the federally occupied area of Louisiana approved a new state constitution, as required by Lincoln's plan of Reconstruction. Under the new constitution, the state superintendency of education fell to John McNair, a protégé of John Shaw and a former principal of the boys high schools in both the First and Fourth districts. But the new state superintendent had little to supervise beyond the New Orleans public school system, which alone had managed to stay open throughout the Civil War.

On June 30, 1864, under the aegis of the new state constitution, the city government once again reorganized the administration of the New Orleans public schools. The new board of directors consisted of sixteen members—thirteen selected by the city council and three appointed ex-officio, the mayor and the chairmen of two city council committees. Under this arrangement, the new board was supposed to set up a subordinate five-man citizens advisory board in each of nineteen school zones newly drawn to give voice to the special concerns of the city's ethnic neighborhoods, but the board of directors itself retained the power to certify teachers and to administer directly the high schools, which they planned to consolidate.[14]

There was considerable continuity of personnel on the new board. All five members of the old military bureau joined the new body, and nine others came from the old boards of visitors. Since seven of the latter group came from the uptown or American section of the city, the school system clearly fell into the hands of moderate, English-speaking white Unionists. They rehired the former superintendent, James B. Carter, at the handsome salary of $5,000 and continued to buy textbooks that were used "in New England, in the schools of New York, Philadelphia, and other prominent cities." Before the school year started they consolidated the eight high schools into four—two uptown and two downtown schools, one in each area for girls and one for boys. Finally, before certifying any teachers for the new year, the board voted to refuse certificates "to those who have not given satisfactory evidence of loyalty to the U. S. government."[15]

The loyalty oath posed no obstacle for obtaining teachers in New Orleans. The prewar high schools and the city normal school had produced a surfeit of teachers in the city, so many that the antebellum superintendents had stopped recruiting teachers from outside the city. These teachers, largely young women, showed little reluctance to teach in the Unionist schools; in fact, 434 qualified for about 175 teaching positions in the 1864-65 school year. Those unable to obtain regular posts took appointments as "supernumeraries" or substitute teachers.[16] By mid-year, about 11,000 students were in regular attendance. The decline from the antebellum peak of attendance, about 12,000, resulted not so much from transfers to private schools or the refusal of students to attend any school as from an almost complete halt of both foreign and domestic migration to the city. Indeed, many resident alien and Yankee families fled from the city after river and ocean vessels reopened regular operations to New Orleans during the fall of 1863.

Even before the war, the city's declining economy had made it increasingly difficult to support its ambitious public school program, the largest system in the entire South. In the late 1850s, the local boards had cut teachers salaries, and the city council had also refused to match the state grant for a normal school in the First District and stymied the construction of a new building for the teacher training institute in 1859. Strapped for funds, the city government had absorbed over half a million dollars of the McDonogh Educational Fund for military defense of the city in 1861-62, and diverted all interest on remaining funds to the war effort. No further monies from the McDonogh Fund were available therefore to the school system for more than a decade after the war ended.

The commanding generals may have speedily centralized the school system, but, when it came to funding it, they moved cautiously. They were understandably reluctant to divert much money to the school system from their own military coffers. They came to New Orleans, after all, not to run schools but to win a war and restore the Union. The generals also had to face demands not faced by earlier city governments. The collapse of the slave system sent thousands of refugees into the city desperate for freedom, shelter, and food. Both Banks and Butler faced the massive problems of providing relief to both white and black unemployed workers in the city. The black families added a particular burden, when the parents pleaded for schooling for themselves and their children. As Americans, they immediately associated freedom with the opportunity not only for citizenship but also for education.

These demands first became apparent at military posts guarding the outskirts of the city. At one such post, Camp Parapet, which guarded the river road near the present-day intersection of Causeway Boulevard, an abolitionist general, John W. Phelps, decided to recruit some of the freedmen as soldiers. To gain their confidence and to make them efficient soldiers, he began to organize schools for them. When he turned to free black leaders for support, both French-speaking Catholic creoles and English-speaking Protestants offered to teach the slave refugees who included both French and English speakers. Robert Isabelle, an English-speaking Protestant, later claimed to a New York newspaper that he had begun the first English-speaking Protestant school for black people in the history of New Orleans. He may have been too expansive in his claims, but his announcement symbolized the beginning of a vast upheaval in New Orleans and other areas of the South.[17]

Butler initially opposed such radical departures. He had not come to bring liberation to black Louisianians, and he did not wish to touch the dangerous question of arming fugitive slaves. He had, in fact, already rejected the offer of the city's free black leaders to join the ranks of his army. Lincoln had not yet issued the Emancipation Proclamation. Indeed, the cautious president had already fired some of his generals for freeing slaves and had turned down offers from black Northerners to join the U. S. army. Butler therefore immediately ordered Phelps to desist; and, when Phelps demurred, Butler demanded, and got, Phelps's resignation from the army.

When Lincoln reversed his own course, Butler moved with almost equal speed in the new direction. He quickly summoned the free black leaders who had offered their services to him earlier and commissioned some as officers, long before such actions took place elsewhere in the United States. They, in turn, recruited not only free black volunteers but also slaves.

The army then began the first authorized public schooling for black Louisianians.[18]   Every regiment eventually became a school, and a new mood of revolutionary change swept through the city. Free black leaders from the Couvent school began a weekly newspaper, *l'Union*, with support from Butler, and that newspaper began to demand full emancipation and equal citizenship for all black Louisianians.

The demands were already pronounced before Butler left the city at the end of 1862. Some black families even tried to enroll their children in the city's all-white school system, but most local white Unionists resisted such radical change. Enforcing the color line had been difficult enough before the war. Now school officials were uncertain how to react. The board of visitors in the French Quarter warned all principals to check the status of every pupil by demanding birth certificates. Within a week, they discovered that they had even hired a black teacher named Miss Snyder, who in turn had encouraged some of her relatives to send their children to her school on Barracks Street. The principal hesitated to admit the children because they were "very dark."[19]   But the father told her that he had permission from one of the board members to enroll his three daughters. When the principal reported the matter to the full board, they fired the teacher and removed the children. But their problems had only begun.

General Banks, Butler's successor, tried to sooth the anxieties of white New Orleanians by dismissing all black officers from the army and by resisting all further demands from black leaders to take part in the new civil government. But revolution could not be so easily repressed. Within a year, determined black leaders sent a delegation to Lincoln and to the United States Congress to demand equality. Although Lincoln officially denied their request for his personal intervention, unbeknownst to the black leaders, the president sent a confidential message to the new provisional governor of the state, Michael Hahn, asking him to consider granting suffrage to black Louisianians who had served in the army and who could read and write.

The free black leaders wanted more. Before their delegates, Jean-Baptiste Roudanez and E. Arnold Bertonneau, came home, they went on to Boston where, at a dinner held in their honor, they met the governor of Massachusetts and almost every major abolitionist leader, including William Lloyd Garrison and Frederick Douglass. At the dinner, the New Orleanians not only announced their demands for universal male suffrage and civil equality under the law, but they also made a stunning declaration of their dream for public education in Louisiana. Bertonneau declared that their ultimate goal was to change "the character of the whole people" by sending their children to schools "to learn the great truth that God 'created of one blood all nations of men to dwell on the face of the earth'—so will caste, founded on prejudice against color, disappear. . . ."[20]

Bertonneau then turned to Garrison, president of the Massachusetts Anti-Slavery Society, and, to prolonged applause, vowed that he would return to New Orleans and urge his compatriots to fight for the same integration of public accommodations and schools that the Garrisonians had helped to inaugurate a decade earlier in Massachusetts. Once again, another dream for the public schools of New Orleans was evoked by the experience of public education in Massachusetts.

The trip of the New Orleanians had immediate repercussions in Louisiana. The national exposure of the situation in Louisiana embarrassed the commanding general, Nathaniel Banks. Both abolitionists and radical Republican congressmen began to focus their attention on the sensational developments in the Deep South state. Louisiana staged, as one scholar later dubbed it, the rehearsal of the Reconstruction drama later played out in the rest of the South. Banks had hoped that his military and political service in Louisiana would take him to the White House as Lincoln's successor. But suddenly his record became the subject not of national admiration but of abolitionist and Republican scorn. He had accomplished little during his stay as a military leader, and his labor program for the former slaves looked to most outside observers like an attempt to move the freedmen from slavery to an oppressive serfdom. To recover politically, Banks turned over the freedmen's programs in his department to the two abolitionists who were serving in his army. He put Thomas W. Conway, a Baptist chaplain, in charge of the labor resettlement program and made B. Rush Plumly, a fighting Quaker soldier, the head of his education program for black Louisianians.

The education program was already the pride of the operation that Banks had established for the freedmen in Louisiana. The program grew out of the earlier ideas, first of General Phelps, and then Butler. Each regiment had a special officer with a lieutenant's pay and the title of "Regimental instructor." A captain supervised and directed the entire operation in the segregated troops that Banks called his *Corps d'Afrique*. Despite the difficulties of running an educational operation in the midst of a war, the army program began to bring literacy to hundreds of former slaves, a number of whom became leaders after the war.[21]

Banks had not given much thought to black education outside the army until he came under abolitionist attacks in early 1864. With the help of Conway and Plumly, however, he made an impressive beginning—now judged the first major effort in any state in the South. Pressure had also been coming from black parents who besieged the army labor agents with requests for schools for themselves and their children. Even before Banks ordered that special black schools be set up on all plantations controlled by the army, he had allowed some experimentation in the refugee camps of New Orleans.

On March 22, 1864, when Banks set up a separate Board of Education under Plumly to direct the entire program for black Louisianians, seven black schools with twenty-three teachers and 1,422 students had already been operating in New Orleans. Most of these had begun during the previous six months under the direction of Lieutenant William Stickney of the Eighth Vermont Regiment, who had set them up on the New England model. Teachers from these schools came from various sources. Some came from Northern agencies such as the American Missionary Association, but most came from the vast ranks of unemployed teachers in the local area. By the end of the war, 130 of the 162 teachers in the ninety-five freedmen's schools were native Southern women, most probably from New Orleans. These schools enrolled 9,571 students, about half of the estimated 20,000 black youngsters who resided within Union lines.[22]

Without the earlier development of the New Orleans public schools system, such woman power would not have been available for such a massive effort. No Northern agency would have been able to assemble and send a force that large into the dangerous military zone and sickly climate of southern Louisiana.

The freedmen's program, both in New Orleans and outside the city, remained completely apart from the white public school system that had been resuscitated by the reconstructed Unionist government in 1864. With pressure from Banks the constitutional convention's education committee called for a dual, segregated state system, and the convention eventually

22 The Abraham Lincoln School, one of the largest free schools established for black students by the Union army under Gen. Banks during the Civil War. It occupied the former medical school building of the University of Louisiana.

endorsed their measure after turning back a call for an integrated system by a vote of sixty-six to fifteen. But the delegates balked at the idea of giving the new black system any financial support. At one point they voted for each system to be supported by a separate tax on each racial group. The supporters of Banks killed that proposal, but could replace it with only a compromise that left financing to the new state legislature.

Banks reported the result to Lincoln, carefully phrasing his communique so that it appeared that the legislature was required "to provide means for the education of *all* children without restriction as to color."[23] The president knew better and complained that the provision was inadequate. And he was right. Despite the pleas of the new state superintendent of education, John McNair, the legislature, in the fall of 1864, refused even to set up a committee to investigate possible ways to finance black public schools. They voted instead simply to forbid entry of any black children into the white schools.

In the separate, all-white public school system in New Orleans, the local Unionist board made several significant changes during the 1864-65 term. First, it consolidated the high schools. Its ultimate goal was to have just two high schools—one for boys and one for girls—but, because of continued ethnic concerns, it decided to have two such pairs during a transition period, one pair uptown and one pair downtown. It also reopened the normal school to prepare elementary school teachers. Wanting to re-establish the free textbook policy that had operated in the elementary schools while he was a principal before the war, Superintendent Carter helped convince the board to continue the "unusual liberality, contrasted with that of most other cities." The board even extended the traditional policy by instructing high school principals "to furnish gratuitously all necessary books and stationery to those pupils who cannot purchase them." The board streamlined textbook distribution by creating a central depository with a staff in charge of delivering the books to local schools.[24]

Largely because the income of the McDonogh Fund had been depleted by Confederate authorities, no new schools were built during the war. The city owned twenty-eight of the thirty-eight elementary school buildings and rented the rest. The system did not construct a building for a high school until 1912. As before the war, the number of schools always fell short of demand. More than 7,500 students jammed into the available space bringing classroom size close to the sixty-student maximum set by the board. Union loyalty did not change the parsimonious habits of the city council. It increased the appropriation of the previous year by $20,000, to a total of $207,299.10, but it was not enough to run a school system that quickly drew another 2,500 students. Class size began to swell, and many of the primary classrooms had over seventy-five students and several over a hundred.[25]

The superintendent begged for financial help, noting that he was running a larger school system on less money than his predecessors had before the war. He had high hopes for the schools. The reopened normal school enrolled over two hundred teacher candidates, and he wanted to make it coeducational in order to attract men into the profession. He also urged that the high schools be upgraded by modeling them on the Free Academy of

New York and that the girls high school maintain the same standards set for the boys school. But in a flash, everything collapsed as the war ended.

Lincoln's assassination only dramatized the rapid turn of events. The new state governor, J. Madison Wells, turned from his defiant Unionist stance to a warm welcome of ex-Confederate leaders into his administration. He appointed a new mayor in New Orleans, Hugh Kennedy, who quickly attempted to reverse the military's earlier policies. Kennedy closed the normal school, berated the school board for overspending its budget, and moved to return the school board to its prewar managers. Andrew Johnson, Lincoln's successor as president, had his own plans for Louisiana and Reconstruction, quite different from those of his predecessor. He supported Kennedy, dismissed Banks from his command, and encouraged a total dismantling of the military government.

The revolution suddenly appeared to be moving backward. The new school board, appointed under a council ordinance of August 26, 1865, did not undo everything that had been achieved by the Unionist educators. They cut off the small subsidy to the Couvent school but kept much of the teaching staff of the Civil War school system. They simply changed the administrative personnel.[26] The key men put in charge of the new city and state educational programs mostly came from the uptown, American sectors of New Orleans. Both the new state superintendent, Robert Lusher, and the new superintendent of the city schools, William O. Rogers, had played leading roles before the war in the schools of the First District. Lusher had been a leading board member, and Rogers, had served as superintendent of the First District from 1856 to 1862.

Neither Rogers nor Lusher was anxious to return to the antebellum system. True, they were glad to see power restored to their hands, but they found that Union generals had accomplished some changes that accorded with their own ideas about education. Lusher, although a rabid Confederate and outspoken racist, had little sympathy with planters' demands for restoration of the old order which allowed them the use of state funds to subsidize private academies and to draw just a handful of deserving poor whites into their virtually private classrooms. Both Lusher and Rogers took pride in the New Orleans prewar schools and saw them as a model for a reformed public school system throughout the state.

Rogers candidly praised several key changes made by Benjamin Butler and the Unionist boards during the Civil War. When he got word that the city council was considering a return to the "four District organization which prevailed before the war," he pleaded with the mayor to stop and reflect. Rogers recognized that many wanted to do away with everything that was associated with the "military authority." He also knew that some French-speaking proponents wanted to be released from the yoke of "uniformity" that had ended the bilingual educational program of the downtown districts. But he wanted the mayor to judge the Civil War changes upon their "own merits" and to compare them "with that which formerly existed." He frankly confessed his own belief "that the reasons in favor of the present system are more weighty and more numerous than those in favor of the former system."[27]

He noted that the schools had not suffered under the new system. Enrollment had not only matched the figures in the most prosperous prewar years of 1858-1860 but had even surpassed them while costing less money. The savings had resulted, he argued, from reducing the number of superintendents from four to one and of high schools from eight to four. Consolidation had also cut down costs for printing, books, and supplies. Any new funds, he added, could now be applied to the construction and repair of badly needed facilities.

In Rogers' mind, more than savings resulted from the actions of the Americanizing Unionists. Their consolidation of the city's public schools had also produced some "important educational advantages." He thought it wise to apply "the same standard of excellence" to the whole city. For Rogers, the movement toward greater centralization and bureaucratic control reflected what was taking place in "various portions of our country" and resulted from "the science of education" which favored "uniformity in every large system of Public education." He explained his admiration for the new trend of centralized bureaucracy: "Uniformity in the use of text books, in the nature of studies pursued—in the method of instruction, in the end to be accomplished, admits of classification which shall embrace every mental condition, and in the generalization embrace all the essentials of a sound education. Our Public schools under a single direction and a common impulse, are capable of accomplishing these results."[28]

Rogers had already been moving rapidly in the direction he urged upon the mayor. The large system of forty-two schools and 238 teachers made it impossible for the superintendent to visit every school and counsel with individual teachers as John Shaw had done in 1850. To monitor affairs from his central office, Rogers instead developed a reporting system that made every teacher fill out duplicate forms recording the daily progress of each student. In addition, he insisted on standard grade reports for every student. When a principal expressed his reluctance to trouble his teachers with such tedious tasks, Rogers dashed off a stern admonition that "uniformity is desirable" and that "other things being equal, the closer the classification the better the school system." The forms, he insisted, had to be maintained with "accuracy and completeness."[29]

If Superintendent Rogers liked the wartime reforms, many in the city did not. When, John T. Monroe, the recalcitrant former Confederate mayor came back to office in the summer of 1866 from a Civil War prison, his old gang of Know-Nothing extremists stood ready to wipe away as much of the Unionist school system as they could.[30]

In late July 1866, with the help of the police force and a gang of deputized officers largely made up of his pre-war "Thugs," whom he had once used to terrorize immigrants, Monroe unleashed an orgy of violence to stop the 1864 Unionist constitutional convention from reconvening. The ferocious riot resulted in the deaths of several white Unionist delegates and almost fifty black sympathizers who were parading in support of the convention. The New Orleans Riot, as it came to be known, shocked the nation and led, in large part, to the Congressional Reconstruction Acts of 1867.[31]   Many reluctant Republicans came to the conclusion that only the imposition of universal male suffrage and renewed military control would end such persecution of white and black Unionists in Louisiana and other areas of the South. But until Congress reassembled after the fall elections, Monroe and his cohorts were able to have their way with New Orleans and its school system.

Just before the riot, Monroe's administration had passed an ordinance on July 11, which reorganized the school board. His city council ignored the state constitution of 1864 on the grounds that it had never been approved by the U. S. Congress. The councilmen based their reorganization on the earlier state school law of 1855. They kept a single board but expanded it to twenty-four members, six from each of the antebellum school districts, and all appointed by the city council.

Several leaders on the new board tried to reinstitute additional features of the old system by recommending two assistant superintendents—one uptown and one downtown—and by restoring the bilingual program to the upper grades of the elementary schools and to the high schools in the downtown districts. But the board could not reach any unanimity on these old controversies. Not only did most of the Anglo-American members, in concert with Rogers, resist these ideas, but immigrant leaders also opposed such a restoration. One of the latter, E. C. Kelly, protested that "our Public

23 John T. Monroe,
Mayor (1860-1862; 1866-1867)

Schools were established for the purpose of giving a thorough common school English education and nothing more."[32]

After prolonged wrangling, the board compromised their linguistic feuds by hiring the prominent antebellum creole educator, Alexander Dimitry, as the sole assistant superintendent and by having French taught in all of the schools as a required subject but not as a language of instruction. By 1868, however, they allowed the uptown schools to drop French in the elementary schools. They also allowed any dissatisfied, downtown parents to let their children drop French classes and, at the same time, permitted any unhappy uptown parents to transfer their children to the downtown districts for pre-secondary school French instruction.[33]

Financial costs troubled this board just as it had every previous school board in New Orleans. Rogers tried to explain to Mayor Monroe that the schools, even with the inflated dollars of the Civil War era, had less money on a per capita basis than they had before the war, when they had about $20.00 per student, not much less than Northern cities. Teachers' salaries had fallen behind national averages to levels "less than living rates." Meanwhile, school admissions climbed to 15,421 with an average daily attendance of close to 12,000. After the teachers reacted to the low wages with a petition for salary increases, the city council—confident that they had purged all their Unionist enemies—increased the school appropriations by fifty percent, to $360,000.

If the school board fought bitterly over language issues, it found considerable unanimity in attacking the ideology and the personnel of their Unionist predecessors. They straightaway imposed greater sexual segregation on the students. Creole members were especially anxious to end sexual integration in the handful of coeducational primary schools that had come into existence during the war. But it was the issue of subversive Yankee schoolmarms that most disturbed board members. The Committee on Teachers insisted that "the teachers of girls, especially, must be refined in manner and womanly in deportment. We want no masculine women to teach our girls—no advocate of 'women's rights.' We wish our girls to be gentle, delicate and refined—not bold, forward, masculine." They were convinced that such personnel and ideas had infiltrated the system "during the late unhappy struggle" when "the very dregs of society floated to the surface." On this question they were determined: "It behooves us to exert ourselves to bring back our schools to the high position they occupied before the war desolated our land. Let us place in all vacancies those only who possess the qualifications previously enumerated, adding, of course, to those of unswerving loyalty to the United States government as administered by our noble chief magistrate, Andrew Johnson."[34]

The policies of Andrew Johnson had given Monroe's administration a false sense of security. By the spring of 1867, Congress imposed its Reconstruction Acts, and Philip Sheridan, the general placed in charge of Louisiana, proceeded by removing Monroe and other city officials from office. The general's new appointees, Mayor Edward Heath and a new city council, which included several black members for the first time, seemed equally reluctant to take on the issue of the public schools, because they finally had to face the issue of including black children. Congress allowed the Freedmen's Bureau to be phased out of existence as local authorities gave black Southerners civil equality under the new plan of Reconstruction.

Nowhere in the South did the school issue become more central in Reconstruction politics than in New Orleans. The new constitution drafted by the convention that assembled in the city during the fall of 1867 clearly called for desegregated schools. The demands for integrated schools had been framed even before the convention met. During the spring, black leaders had led a series of massive demonstrations that won an end to segregation on the city's streetcars. Following that victory, black newspapers, along with a few white allies, quickly voiced demands to develop schools without racial bars. The daily, black-owned newspaper, the *Tribune*, gave new meaning to the often repeated dream of the city's public school founders. It called for schools that would serve "a rising generation . . . raised as one people."[35]

To thwart the possibility of black students entering the all-white schools, Monroe's school board moved quickly before they could be replaced. In its first meeting following the passage of the Reconstruction Acts of 1867, members endorsed a resolution "to open Public Schools in each District of this city for the education of colored children." When they asked Sheridan's new city council for approval, their request stirred up only a paralyzing debate, with some council members supporting integration and others defending segregation. After Sheridan added black members to the council, the debates became even more heated. When a majority of the council finally agreed upon a segregated system and added $70,000 to the existing appropriation for the public schools, the mayor added to the chaos by vetoing the measure. The ordinance, Heath declared, called for too little funding and too few black members on the school board. The council responded by passing the measures over his veto. General Sheridan had no chance to break the deadlock, for Andrew Johnson, using his powers as commander-in-chief, removed Sheridan from his post.[36]

In the interim, the old school board—still entrenched in office—moved deftly both to maintain its control over the schools and to avoid integration. When the city council tried to set up a new school board, the old board successfully challenged the new board's legitimacy in court. They also had the support of Johnson's new military appointee, General Winfield Scott Hancock, who encouraged other military officers opposed to integrated schools to transfer the already weakened Freedmen's Bureau schools to the control of the conservative school board.

Immediately after the war, Johnson had reduced the once large black school system of the Union army in Louisiana by destroying its basis of support. In July 1865, when General Banks turned his freedmen's schools over to the army's newly organized Freedmen's Bureau, his former assistant, Thomas W. Conway, became the military commissioner in charge of the bureau's operations in Louisiana. Conway initially supported the schools by using rents collected from plantations that he had confiscated from rebel planters during the war. But in the fall of 1865, Andrew Johnson removed Conway from his command, ordered an end to the taxes imposed by the Banks administration, and returned almost all confiscated lands to former owners whom he had pardoned for acts of rebellion. Thereafter only those black parents who could afford tuition managed to send their children to school. An effort to maintain the remaining Freedmen's Bureau schools by a voluntary taxation scheme among black New Orleanians failed both because most were so poor and because many black leaders also felt that they should press instead for government support of integrated schools. As a result, by 1867, less than a dozen of the Freedmen's Bureau schools survived in New Orleans.[37]

The school board wanted to absorb these remaining schools to keep them all-black. Before they agreed to rehire any of the former teachers, they set up a special committee to investigate the teachers' political views, especially about racial integration. Since the teachers understood that their views might affect their continued employment, some almost certainly hedged their convictions.

All of the white teachers in the uptown schools supported segregation and insisted that the black parents wanted black schools. Black teachers in uptown schools were more circumspect, but they too voiced support for separate schooling. Almost all were associated with black Baptist or Methodist churches which had already accommodated to the color line.

When the investigators crossed into the downtown areas of New Orleans, they found the stronghold of integrationist sentiment. A free black teacher from New York, Edmonia Highgate, refused to consider accepting any position in legally segregated schools. The leaders of the Couvent school refused even to discuss the matter with representatives of a board that they considered illegitimate. Foreign white parents and teachers from France and Italy had already been experimenting with integration in private schools. Such black and white leaders had encouraged Paul Trévigne and other editors of the *New Orleans Tribune* to declare that the time had come to end the divisions of race in the public schools. "When will the right time come? It is, per chance, after we have separated for ten or twenty years the two races in different schools, and when we shall have realized the separation of this nation into two peoples? . . . It will, then be TOO LATE."[38]

No other city in the South could have mustered the determination and spirit to evolve such an experiment with integrated public schools. That unique support for a unitary public school system in New Orleans deserves some explanation. It stemmed from some peculiar qualities and characteristics of the black community in New Orleans. Many of that community's leaders, particularly those with French-speaking, creole backgrounds, had much broader world experience than either the state's conservative white elite or the cautious white Republicans. They had seen alternative ways dealing with racial differences in France, Massachusetts, Mexico, and the West Indies.

Many had also absorbed the revolutionary ideology of republican France rather than the racist thinking of Anglo-America. They had, moreover, by their own educational achievements, defied the assumptions of local racists about limited capabilities of men and women of African ancestry. And finally they had the raw courage to push for a realization of their radical vision of a racially blind public order. Because their daring had already won emancipation and enfranchisement for black Southerners, they now stood ready to try for still greater gains. Their efforts in the constitutional convention of 1867 produced provisions that stipulated that there be "no school established for any race" and that no official could deny admission to any public school on the grounds of race or color.

The 1867 actions of the conservative school board in setting up segregated schools had given the integrationist leaders little hope for justice from that quarter. The board members had sponsored black schools, in the first place, only under the threat of more sweeping action by

Radical Republicans in Congress. And the meager achievements of that board during the next two years only added to the black leaders' dissatisfaction with halfway measures. Ten black schools which first opened on October 14, 1867, eventually took in about 3,000 pupils, after absorbing four more schools from the American Missionary Association in 1869. They were scattered across the city, all housed in substandard facilities. The board limited them to primary grades and refused to open any evening schools for black adults. When the large white majority of voters in New Orleans elected a new city government under the 1868 constitution, the council still refused to grant any funds for the new black schools and held to racial segregation in the schools. Embarrassed Freedmen's Bureau officials began to reopen schools for the unmet needs of black children.[39]

Since the new state constitution clearly outlawed segregated schools, black parents immediately tested the legitimacy of the local school board's policies in New Orleans. When their well-publicized efforts gained admission of twenty-eight girls to one white school, the board reacted by chastising the principal for violating "a cardinal rule" of their system and threatening to dismiss her.[40] The board removed the twenty-eight girls and issued defiant orders that all principals of white schools had to bar "any children of color."[41]

The school board's recalcitrant stance on segregation brought a heavy cost. In order to maintain a dual racial system without any major increase in their funding, it had to make financial cutbacks in other areas. The board dismissed the assistant superintendent, cut staff salaries, and fired a number of teachers. It also transformed the once proud normal school into a simple institute offering only those pedagogical courses that the private Peabody School Fund was willing to support. In their most damaging moves, the board members also ended the system's famous free textbook policy, shut down the school library, and cut teachers' salaries five to fifteen percent, depending on their rank.[42]

When the Republican governor, Henry Clay Warmoth, refused to enforce the state constitutional and legislative mandates requiring desegregation of the public schools, more assertive Republican legislators took unusual measures to sidestep the entrenched New Orleans school board. In March 1870 (after a bungled effort in 1869), the radical Republican leaders passed an act that totally revamped both the state and city school systems. The new law divided the state into six divisions supervised by a state board made up of Thomas W. Conway, the state superintendent elected in 1868, and the six superintendents whom he appointed to supervise each of the

24 Black leaders from the Constitutional Convention of 1867-1868 and the Louisiana legislature. Note the prominence given to the measures for desegregation of the public schools.

districts. The new all-powerful superintendent also appointed members of the local boards, which were limited to managing the daily affairs of the schools within their own divisions.

The Sixth Division, which comprised New Orleans, went into operation only after a court order finally forced the stubborn, old city board to disband. When the new authorities began to desegregate the schools, many white parents removed their children and enrolled them in the private and parochial schools that rapidly proliferated throughout the city. Until 1867, the Catholic church had established no more than a dozen schools in New Orleans. But even before the old board was disbanded, some parents had already begun to remove their children to Catholic schools, which jumped in numbers to thirty-four by 1871 and forty-nine by 1874. Despite this exodus, many whites remained in the system, and after the initial shock of 1870-71, many others returned, largely because of the prohibitive cost and poor quality of the private schools.[43]

Since the new school system dropped all racial designations in its records for its students and staff, it is difficult to gauge the level of integration that the school system reached. Most of the desegregation resulted, moreover, from parental initiative rather than school board directives. The best estimates suggest that about a third of the schools remained almost all white, a third virtually all black, and a third integrated. Almost a thousand, or about a quarter of the black students, attended integrated schools, and the number grew each year because the integrated schools were judged the best in the system. Most of the integrated schools were in the downtown creole and German neighborhoods. Virtually every school had some black children. The assertiveness of the black creole families rather than the tolerance of the so-called Latin white community explains the achievement.

Some desegregation also took place in the uptown, American sector. Newspaper reports noted at least six integrated schools in those districts after the black lieutenant governor, Oscar J. Dunn, led the way by enrolling his four adopted children in a formerly white school. P. B. S. Pinchback's newspaper, the *Louisianian*, promoted the new system and noted that several black children made top scores in the annual examinations given in the prestigious Fisk school of the First District.[44]

The record demonstrates that, after the first year, desegregation proceeded rather peacefully for the next three years. The success confounded the assertion of the local naysayers, led by the New Orleans *Picayune*. It declared that "the colored race must be considered as a nation by itself so far as relates to education. It is a fact most thoroughly fixed in human nature and in our condition, that the children of whites will never be

25 Henry Clay Warmoth.

mixed in private or public schools with the children of the colored." And it went on to pronounce that "enthusiastic visionaries, educational quacks and political monntebanks may scheme, and croak, and manoeuver as they may, but the result will not be changed . . . . the commingling can never be completed."[45]

Nearly 5,000 white students, or twenty percent of the 24,892 students in the schools, left during the first year of integration, but by 1875 the city's public schools enrolled 26,251 pupils. Some of the 1875 total came from the school system of the town of Carrollton that was annexed to New

26 Lower Girls High School. This rented building at the corner of Royal and Gov. Nicholls streets housed the first desegregated public high school in the South.

Orleans in 1872, and some also reflected greater black student enrollment, but all sides generally conceded that white students returned to the public schools despite desegregation. The private schools could not match the quality of the public schools or raise the funds necessary to maintain themselves. Former state superintendent Robert M. Lusher lent his prestige to a fund-raising drive for a set of private schools, but even he finally acknowledged that not enough money could be collected.[46]

Good management and substantial new funding helped the public schools prosper until 1875. James B. Carter, the former Civil War superintendent, got the new system off to a good start, and his replacement in 1873, Charles W. Boothby, "conducted a school system good enough to win loyalty from the teachers and even occasional compliments from the opposition."[47] The presence of several prominent and moderate white Southerners on the local board also helped, particularly that of the famous Confederate general James Longstreet, who felt it was time for the South to heal racial divisions and move forward. For a while, a substantial group of New Orleans businessmen also proved brave enough to step forward and join key black leaders in public statements supporting desegregation of the public schools as well as the public accommodations of the city.[48]

As had been the case throughout the tumultuous era, the teachers and principals showed remarkable fortitude in maintaining classroom order and efficiency. George Washington Cable, a former Confederate soldier, who was assigned by his newspaper, the *Picayune*, to expose the expected ills of the system, instead came away impressed by the camaraderie of the black and white teachers in the schools. At the highpoint, black teachers made up about eleven percent of the teachers (48 of 440).[49] Cable wrote: "I saw, to my great and rapid edification, white ladies teaching Negro boys; colored women showing the graces and dignity of mental and moral refinement, ladies in everything save society's credentials; children and youth of both races standing in the same classes and giving each other peaceable, friendly, effective competition."[50]

Some of the staff morale of the teachers stemmed, no doubt, from the Republicans' success in gaining substantial new funds for the school system, funds that allowed them to increase teacher salaries and upgrade facilities. An increase of the state millage formed the major source of new funding. In New Orleans, the appropriation jumped from the $360,000 high point under the old board to over $480,000 in 1874. In addition, the local school board uncovered a surplus in the McDonogh School Fund that permitted construction of five more McDonogh elementary schools, the star facilities

74

27 General James Longstreet. This former Confederate officer served as a board member of the New Orleans public schools from 1870 to 1877.

28 George Washington Cable. The famous New Orleans writer defended the integration of New Orleans public schools.

of the New Orleans system.[51]   Even the election of a black state superintendent of education, William G. Brown, did not cause any immediate
disturbance. Indeed, his efforts capped off the city's public educational
system in 1873 by setting up the Agricultural and Mechanical College with
federal land grant funds. This college maintained an integrated student body
and produced both black and white graduates before it was moved to Baton
Rouge and made part of the all-white Louisiana State University after
Reconstruction.[52]

It was not educational failure that eventually ended the daring experiment
in New Orleans, which had all the elements of a model school system. It
was rather new national and local developments that led to a change of
mood. The heavy taxation undoubtedly became burdensome after the severe
depression of 1873 cast the national and local economies into ruinous
decline. Corruption in both the national administration and the state
government also helped undermine what little white support the
Republicans had in Louisiana. But the turning point came when the federal
government seemed to signal its unwillingness to enforce the Reconstruction Amendments in the South.

First in isolated North Louisiana and later in New Orleans, influential
leaders of the terrorist, paramilitary White League instigated well-
orchestrated violence against the state government in September 1874.
Federal troops put down that attempted *coup d'etat*, but two months later, in
December, the same leaders initiated another wave of violence, this time
directly against the integrated schools. Republican loss of the U. S. House
of Representatives in the fall elections gave the conservative Louisiana
leaders renewed hope. Indeed, the action of the Republican lame-duck
Congress in December to exclude public schools from the mandates of
integration in the Civil Rights Act, passed in 1875, reopened, in the local
press, a shrill debate over the New Orleans schools.[53]

The debate, local and national, coincided with the entrance of the first
black students into the prestigious and still lily-white Upper Girls High
School. Black girls and boys had already been attending the other two high
schools in downtown New Orleans. But the timing of the desegregation of
the Upper Girls High produced three days of rioting, during which white
high school boys, cheered on by the newspapers, raced through the
integrated schools of the city, intimidating teachers and physically evicting
black children. In the process, they mistakenly expelled some swarthy
Jewish students. At first, some whites of the city applauded their
"chivalrous" actions in saving white girls from integration. But when the
youths also smashed over 350 windows and killed a black man and child,

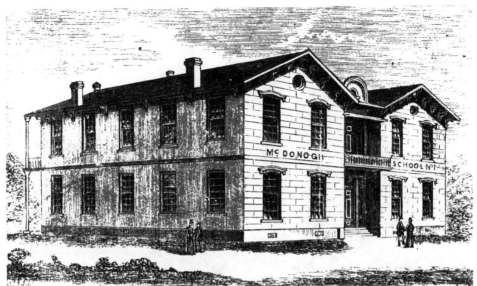

McDonogh No. 1 Public School.

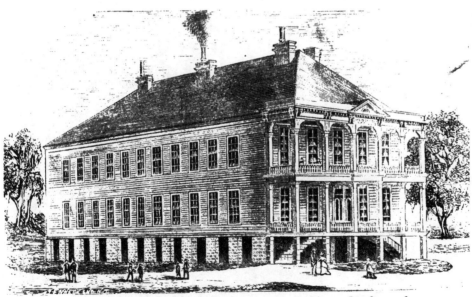

McDonogh No. 2 Public School.

29 The first six McDonogh schools. The Reconstruction school board uncovered the misuse of the McDonogh Fund by Confederate authorities and reestablished the legacy on a sounder basis. The board, besides building five of the schools, began naming all after the benefactor and numbering each of them. Reconstruction leaders also brought to the public's attention that John McDonogh wished to educate both black and white students.

78

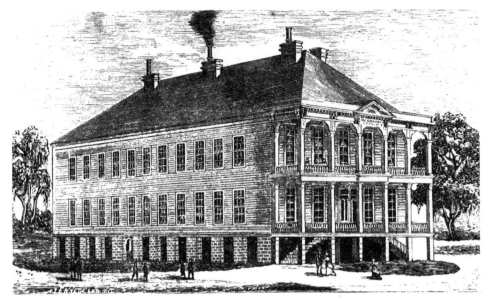

McDonogh No. 3 Public School.

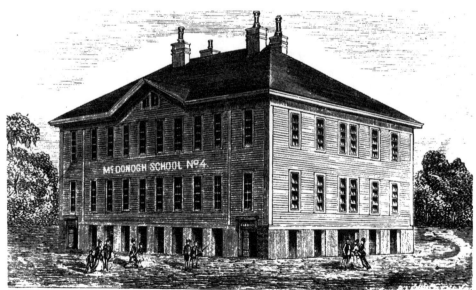

McDonogh No. 4 Public School.

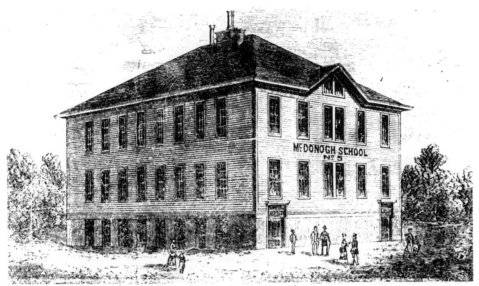

McDonogh No. 5 Public School.

McDonogh No. 6 Public School.

30 William G. Brown, State Superintendent of Education, 1872-1876. The only African-American ever to have served in that post, Brown was born in New Jersey and educated in the British West Indies.

even the White League leaders called a halt to the violence. To help calm the mayhem, the school board shut down the schools a week early for the Christmas holidays.[54]

The rioting, which continued on and off, did not halt integration. The schools reopened and continued on their old basis for another two years. All of the high schools finally accepted black students. The last furor occurred when a black mathematics teacher, E. J. Edmunds, joined the faculty of the elite Boys Central High School. Despite his credentials as the fifth ranking graduate in class of two hundred students at the famous Ecole Polytechnique in Paris, and a distinguished record as an officer in the French army, the newspapers of the city judged the New Orleans native incompetent to teach until he publicly challenged any white mathematician to meet him at the blackboard in a contest of abilities.[55]

The integrated schools ultimately collapsed not because teachers and administrators proved unable or unwilling to educate children in racially integrated classrooms. Indeed, if anything they demonstrated considerable success. As the careful scholar Louis Harlan concluded, the remarkable experiment ended only because it "depended too heavily on one *sine qua non*, the temporary sojourn of federal power in the South."[56] And that sojourn ended with the contested presidential election of 1876, which was marred by Republican corruption and Democratic violence. To resolve the disputed election, which depended upon the contested electoral votes of Louisiana, national Republican leaders cynically agreed to turn the state government over to the white Redeemers in return for an agreement to have Louisiana's electoral votes cast for Rutherford B. Hayes as president.

The bargain, worked out finally in the Compromise of 1877, led to the appointment of a new school board which not only ended school desegregation in New Orleans but also brought about the steady deterioration of public education in the city and the state generally, both for black and for white students. The new Bourbon leaders who gained control of the state had never shown much interest in public education either before or after the Civil War. During the next quarter of a century, their actions would almost completely undermine the proud accomplishments of the public schools in New Orleans.

III

Reaction and Failure

During the late nineteenth century, public education in New Orleans spiraled downward as city leaders—both black and white—waged a raging battle for political control of the city and state. The competing groups camouflaged themselves with party labels, but the primary issue was clear. They fought to decide whether the newly enfranchised black voters would or could continue meaningful political participation. Led by such stalwarts as P. B. S. Pinchback and C. C. Antoine, the black community eventually lost the battle for political influence and, with it, much of the educational initiative generated between 1868 and 1876.

The political reaction was not sudden, nor was the educational loss immediate. True, in 1877, the removal of federal troops and the return of the Democrats to power ushered in dramatic change in Louisiana, but black Louisianians, especially those in New Orleans, continued to vote until the end of the century. Because they actively resisted the decision to reduce them to an inferior status in society, they lost civil rights and privileges in small, significant increments, not in one climactic fall. White Louisianians frequently disagreed about the educational agenda for black New Orleanians. As a result, the nadir in black schools came not in 1877, but at the opening of the twentieth century, soon after Louisiana officials finally disfranchised almost all black voters in the city and state.

The educational collapse may have been most dramatic for black New Orleanians, but all groups suffered after Democratic Redeemers launched their determined attack on the reforms in public education that had occurred during Reconstruction. Between 1877 and 1900, the quality of public schools declined drastically. By the early 1880s, the school board had to close the schools for several months of the year and even beg Northern foundations for outright charity. It was a humiliating and sad spectacle for an urban system once ranked among the nation's best.

Problems began soon after a new twenty-member school board took office on April 4, 1877, and moved quickly to elect Thomas J. Semmes as president and to restore William O. Rogers to his former position as

31 P. B. S. Pinchback. Lieutenant governor of Louisiana, 1868-1872. He also served as governor of the state in 1872 and as a member of the New Orleans school board from 1872 to 1877.

32 C. C. Antoine. Lieutenant governor of Louisiana, 1872-1876.

superintendent of the New Orleans public schools. The new leadership resulted from the complicated bargaining between the national Republicans and the state Democrats. In early 1877, both sides acceded to the election of Rutherford B. Hayes as president and to a Democratic takeover in Louisiana. Francis T. Nicholls, the new Louisiana governor, negotiated with P. B. S. Pinchback and other black leaders for their support of the new arrangements. Among other requests, Pinchback asked for black appointments to the city school board, and the new state superintendent, Robert M. Lusher, used his share of the appointments that the state legislature had divided between his office and the city council to name four black leaders: Louis A. Martinet, Joseph A. Craig, George H. Fayerweather, and Pascal M. Tourne.[1]

Many black Republican leaders criticized Pinchback's cooperation with the Democrats, but none showed a way to reverse the actions of the new Democratic board. Only a major commitment by the federal government could have sustained the Reconstruction school system in the face of the massive white hostility and violence that reigned in Louisiana. Within two months of their appointment in April 1877, the new school board members sought to codify the sentiments of the white community for a racially segregated school system. A three-member committee led by Archibald Mitchell, outlined the rationale for a such a system. Defying reality, they insisted that "personal observation and universal testimony concur to establish the fact that public education has greatly deteriorated since colored and white children were admitted indiscriminately into the same schools."[2]   And to give added sanction to their proposal for segregation,

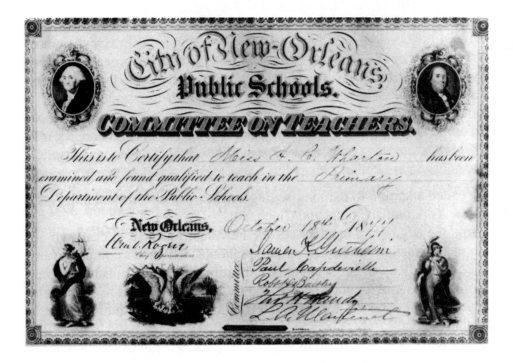

33 Note the signature of Louis A. Martinet, a black member of the board who opposed resegregation of the New Orleans public schools in 1877. He later served as a key proponent of the *Plessy* v. *Ferguson* suit during the 1890s to stop segregation on state railroads.

34 Governor Francis T. Nicholls.

they called attention to the long-segregated schools in Northern cities such
as New York, Philadelphia, and Cincinnati.

From the beginning, members of the new board wanted to change more
than racial practices of the city's public schools. Mitchell's committee also
called for the end of all secondary education; members considered high
schools a waste of public funds. The two recommendations must have
stunned the new board, for they deferred action on both until their next
regular meeting.

When the board met on July 3, 1877, a large delegation of black New
Orleanians presented a petition against reestablishing separate schools.
About a week earlier Governor Nicholls had already rebuffed their demands

that he live up to his public pledge to protect the civil rights of black Louisianians and enforce the integration provisions of the 1868 constitution. Now the same group, led once again by the black businessman, Aristide Mary, took their case directly to the school board. The board listened to the appeal but quickly passed the earlier resolution of Archibald Mitchell:

> Whereas: This board, in the performance of its paramount duty; which is to give the best education possible with the means at its disposal to the whole population, without regard to race, color or previous condition, is assured that this end can be best attained by educating the different races in separate schools.[3]

The proposal to resegregate the schools passed by a vote of fifteen to three. Joseph Craig, a member of a "colored conservative club," broke with his three black colleagues and supported the resolution. His vote made little difference in the outcome, but it foreshadowed a long debate among black Southerners about how to respond to the new Democratic regimes in the South. Many, like Craig, thought that accommodation to segregation would protect other civil rights, bring social peace, and perhaps even promote some advancement in black public education. Eventually similar views would be championed by Booker T. Washington, but he was not the first to evoke such a benign vision of a New South.[4]

In bold contrast to Craig, other black New Orleanians marshaled what became the most assertive resistance to segregation anywhere in the South. Their counterattacks began with opposition to the resegregation of the New Orleans schools and lasted until the end of the century when, in the 1890s, many of the same black leaders took a suit against railroad segregation to the U. S. Supreme Court. True, they lost the famous *Plessy* v. *Ferguson* case in 1896, but they left a legacy of protest not just for New Orleans but for the entire nation. Few have tried to understand their reasoning or their motivations.

In 1877, Robert M. Lusher, the new state superintendent of education, publicly speculated that the black leaders who protested segregation merely wished to defend a caste of racially mixed people who had been free before the Civil War. He thought that they did not want to go to school with the darker-skinned freedmen. To mollify them, Lusher even proposed offering a tripartite system of segregation. Nowhere, however, did the black protest leaders ever make such a suggestion. Instead, they saw the

35   Robert M. Lusher

school issue in a much larger context. They fought against the very notion of racial caste and recognized, well before most other Americans, that legalized segregation in any form would promote total subordination of black Americans and inflict the whole community with unending social problems.

In 1877, these leaders tried valiantly to mobilize resistance to what may have seemed inevitable to others. According to the *Weekly Louisianian*, a local black newspaper, attendance at their protest rallies was "large and enthusiastic." The participants adopted resolutions condemning the school board for violating the 1868 state constitution that prohibited the establishment of separate schools. After the board rejected their petitions in its July 3 meeting, attorneys for the black leaders filed a constitutional suit in the state courts on behalf of Paul Trévigne, a prominent Reconstruction journalist, who had once served on the school board. At first, the judge issued a temporary injunction that stopped the school board from proceeding with the resegregation plan, but later lifted the restraining order and dismissed the entire suit on the grounds that Trévigne failed to show any personal injury and that he had filed the suit too late, after the board had begun resegregating the schools.

Since the judge had skirted the central constitutional question, another of the Reconstruction stalwarts, Arnold Bertonneau, filed a second suit. Bertonneau may have been the first Louisianian to make a public call for integrated schools during the Civil War, and, it had been he, who as a delegate in the Constitutional Convention of 1867, had shaped the disputed Article 135, which declared that "there shall be no separate school or institution of learning established exclusively for any race by the State of Louisiana."[5]   In defending his threatened achievement, Bertonneau tried to avoid the technical issues of the Trévigne case by registering his own children at the all-white Fillmore School. Rebuffed in his efforts by the principal, he charged the school board and its agents with violating his civil rights as outlined in the Fourteenth Amendment of the U. S. Constitution and in the famous Article 135 of the Louisiana constitution.

Judge W. B. Woods waited until February 1879 to reach his decision. In his opinion, he noted that the federal courts had already permitted school segregation in the North, rejected the argument that such a practice violated the Fourteenth Amendment, and insisted that the New Orleans school board had adopted policies which insured that "both races are treated precisely alike."[6]   The judge simply ignored the clear mandate of the Louisiana constitution.

Before any further action could take place, the state drew up a new constitution, in 1879. It eliminated the provisions of Article 135 and removed another provision that required public schools in every parish of the state.   The Redeemers thus brought to an end the "only serious experiment with public school integration in the postwar South."[7]   In addition, they almost destroyed the foundations of all public education in the state.

The new school board in New Orleans had not bothered to wait for the outcome of the court challenges to resegregate the school system. The board ignored the initial injunction and, under the leadership of the veteran superintendent, William O. Rogers, moved quickly to accomplish its objective. During the rapid reorganization in the summer of 1877, Rogers went beyond racial segregation. He was also personally opposed to the sexual integration of the schools that had been implemented by his Republican predecessors. Although the board had spoken its mind only on racial separation, Rogers wanted to end "both mixtures." He dismissed the argument that "the co-education of the sexes" only mirrored the experience of the family where boys and girls were reared together in the home. "Children thrown together in a large public school," he countered, "are not members of the same happy family and never will be this side of the millennium."

His condemnation of coeducation reflected his larger opinions about the place of women in the society. He found "the characteristics of the female mind . . . distinct from those of the other sex." That conviction as well as other, undisclosed "sound reasons based on physical, mental and moral grounds" convinced him that "the education of the sexes should not be run in the same groove." He decided therefore that, as he carried out the board's demand for a color line, he would also draw "a line between the sexes."[8]

Although coeducation had never begun in the public high schools and separate education of the sexes had always been deeply rooted in the Catholic schools of the city, no significant outcry had challenged the move toward coeducation in elementary schools during the early 1870s. The return to sexual segregation stemmed purely from the stubborn conservatism of Rogers, and it reflected more than pedagogical theories. Rogers simply believed women should be subordinated within the entire school system. Despite the great numerical predominance of women teachers, who made up almost ninety-five percent of the staff of the New Orleans public schools, Rogers felt that men had to retain total control of the system. He had made his position clear some years earlier when he opposed the growing presence and influence of women teachers at the conventions of the National Education Association. He told one of the officers of that influential body that, despite "the great work done by the women in the education of youth," he believed that "man is the proper representative of women in all public assemblies. I do not believe in 'women's rights conventions' in any form."[9]

Rogers' decision to restore sexual segregation in the elementary schools added considerably to the expenses and the disruption of the schools for the next decade. In every former municipal district, the system not only had to find separate facilities for black and white children but also for the boys and girls of each racial group—four schools in place of one.

The reversal of coeducation in 1877 had a lasting impact on the schools, for New Orleans held on to the policy much longer than any city in the nation. The policy also subordinated women educators and laid the basis for bitter and disruptive feuds between the dominant male managers and the increasingly restive female teachers that lasted well into the twentieth century.

Deteriorating financial support from the state legislature and the city council created further havoc. Immediate and severe reductions forced the officials of the public schools in New Orleans to make painful choices. Revenues for the schools came from state and city appropriations and from a special state poll tax. State legislation in 1877 reduced the five-mill school tax established by the Republicans to just one mill. The share for New Orleans, based on its percentage of educables, represented a mere pittance. New Orleanians complained, moreover, that they paid more than half of what the state collected in property taxes but got little more than a fifth of the state funds. The state poll tax of one dollar per voter not only cost the school board time and money to collect, but it also brought little revenue since the tax was voluntary and not a requirement for voting. The board received less than $750 from that source in 1878 and during the rest of the century never more than $5,000. Even after the depression of the 1870s ended, appropriations from both the city and the state continued to decline. Finally they sank to less than half of the Reconstruction peak. Indeed, as Superintendent Rogers pointed out, funding fell below the levels maintained during the 1850s.

It was more than the state's declining economy that created the fiscal crisis. The planters and merchants who dominated state politics after 1877 wanted to keep taxes in the city and the state extremely low. In New Orleans, they were joined by urban politicians who traded low assessments for the votes of small property owners. Many in the city's large Catholic and Lutheran population, moreover, tolerated the sorry state of public schools because they were sending their children to the sixty or so parochial schools that had been established by the end of the 1870s.[10]

The aftermath of Reconstruction revealed that Louisiana had generated little support for public education among its native white citizenry. Before the Civil War, public education never extended much beyond the confines of the school system of New Orleans, which had been founded by a commercial elite originally from the Northeast. The turmoil of Reconstruction only disguised that reality. After the downfall of the Republican party diminished the influence of black leaders, just a handful of Democrats who had been officials in the antebellum New Orleans system took up the advocacy of public schools. Despite their conservatism on racial matters, their defense of public education made them a beleaguered minority among state leaders in Louisiana.

In 1877, the call for the elimination of the high schools by Archibald Mitchell's committee exhibited the ambivalence about public education even on the New Orleans school board. To be sure, the committee had to face tough choices posed by a forty-percent cut in the city's public school budget. Mitchell informed the board, however, that more than a lack of funds guided the outlook of his committee: "We do not regard our High Schools as indispensable requisite to an efficient system of public education, and are inclined to believe that teaching advanced studies at the public expense is an abuse of our educational system."[11]

Superintendent Rogers tried to preserve as much of the school system as he could while trying to maintain some semblance of equity in the segregated system. He had to make cruel choices. He closed one of the two girls high schools and drastically cut remaining enrollments by raising examination scores required for entrance. But his efforts salvaged only a two-year secondary school curriculum.[12] He understood that the high schools, especially the girls high school had provided the city's public school system with almost all of its teachers. Indeed, in November 1877, he even managed to open a tiny high school program for sixteen black girls in order to train black teachers for the segregated system and to give the appearance of a separate-but-equal system. To find funds to operate the schools, he cut teachers' salaries by forty percent.

The savage cuts in 1877 and 1878 were only the beginning. When the constitutional convention met in 1879, the delegates placed draconian restrictions on all public expenditures. They limited the state legislature to six mills of taxation for all purposes and insisted that no more than one-and-a-half mills could be spent on all levels of public education. They also crippled educational leadership in the state by setting a cap of three thousand dollars for the entire operation of the state superintendent's office and two hundred dollars for the salary of a parish superintendent. Special provisions exempted the Orleans Parish public schools from most restrictions, but another section of the constitution inflicted an almost fatal blow to New Orleans. The convention lowered the city's power to tax from fifteen to ten mills, at the very time local assessors were dropping property assessments.

Educators quickly recognized the terrible prospect they faced. Both Robert Lusher, the state superintendent, and William O. Rogers, the city superintendent, had expected the constitutional convention to promote "the cause of popular Education." Their new co-edited magazine, the *Louisiana Journal of Education*, initially greeted the assembled delegates with high hopes: "We confidently look to this Convention . . . to place our state system of public Education upon a firm, liberal, and permanent basis." The outcome of the convention, however, made Lusher and Rogers warn of "the possible disintegration of institutions which have prospered through

36 William O. Rogers.

many years." Experience under the new constitution only heightened their fears. During the first school year after the constitution was adopted, the editors complained that the entire public school system had fallen into a "slough of despondency." And by 1882, they were openly condemning the 1879 constitution as "a standing menace to public education in this state."[13]

Neither Rogers nor Lusher, who was dismissed as state superintendent in 1880, could argue with the much harsher condemnation of a former Republican school board member in New Orleans, the Rev. Joseph C. Hartzell. He used the editorial page of his Methodist weekly paper to excoriate his old Democratic foes:

> To such straits has Bourbon ignorance, stupidity and folly brought the late bountiful system of free schools established and maintained during the existence of a republican form of government.
>
> The minority, now in power by virtue of stuffed ballot boxes, and the physical enforcement of their rule in defiance of the laws of the land, have shown themselves to be incompetent to deal with any great measures of public welfare dictated by enlightened statesmanship. Repudiation of the state debt, destruction of the school system, and the exodus of thousands of her people from misrule, are the manifest results of White League supremacy in Louisiana.[14]

Under the constitution of 1879, each year seemed to bring tougher choices for the New Orleans school board, as the city government cut deeper into its already meager appropriations for the public schools. Usually black students and female teachers had to bear the brunt of the board's decisions. By the 1881-1882 school year, Rogers managed to restore a three-year secondary program with one high school for boys and another for girls. But after the removal of all black appointees on the board in 1881, the board ended all classes for black students after the sixth grade. They took the action, in part, because P. B. S. Pinchback had won a concession in the Constitutional Convention of 1879 that promised a black college in New Orleans. Southern University opened its doors in 1881 and partially compensated for the loss of educational opportunities several years earlier in the public schools of New Orleans. The necessity to run both elementary and secondary classes on its tiny state appropriation of $10,000, however, kept Southern from becoming a real institution of higher education.[15]

Financial cutbacks seriously eroded elementary public education in New Orleans for many poor white and almost all black students by ending the Reconstruction policy of free textbooks for indigent students. Recognizing

37 Southern University. After this black state college closed in 1913, its campus became the site of Xavier Preparatory School, a Catholic high school for black students. Xavier opened in 1915 and continues to occupy the site.

that only "about ten per cent of the colored children in our schools are able to obtain a full supply of books required for their daily lessons," Rogers had to beg the Yankee philanthropists of John F. Slater Fund for their help: "While conscious that this statement is not a flattering or pleasing exhibit of our educational work, I can only say that we cannot help it, and that our teachers are doing the best they can . . . ." Despite his steadfast defense of segregation, Rogers showed some genuine concern for the education of black children. He wrote the Slater Fund officials of his own desire "to further the noble cause which you have undertaken—the amelioration of the present condition of the colored people and their advancement in intelligence, virtue, and useful citizenship." A year later, after the Slater Fund failed to help buy textbooks, Rogers excused the teachers in all of the system's eleven black schools from keeping up with the prescribed curriculum, thus ending all appearance of equal education for black pupils.[16]

By 1883, after the city and state cut their appropriations even further, problems grew so desperate that the school board closed the schools for most of the first semester because it had no money to pay its teachers. That action marked the lowest point in the history of the public schools of New Orleans since their founding in 1841. Public education was shut down.[17]

The closure returned the public schools of New Orleans to the indigent system that had prevailed in the state before 1841. During the fall of 1883, the board authorized teachers to conduct classes only for those children whose parents could afford to pay tuition. In the past, the board had allowed teachers to conduct private evening and summer classes so that the teachers could supplement their meager salaries.[18]

Only about 5,000 students attended the private classes. Most students, whose parents could not afford the tuition, went without instruction during the forced school vacation. In a candid appraisal made to an agent of the Peabody Educational Fund, Rogers admitted that "only a very small number" of black students showed up for classes because of the poverty of their parents.[19] Worse still, many of the children of the black and white poor failed to return when the schools reopened in December. School officials estimated that only a small number of the missing students transferred to private schools. They thought that some of the youngsters found jobs but that others joined the "ungoverned *gamin* of the streets."[20]

Rogers and other officials of the schools hoped that the closing of schools would shock the city into greater concern for public education. But they badly miscalculated the public mood. The city council paid no heed to the board's elaborate printed appeal. Indeed, the council stubbornly refused to raise its appropriation.[21] Political leaders had other matters on their minds, specifically the costly World's Industrial and Cotton Centennial Exposition, which they promoted as a means to stimulate the economy of the Deep South.

When Major Edward A. Burke, the state treasurer and leading Regular Democrat, first ballyhooed the idea of the Cotton Exposition, Rogers himself got caught up in the New South mood and tried to use the extravaganza to promote public education in Louisiana. While the schools were closed in the fall of 1883, he urged Burke to set up an exhibit on education in the South and particularly in Louisiana. He tried to explain that education fit into the New South agenda because it lay "at the

38 E. A. Burke. After the Cotton Centennial, but while still state treasurer, Burke was accused of taking more than $700,000 in state funds under his control. He avoided prosecution by remaining out of the United States.

foundation of individual progress and public prosperity." Recalling the American Centennial Fair at Philadelphia in 1876 and the Paris Exposition of 1878, he pointed out how those fairs had stimulated educational progress in both Europe and the United States. He felt that exhibits about the "art and technical schools of St. Louis, Philadelphia, New York and elsewhere might be of practical advantage in this section." He noted that he had just used the enforced holiday of the New Orleans public schools to visit "some of the school systems of Northern cities" and had convinced leaders in the National Education Association to appoint a committee to promote an educational exhibit at the Cotton Exposition.[22]

By the spring of 1884, Rogers still had no positive response from Burke. He had already secured the promise of a mini-convention while the fair was open, to be attended by fifty leading superintendents of the National Education Association. In addition, he had organized the Louisiana Educational Society, made up of leading educators and businessmen who agreed to serve as a lobbying group for public education. With the help of Warren Easton, one of his former elementary school principals who had become state superintendent of education in 1884, Rogers also organized the State Teachers Association. As the first president of the teachers group, he planned for a joint meeting with the N. E. A. superintendents during the fair in late February 1885.[23]

Well before the fair opened, however, Rogers gave up. The corrupt managers of the exposition proved unable to raise enough money to open their extravaganza on time. They also left Rogers to scramble alone for money to display the work of the New Orleans public schools. Since the school board faced another bleak round of appropriations for the 1884-1885 term, Rogers had to beg Warren Easton, the state superintendent of education, for $250 or $300 to install an exhibit on the city's own schools at the New Orleans fair. Although his local board had promised the funds earlier, he confessed to Easton that he feared "to bring up the matter again before the new Board in the present condition of our finances."[24]

Before his promising assemblage of educators converged on New Orleans, Rogers suddenly resigned as superintendent of the public schools in New Orleans. Because the city council made its appropriations on a yearly basis from January to December, he always had to face uncertainty for the second semester of any school year. When the city council refused to remedy the budgetary straits in their annual appropriations for 1885, the veteran superintendent balked at facing another round of budgetary cuts in mid-year. He had had enough.

Jumping at the opportunity of a job as secretary of the recently established Tulane University in the city, Rogers informed his board in late November that he would begin his new post in January 1885. It was a particularly low point for public education in New Orleans. The Tulane corporation took over all property in the city formerly belonging to the University of Louisiana and the Agricultural and Mechanical College, which had been moved to Baton Rouge and made a part of L. S. U. Rogers was not the only public educator to sense the terrible prospect for public education in the state. The president of Louisiana State University, William Preston Johnston, had also left public education to take over the presidency of Tulane University.[25]

In his last appearance before his board, Rogers referred to the "privations and embarrassments" in the city's public schools. Unlike other educators in the state, he knew that Louisiana Democrats could no longer blame the collapse on the specter of integration or on corrupt Republican officials. Indeed, in his educational journal, he frequently chastised leaders for blaming the state's educational problems on flawed Northern ideals or Republican scapegoats. Both he and his successor, Ulric Bettison, acknowledged that the cause for "the cloud" which had so long hung over the schools resulted from the refusal of officials of the city and the state to provide the resources necessary to carry out a decent system of public education in Louisiana.[26]

When the school superintendents from other cities in the United States showed up at the fair in late February 1885, they tried to be generous with their colleagues in Louisiana and other areas of the South. In reports to the N. E. A. convention later that summer, Warren Easton declared that the New Orleans exposition demonstrated that "old prejudices were passing away" in the South and that a "new era" was dawning for public schools. A northern educator from Boston, A. D. Mayo, who edited the *National Journal of Education*, was less sanguine about what he had seen. Reflecting the growing racism among even the national education hierarchy, he evoked the bond felt, he said, by many Northern white leaders for the problems that those of "Anglo-Saxon descent" faced in dealing with "freedmen, of another race, in an almost complete state of ignorance of the very elements of knowledge." He called upon "the foremost people of the North to strike hands with their brethren of the South" and to give them "the aid and comfort that comes from hearty sympathy and appreciation." Aware of the economic and political problems of states like Louisiana, he advocated the remedy that many in the N. E. A. had championed since the Civil War. He

39 Ulric Bettison. After his service as superintendent, he became a
professor of education at Newcomb College in New Orleans.

called upon "the whole body of American teachers" to demand that Congress and the president "enact a law for national aid to education."[27]

Teachers in the public schools of Louisiana demonstrated their own willingness to seek national help by endorsing the call for a national educational bill which would appropriate funds on the basis of the number of illiterates in each state. At one point or another, both Louisiana senators voted for national educational bills, but Democratic politicians elsewhere in the South resisted such remedies because they feared renewed federal interference in the region's racial order. Until the late 1890s major leaders in the national Republican party continued to threaten to enforce the voting rights of black Southerners. And for most white Southern leaders, including those in Louisiana, the subordination of black Southerners remained a higher priority than the improvement of public education.

Ulric Bettison, the new superintendent of education in New Orleans, had risen from the ranks of teachers in the city's public schools and served as principal of an elementary boys school before and during Reconstruction. Throughout his four-year term from 1885 to 1888, he had no greater success in raising the funding for the school system. Reluctantly he allowed the teachers to continue the practice of private classes after school and during the summer. A series of reports that he issued revealed, however, that such private tutoring benefited only a small group from the more prosperous neighborhoods of the city. Only seventy-three of approximately four hundred teachers conducted evening classes, which enrolled just 641 students. He tried to regulate the practice and to guard against abuses, such as teachers recruiting students by stressing the need for the classes to worried parents.

Like Rogers before him, Bettison realized that he could accomplish little without some basic reforms in Louisiana policies. In his estimation, the educational exhibits at the Cotton Exposition clearly proved how far New Orleans had fallen behind other major American cities. Although the post-Reconstruction superintendents took part in the Southern Educational Association, they maintained their national contacts and continued to look to Northern school systems for their educational models. Bettison complained that New Orleans had failed to develop any technical training in its schools or to adopt the popular kindergartens already widely used in "Northern or foreign cities." More troublesome to him was the low quality of the elementary students' work in the various exhibits at the fair. An honest comparison, he thought, attested "the deficiencies of our system."

He was careful, however, not to exaggerate the educational problems of the city. He made the first reliable survey of education in the city during the mid-1880s and discovered 205 private schools, including ninety-five parochial schools. The private schools enrolled 16,400 students, or about two-thirds the enrollment of the public schools. Of the approximately 26,000 school-age children of the city who were not in any school he estimated that most were over twelve years old and had attended some early primary grades. He judged that relatively few, including black children, were totally illiterate. Despite this basic achievement, he pointed out that New Orleans was still falling behind other cities in educating its population. "No American city," he warned, "can enjoy permanent prosperity without a well-sustained system of public education."[28]

He scorned city officials for insisting that "inadequate support" was the "natural and inevitable result of the poverty of our city." He noted that, in every retrenchment during the previous fifteen years, city officials made the schools "suffer more than their share of the reduction." He compared appropriations for the more favored police and fire departments to show that both agencies had received more funding than the public schools. He used six other cities in the North and South to show that other school systems normally obtained two or three times the funding of their fire and police departments.

He wisely avoided comparing the current state of affairs to funding levels during the Reconstruction period. Instead, he used the city budget of 1858 to show that the schools received less during the 1880s than they had before the Civil War, despite a population increase of fifty-four percent and a doubling of the public school enrollment. During the same period, he noted, the funding for schools diminished thirty-two percent, while the budget of the fire department increased 219 percent. To counter the shopworn argument that the city had inherited a disabling debt from Reconstruction carpetbaggers, one of his bold reports showed that other cities apportioned a greater percentage of their budgets to schools even after all debt payments were excluded.[29]

In his last published report, Bettison got to the heart of the problem: "As long as the state government doles out to the parishes an annual pittance for education and assumes control of their schools, so long will the people sit with folded hands and complain of the inefficiency of their schools and the shortness of the school term. If good work is to be done, local responsibility must be felt and local pride aroused. Let the parishes be free to levy their own tax for local schools, and an eight-month session would soon become the rule rather than the exception."[30]

Such outspoken views must have made Bettison's an unwelcomed voice among local politicians. In 1888, he failed to win renewal of his contract and lost the city superintendency to Warren Easton, who had just ended his elected term as state superintendent. Nonetheless, Bettison's agitation, along with that of Rogers before him, may well have helped bring about some change in the state tax laws that took place several years later.

During the troubled post-Reconstruction era, the New Orleans school system had two key assets that kept it from crumbling, as did education in the rural areas and small towns of the state. First, the McDonogh endowment provided the school system with almost all of its facilities. Between 1862 and 1893, no tax funds financed any new school building. By 1894, twenty-six of the fifty-four schools were housed in McDonogh buildings.[31] Most of the other facilities either predated the Civil War or had been other kinds of structures converted into school buildings. The commissioners of the McDonogh fund also paid for repairs to the buildings they had helped construct. Private charity, not public concern, kept the schools afloat.

New Orleans' other key asset was its teachers. Perhaps the most remarkable story during the difficult years of the late nineteenth century was the loyalty, competence, and initiative of the almost totally female teaching staff. By 1886, not a single male teacher remained in any classroom except at the boys high school, and only about a dozen remained as principals, mostly in the male elementary schools of working-class neighborhoods. But even there, more and more women were taking over as principals.

During Reconstruction, many white women had taught in integrated schools with little complaint, and subsequently some volunteered, because of the lack of certified black teachers, to teach in all-black schools. In 1886, only nineteen of seventy-three teachers in black schools were black men or women. The white women worked in segregated staffs at the individual schools, but they attended training sessions together with black teachers until the early twentieth century. In the schools of poor neighborhoods, teachers often had to devise special methods of teaching students. Some encouraged black girls to sew while they read to them aloud; others conducted spelling bees and group recitals when their students could not afford to buy textbooks.

104

40 The John McDonogh Monument in Lafayette Square. After the New Orleans
School Board began Founder's Day on May 1, 1891, to honor John McDonogh, it
approved the construction of a monument to be paid for, in part, by the
contributions of public school children. The sculptor, Attilio Picirilli, used two
public school pupils as his models: Edward White of McDonogh No. 9 and Lucy
Toujan of McDonogh No. 15. It was formally dedicated on December 29, 1898.

41 The teaching staff of McDonogh No. 13. Standing left to right: Anna Conway, Annie Sinclair, John Heslin, Annie Macken, Teresa Sbisa, Julia Donavan. Sitting left to right: Alice Hamilton, Anna Louise Miller, Marion C. Hewitt, Maria Mulvey, Emma Lived. Inset: Isabella B. Grant. These dedicated teachers stayed on after several pay cuts and the closing of the schools in 1883.

The career of Eveline A. Waldo revealed the resourcefulness of many of the unmarried women who dedicated their lives to public education. Eveline Waldo can only be described as a secular nun. In fact, she spent four years at the city's Dominican Convent before she used her fluency in German to study the methods of the founders of the kindergarten movement. After a personally financed tour of kindergartens throughout the United States and Canada, she returned to New Orleans determined to set up a kindergarten system in the public schools. To help her, she brought together over five hundred young Catholic women like herself and formed them into the Association of St. Margaret's Daughters. Their efforts not only fostered the development of kindergartens but also led to the first free night school for girls. And by the early twentieth century, Waldo spread her influence beyond New Orleans to help create kindergartens in other areas of the South.[32]

For the most part, women also trained the teaching staff. Until 1886, they recruited and prepared young women in the girls high school. True, male

42 Eveline A. Waldo, the founder of the kindergarten program in the New Orleans public schools.

instructors dominated the two segregated, Peabody-sponsored normal schools that provided advanced training in pedagogy—the first had opened in the late 1860s for white teachers and the second in 1877 for black teachers. After state cutbacks led to the closing of these two institutions in 1883, State Superintendent Warren Easton helped the New Orleans school board reopen its own normal school in 1886. From then until the normal school closed in 1940, women had almost full charge of the teacher training program. Two strong-willed women principals dominated the normal school during most of its existence—Marion Brown and Margaret C. Hanson. They shaped the careers of several generations of white women who taught in the public schools of New Orleans.[33]

The normal school concentrated on content courses and offered only a few courses in pedagogy. For practical training, the normal staff conducted a laboratory school where every trainee worked with an experienced teacher. And after the normal school training, individual school principals continued to guide the new teachers. Because the superintendent's office

43   An early kindergarten class at the William O. Rogers School.

108

44 New Orleans Normal School, 1532 Calliope. Founded in 1858, the school remained in operation at different sites until 1940.

45 Normal School classroom in 1904.

46 A teacher training session at the all-boys Paulding School, which was used by master
teachers to help prepare normal school students.

had no professional staff, neither Rogers nor his successors could do more
than draft occasional memoranda to the principals. Prescribed textbooks
and curriculum guidelines created some uniformity, but beyond that,
individual school principals conducted their operations largely on their own.

The structure of the New Orleans schools changed very little after John
A. Shaw first introduced the Massachusetts graded system. Emphasis
remained on primary education. Most pupils, white and black, seldom
went beyond the third or fourth grade. In the upper elementary grades,
which were called grammar schools, teachers saw themselves training
students for entry into high schools. Such a pyramided system generated an
elitism among both the students and the teachers.

New teachers started at the lower grades and worked their way up, by
means of seniority and favoritism among superintendents and key board
members. Many young women stayed in the system for only a few years.

Large classes, poor equipment, and low pay drove many away. Others left to get married. A surprisingly large number, however, remained unmarried and worked their way upward in the system to higher grades and salaries.

Success in preparing students for the rigorous tests that determined promotion of students through the grammar grades and admitted them to the high schools gave certain teachers and their schools prestige within the system. The tests, difficult even by twentieth-century standards, kept classes small in both the grammar grades and high schools. In December 1885, applicants for the high school faced the following questions in their battery of tests:

History of the United States and Geography

1. Define Latitude, Axis, Poles, Prime Meridian.
2. Through what waters would you pass in going from London, England, to Melbourne, Australia?
3. For what do we remember Columbus? Ponce de Leon? John Smith?
4. How are United States Senators chosen? How many Senators from each State? How many representatives from each state?

Grammar

Write two sentences, the first containing a relative pronoun in the nominative case; the second a relative pronoun in the objective case.

Language

Complete the following sentences by supplying adjective clauses:

This is the time . . . .
He is the largest boy . . . .
Who is he . . . .
We all honor the man . . . .
The day has come . . . .

Probably not by accident, the girls outperformed boys in the high school exams well into the twentieth century. Because so many of the women teachers had passed through the system themselves as favored students and found employment as teachers in the New Orleans schools, they seem to have encouraged protégés among the girls to follow in their footsteps. Whatever the reason, the results of an entrance test in the spring of 1887 gave typical results. Of the 137 boys who took the high school entrance test, only seventy-nine passed, for a success rate of 57.6 percent. The girls fared better: of the 232 who took the test, 198 passed, for a success rate of 85.3 percent. Such a differential in New Orleans, quite rare in American secondary schools, insured that until the 1930s about twice as many girls attended the city high schools as boys.

Lack of physical space and teachers made it impossible for the New Orleans schools to accommodate any more students. Indeed, to keep enrollments at a manageable size, officials from time to time raised the cut-off scores on the annual examinations, particularly on the high school entrance test. And the superintendents never pressed for compulsory education because they simply could not accommodate any more students. Haphazard attendance of poor white and black students insured that only a few of them ever made it into the upper grades of the elementary schools, much less into the high schools. Thus the whole school scene in New Orleans remained stratified for nearly twenty-five years after the resegregation of the schools.

47 George Washington Girls School, 1894. This school was directed by Lucretia Wilder, its principal, from 1859 to 1908. She trained many girls who later, at her urging, became teachers and principals in the New Orleans school system. Parents at this downtown school steadfastly resisted the admission of boys.

New Orleans Public School Enrollment

Year	Black	White	Total
1877	4,338	15,169	19,507
1878	6,856	17,294	24,150
1879	6,654	17,670	24,324
1880	5,595	15,316	20,911
1881	5,473	18,928	24,401
1882	5,540	19,427	24,976
1883	4,511	17,130	21,641
1884	4,955	18,227	23,182
1885	4,752	19,579	24,331
1886	5,306	19,555	24,861
1887	6,029	19,620	25,649
1888	6,042	20,930	26,972
1889	4,858	16,278	21,136
1890	5,426	17,974	23,400
1891	5,592	17,617	23,209
1892	5,436	18,454	23,840
1893	4,929	18,559	23,488
1894	5,441	19,829	25,270
1895	6,126	21,274	27,400
1896	5,855	22,673	28,528
1897	6,117	23,597	29,713
1898	6,013	23,509	29,522
1899	6,221	24,549	30,770
1900	6,662	24,859	31,521

Source: Louisiana Biennial Report of the State Superintendent of Public Education, 1899-1900.

No fundamental change came until the early 1890s. At that point a powerful combination of city and state Regular Democrats finally came to the rescue of the New Orleans school board. A leading corporation lawyer in New Orleans, Ernest B. Kruttschnitt, was the central figure. Appointed to the school board in 1884, Kruttschnitt became president in 1888 and held that position for the next fifteen years. When he also became chairman of the Democratic State Central Committee in the early 1890s, he was able to fashion an alliance with the city machine of John Fitzpatrick, the mayor of New Orleans, and with that support, to help the schools.

48 Belleville School. This upper level grammar class captures the "finishing school"
quality of the public girls schools in New Orleans at the turn of the nineteenth century.
Many more girls than boys reached the upper grades and went on to high school.

Kruttschnitt focused on the money problem. First, he and his powerful
business and political allies persuaded the state legislature to pass a law
which compelled the city council to appropriate at least $250,000 for the
city schools. After taxpayers won a suit declaring such a law
unconstitutional, Kruttschnitt secured a state constitutional amendment that
allowed a separate New Orleans agency, the Board of City Debt and
Liquidation, to pass another one-mill tax on property in order to pay the
city's debt and to raise public school funds. By 1895, the new measures had
almost doubled the board's income.

The new money permitted the board, for the first time since the Civil
War, to build new schools without the aid of the McDonogh Commission.
Increased space spurred enrollment, which quickly outpaced population
growth in the city. Warren Easton, the new superintendent hired in 1888,

found it possible to double the teaching staff, raise teachers' pay, reorganize the curriculum, expand the normal school, and introduce more kindergarten classes. He also ended the private, after-hour classes, restrained corporal punishment, and introduced special classes in music and drawing.[34]

Few of these reforms, however, reached the black schools, which most desperately needed improvement. Just at the time the school system obtained more money, a new wave of anti-black legislation hit the state, and the genteel paternalism that had existed during the 1880s all but disappeared.[35] Most of Louisiana's state legislators joined the rush to Jim Crow in 1890 and passed a railroad bill mandating separate but equal seating for blacks and whites. Other segregation laws followed, forbidding interracial marriage and segregating or excluding blacks in streetcars, railroad terminals, hotels, and all places of entertainment.[36] The new laws, in fact, changed few existing patterns of behavior, for blacks and whites usually congregated separately in their daily affairs. But the new measures represented an attempt to nail down, in law, absolute white domination and supremacy.

Louis A. Martinet, the last black member of the New Orleans school board and a former teacher at Southern University, emerged as one of the chief opponents of the new wave of segregation sentiment. He used his newspaper, the *Crusader*, to rally a citizens' committee to challenge the new Jim Crow laws. Their most famous suit, *Plessy* v. *Ferguson*, fought segregation on railway cars. Between 1892 and 1896 the case moved slowly through the judicial system before the United States Supreme Court finally rendered its decision on May 18, 1896. The court sanctioned the "separate but equal" doctrine not just for railroads but for all public facilities, including schools.

About the same time, the regular Democrats of New Orleans under the leadership of Ernest B. Kruttschnitt joined with almost all other white political factions in the state to disfranchise black voters. To that end, they called a constitutional convention to meet early in 1898. When the convention convened in New Orleans in February, they unanimously elected Kruttschnitt chairman. In his opening speech, he unabashedly told the delegates that they had come together to eliminate "the mass of corrupt and illiterate voters who have during the last quarter of a century degraded our politics." He called for only one other major change, a constitutional mandate for public education. He urged the delegates to insure that "every man shall have the power to educate himself if he so desires."

AN APPEAL!
To All Whom it May Concern:

PREAMBLE.

Feeling the great necessity of an organization for the purpose of uniting and protecting ourselves and the promotion of our intellectual welfare, both social and moral, thereby inculcating a true sense of the importance of education. Uniting ourselves politically, that our support and influence may be brought only where our interest and welfare is protected, where our rights as citizens of the State, and the United States respected.

THEREFORE, We, the undersigned, do hereby agree to unite in an organization, which shall be known as

JUSTICE, PROTECTIVE, EDUCATIONAL AND SOCIAL.

First—Its object shall be for the protection of the class where injustice, partiality or misrepresentation are made, either by members or otherwise. We shall select for said purpose only the most intelligent, possessing both honesty and integrity, whose duty it shall be to fully demonstrate and respond to same, and to expose publicly all dishonesty or frauds, and shall further protect ourselves in all our lawful rights.

Second—We shall promote education by all the limiting means in our power; we shall try and collect a Library, to be located and placed at our convenience; and shall make lawful demand to the Government for our share of public education; and ask that same shall be protected and placed in the hands of proper representatives, proofs against frauds and manipulations, thereby insuring good teachers, a full term and all the necessary articles for the maintenance of schools, which at this moment we have not.

Third—We shall build a Social Circle, where our intellectual welfare, both social and moral, will be promoted by inculcating the best principles and virtues.

Fourth—We shall unite ourselves and bring our support and influence to bear in one solid mass, only where we are respected, our rights protected, and our interest and welfare connected.

Then our support will be given by a solid pledge and guarantee in denouncing all treachery, and the protection and rights of Labor.

With these principles in view, we demand the unanimous aid and support of the class and the approbation of all honest, intelligent and just men.

We, members of the JUSTICE, PROTECTIVE, SOCIAL AND EDUCATIONAL CLUB, appeal for co-operation, aid and protection to every promoter of education, organization, or individual, irrespective of religion and race.

Our appeal is particularly in behalf of that class of people, to which we belong, in the boundaries below Canal street to the Barracks, from the river to the woods, known as the 2d and 3d Districts, Parish of Orleans, State of Louisiana.

We claim of not having sufficient of Public Schools, or any suitable institution of learning within easy reach. Our population of school children exceeds twenty (20) thousand in the Districts. And of the eighteen (18) Public Schools we cannot claim five (5) for one class, of which the accommodations are good. We claim at least from eight to ten thousand children, of school age, that is unprovided, growing in idleness and ignorance.

We, therefore, seeing the horrible state of affairs, and feeling that, unless we appeal for co-operation, aid and protection, our young men and women will grow up in ignorance and immorality, thereby crumbling our societies, and prove themselves unworthy citizens of the State and the United States.

We, therefore, for the purpose of bringing these measures before the people, unite in an organization known as the JUSTICE, PROTECTIVE, SOCIAL AND EDUCATIONAL.

PREAMBULE.

Ressentant la grande nécessité d'organization; afin de nous unir et nous protéger intellectuellement, socialement et moralement, inculquant une vraie idée de l'importance de l'éducation. Nous nous unissons politiquement, afin que notre support et influence puissent être resentis où nos interets et notre bien être sont protégés, où nos droits comme citoyens de l'Etat et des Etats Unis sont respectés.

Nous soussignés par entente générale, nous unissons, par cette organization, qui sera connue et désignée sous le nom de "LA JUSTICE," CLUB PROTECTIF, SOCIAL, ET D'EDUCATION.

I—L'objet de cette organization sera de protéger la classe chaque fois qu'il y aura injustice, partialité, où qu'elle sera mal représentée par ses membres, ou par d'autres. Nous choisirons à cet effet les plus intelligents, mais honnêtes et intègres; leur devoirs seront de démontrer clairement de répliquer et d'exposer publiquement toute action déshonnête, et devront nous protéger dans tout nos droits.

2—Nous encouragerons l'éducation par les faibles moyens que nous possédons.

Nous éssaierons de recueillir une Bibliothéque, qui sera placée à l'endroit le plus convenable à notre organization. Et demanderont légalement au gouvernement notre part de l'Education publique, dont la charge sera remise, pour sa protection, entre les mains de dignes représentants, éprouvé contre les fraudes, et les manipulations. Nous aurons par ce moyen de bons professeurs, l'année scolaire, accomplis du combustible et tout ce qui est nécessaire à l'entretien des écoles: ce que nous n'avons pas en ce moment.

3—Nous formerons un cercle social où notre progrès intellectuel, social et moral sera encouragé par l'incucation de bon principes et des vertus.

4—Nous nous unirons et n'apporterons notre support et influence pour former une masse solide, que l'à seulement où nous sommes respectés, où nos droits sont protégés, et nos interets et notre bien être, unis.

Alors notre support sera donné par un gage solide, en dénonçant toute fourberie, et en protégeant les droits du travail. Avec ces principes en vue nous demandons l'aide et le support unanime de notre CLASSE, et l'approbation de tous ceux qui sont honnêtes, juste et intelligents.

Nous, membres de la JUSTICE, CLUB PROTECTIF, SOCIAL, ET D'EDUCATION, fesons appel de co-opération, aide, et protection, à tout partisans d'éducation, d'organisation, où individus, sans égard de religion, où race.

Notre appel est particulièrement fait pour la classe, à laquelle nous appartenons, comprise entre la rue du Canal et les Casernes, et de la Rivière au bois, connus comme 2me et 3me Districts de la Paroisse d'Orléans, Etat de la Louisiane.

Nous prétendons ne pas avoir assez d'écoles publique où institutions, à proximités, pour l'instruction de nos enfants, jeunes gens des deux sexes, etc., etc. Notre population en enfants est au dessus de vingt (20) milles. Et de dix-huit (18) écoles publique, dans les dits districts, nous ne pouvons en compter cinq (5) pour notre classe, avec accommodation satisfaisante.

Nous comptons au moins de huit (8) à dix (10) milles enfants, à l'âge d'instruction qui n'y sont pas pourvus, et qui sont élevés dans la fainaiantise et l'ignorance.

Voyant la grande nécessité, et l'état horrible où nous nous trouvons; sans appel de co-opération, aide, où protection, nos jeunes gens seront élevés dans l'ignorance, et l'immoralité, et deviendront une honte à la Société, et seront des citoyens indignes de l'Etat, et des Etats Unis.

Nous nous sommes unis dans le but d'exposer ces mesures au devant du peuple, sous le nom et titre de la JUSTICE CLUB SOCIAL ET D'EDUCATION.

OFFICERS.

L. J. Joubert, ...President.
H. A. Plessy, ...Vice-President.
J. Tournois, ...Corresponding Secretary
T. Griffin, ...Commissary.
I. J. Boise, ...Recording Secretary
H. Lalonier, ...Financial Secretary
L. N. Deguerey, ...Treasurer

MEMBERS.

F. Sigg,	P. Lalonier,	W. Lalonier,	F. Gaillot,	J. P. Meteye,	P. Avril,
A. L. Veroslon,	E. F. Urquhart,	J. B. Defillo,	A. Angellet,	M. Camps, Jr.	F. Queretque,
O. Pavajeaud,	K. Dupuis,	J. Robert,	C. Populus,	T. Dutillyet,	L. D. Thompson,
E. Casino,	E. Brulé	A. Dorville,	E. J. Palao,	J. M. Morris,	L. Plessy,
L. Surle,	A. Guyot,	N. M. Maquet,	J. Rixner,	A. Moret,	Rev. C. B. Masse,
H. Learson,	H. Armand,	J. B. Roman,	H. Bruyard,	Jos. Mansion, Jr.	P. Rivarre,
		Dr. E. Dorien,	Dr. E. Milanes,	O. Piron,	

49 A copy of a protest in 1887 from the French-speaking, black community in downtown New Orleans. The French on the bi-lingual appeal is much better than the English. Note the presence of Homer Adolphe Plessy's name among the officers at the bottom. He later became the plaintiff in the famous suit against railroad segregation, *Plessy* v. *Ferguson*.

50 McDonogh No. 6. Black students obtained none of the eighteen McDonogh schools
built between 1877 and 1889. Only McDonogh No. 5 in Algiers and McDonogh No. 6 on
Camp Street, both built during Reconstruction, remained as black schools. In 1888, the
school board transferred McDonogh No. 6 to white children. The resulting uproar from the
black community, then still able to vote, led not only to its restoration but also to the
building of McDonogh No. 24 for black residents in Carrollton.

It was a strange combination of goals, but in Kruttschnitt's mind public
education was "a corollary of the suffrage question." Both somehow were
connected to his vision of a new racial order in the state. He made that clear
in his concluding appeal: "May this hall, where, thirty-two years ago, the
negro first entered upon the unequal contest for supremacy and which has
been reddened with his blood, now witness the evolution of our organic law
which establish the races upon an everlasting foundation of right and
justice."[37]

51 Ernest B. Kruttschnitt. He hoped to become a U. S. Senator like his famous antebellum uncle, Judah P. Benjamin. But shortly after he retired from the presidency of the school board in 1904 to prepare for his candidacy, he died quite suddenly.

When the convention finished rewriting the state's constitution, which included arbitrary literacy tests and the infamous "grandfather clause," black voter registration dropped from about 154,000 to less than 500. Robert Ewing, who had been one of the New Orleans delegates, later recalled that the disfranchisement "in large measure was due to the influence and advice of our great president, Mr. Kruttschnitt."[38]

Less well known is Kruttschnitt's role in reshaping the New Orleans school system. At the dawn of the twentieth century, he did more than insure that the new constitution clearly mandated "public schools for the white and colored races, separately established." Following the convention, he and the New Orleans School Board, which remained under his direction, completely refashioned the city's black education, plunging it to its post - Civil War nadir.

Few apparently anticipated the change. Indeed, the improved financial condition of the city's schools brought some momentary optimism for black schools. A prominent white women, Mrs. H. S. Forsyth, led a delegation of black leaders to the school board where they urged Kruttschnitt and his associates to extend kindergartens to the black schools. But to the delegation's utter dismay, the school board brushed aside their petition and announced, instead, a massive cutback in educational opportunities for black children. They limited all black schooling to the first five grades, thereby effectively shutting off any publicly supported route to the city's private black colleges.[39]

The radical plan was not the result of any financial crisis. In fact, the school board had just begun to receive a new infusion of property taxes after the 1898 constitution had brought higher taxes and rising assessments. The board acted rather on the basis of long on-going discussions about the future of black people in the city and in the South. The board's chief educational committee reported on June 29, 1900, that "it was probably a mistake in the early organization of these schools to attempt so much, or expect so much of colored pupils." They announced that they were giving up all pretense of creating separate schools "identical with that of white schools."

The committee took note of developments in other Southern states where educational opportunities for blacks had seldom reached the levels that they had in New Orleans. They felt it was time for New Orleans to join the "trend of education for the negro to-day in the South . . . and to fit him and her for that sphere of labor and social position and occupation to which they are best suited and seem ordained by the proper fitness of things." Without any further discussion, the board accepted the committee's recommendation.[40]

The decision shocked the black community. The local Methodist newspaper, the *Southwestern Christian Advocate*, immediately recognized the larger implication of the action and bemoaned that "disfranchisement is evidently the gateway to complete subjugation." The editors noted that fairness should have made the board open a high school rather than eliminate three elementary grades. "Think of such a thing," they exclaimed, "in a great city like New Orleans! There is no Southern city of even 50,000 inhabitants that deals so niggardly with its colored inhabitants."[41]

The *Advocate*, then the last black newspaper in the Deep South, managed to evoke a national response to the action of the New Orleans school board. The *Boston Herald* picked up the story and declared that the educational cutback was "the most discouraging blow to the race that has been struck anywhere—worse than disfranchisement."[42] Even white leaders in New Orleans found it hard to believe that their school board had taken such a backward step. The *Picayune* mocked Northern papers for spreading such a ludicrous tale before its editors learned the truth. For several weeks after the board's action, the newspapers in the city carried on a civic debate. One newspaper even asked Booker T. Washington for his opinion on the proper education of black youngsters. In addition to his usual nostrums about the importance of manual and industrial training, Washington offered his advice that "the South has nothing to fear from the thoroughly educated Negro." He tried to make the leaders of New Orleans understand that "ignorance in the end is always more costly to the State or Nation than intelligence."[43] Unfortunately, his letter was never published, because matters grew worse before it reached the city.

In late July, after a black Mississippian named Robert Charles resisted harassment by New Orleans policemen and, in the scuffle that followed, shot one of them, the city broke into a terrible race riot. Mobs pulled black passengers from the streetcars, beat them, and, perhaps influenced by the newspaper debate over the schools, torched the Lafon School, the city's largest black elementary classroom building.[44] Racial violence reached unimagined levels of outrage. Thereafter no white leaders spoke out against the school board's actions.

Some black leaders tried to protest, but were soon reduced to mere begging. They quickly realized that they no longer had any legal recourse, not even to the Plessy doctrine of "separate and equal facilities." Kruttschnitt and the board had fashioned their actions in accord with a recent Supreme Court decision, *Cumming* v. *School Board of Richmond County, Georgia*, which permitted the school board of Augusta, Georgia, to close its black high school while it kept its white high school.[45]

The reasoning of the superintendent of the Augusta schools was that white educators should avoid equalization out of fear of elevating "the educated negro . . . until he has the instincts and desires of a white man."[46] Although none of the New Orleans school board members ever agreed with the Georgia superintendent, at least in an open meeting, they came very close. When a delegation of New Orleans black ministers asked the board whether the decision would allow at least some vocational education beyond the fifth grade, the board responded that it intended no technical training for black students beyond simple manual training in the primary grades.

Later, in response to the last organized black petition on the issue, the board members reasserted their stand, insisting that they saw "no reason for reversing our policy, or reinstating those grades." With a dramatic flourish, they closed out the long struggle for equal education in New Orleans and opened a new era: "It seems to us the right thing to have done, to start over again in the work of educating the negro. Where the start should have been made in 1863 we are starting in 1900, commencing at primary education."[47]

IV

White Schools, 1900-1945

The twentieth century brought a new era for public education in New Orleans and, indeed, for much of the rest of the American South. Until World War II, local white officials had total control of the region's public schools; no one feared any threat of federal intervention. As a result, while black schools remained throughout the period victims of a studied policy of neglect, white schools underwent major improvements that reversed many of the earlier patterns of poor attendance, inadequate facilities, and meagerly trained teachers.

The Constitutional Convention of 1898 had given the New Orleans school board special privileges that virtually freed it even from state regulation. The board relied on the state only for the power to collect special city taxes which it used to fund their school system. As a result, New Orleans teachers and school officials increasingly turned inward. Neither Warren Easton, the superintendent, nor the board members showed much interest in the South or Louisiana beyond New Orleans. After the 1890s, they played only minor roles in the Southern Educational Association and offered little leadership for the Conference for Education in the South, which later gave birth to the Southern Education Board. Some of the New Orleans educators attended the meetings of these Southern agencies, but none played any major role in those bodies.

Ignoring their black schools after 1900, New Orleans school officials concentrated on improving their white schools. Warren Easton wanted to bring them up to what he considered the best standards of public schools in Northern cities. He regularly attended the annual conventions of the Department of Superintendence of the National Education Association (N.E.A.) and, in 1902, served as its second vice-president. He looked upon the N.E.A. Department of Superintendence as the "body that largely molds the thought on educational matters in this country, and controls the trend of progress and development."[1]

About the time Easton became an official in the N.E.A., he also developed a set of goals for the New Orleans white schools. In 1901, the school board

52 Warren Easton

permitted him to expand his administrative staff by adding two new
assistant superintendents, John R. Conniff and Nicholas Bauer. They took
over routine office matters and visitations to the now more than seventy-
five individual schools in the system. Easton was freed to concentrate on
ways to implement what he considered essential reforms: improved teacher
salaries, smaller classes, and elective secondary curriculum, vocational
training, compulsory education, and free textbooks. Though all important,
none were imaginative or original ideas. Easton simply wanted to catch up
with Northern innovations that had taken place during the last quarter of the
nineteenth century, while the New Orleans schools were in the doldrums.
His campaign for reform, however, produced an unusual confrontation in
local politics.

To generate public support and increased revenue for his goals, Easton
organized his teachers into the New Orleans Educational Association and
then joined them in an appeal to the city council for salary increases.
When that approach failed, he invited prominent leaders in the city to help
the teachers and, in 1905, formed the Public School Alliance. For the next
twenty years the PSA would be the chief advocate for the city's public
schools. Such an approach fit Easton's conception of educational reform.
In a speech at Tulane University in 1901, he scoffed at the idea that an
"organized crusade" of criticism directed against the troubled public schools
would do any good. Instead, he urged his privileged audience to "cooperate"
with him.[2]

In its first assembly, the Public School Alliance pulled together a
coalition of eleven well-to-do, uptown organizations. Unlike similar efforts in the past, however, the PSA brought large numbers of women into
the public arena. True, women had always dominated the membership of
earlier teacher groups, but during the nineteenth century, influential men
had always handled public advocacy for the schools.[3] The Public School
Alliance drew the usual quota of men from such business groups as the
New Orleans Progressive Union and the Algiers Improvement Association,
but it also recruited women from the Local Council of Women and the
Local Council of Jewish Women. Indeed, women outnumbered men in the
Alliance, and included some outspoken feminists and suffragettes from the
city's Era Club. After 1905, it became difficult in New Orleans to separate
the women's suffrage cause from that of educational reform.

At first, the men who held the key offices of the PSA dominated the
group. Most came from either Tulane University or the circles of "good
government" reform politics. Its first president, John Clegg, had been like

53   James H. Dillard

Warren Easton, a member of the Citizens League which had scored one of
the few good government victories during the nineteenth century when it
took over city hall in 1896. And at the start, the PSA drew its educational
reform ideas largely from James H. Dillard, a Tulane dean, who simultaneously worked for the Southern Education Board. His prestige provided
an immediate elan.

Behind that thin line of male leadership, however, stood a veritable army
of women, particularly after the PSA began organizing at individual
elementary schools in order to form its auxiliary "cooperative clubs."
These parents' clubs drew so heavily upon women that the press usually
referred to them as mothers' clubs. The more than 5,000 women in the
cooperative clubs shortly created their own umbrella organization called the
Presidents' Cooperative Club. It was dominated by Mrs. Adolph
Baumgartner and Mrs. Jessie Goetz Skinner. With their help, New Orleans
women finally began to speak for themselves in the public arena. Together
with the High School Alumnae and the New Orleans Education
Association, the two new citywide coalitions formed an engine of reform
for the city's public schools.[4] But almost immediately the ladies found
themselves on a collision course with the city's boss, Mayor Martin
Behrman, and his powerful political machine.

Since the end of Reconstruction, politics in New Orleans had degenerated
into a struggle between the city's Anglo-Saxon Protestant elite from the
prosperous uptown neighborhoods and the sons of Irish and German
immigrants who lived close to the wharves all along the river and in the old
downtown Catholic neighborhoods. Class as well as ethnicity fostered the
political antagonisms. When the state constitution of 1898 removed black
voters as well as a number of poor whites from the rolls, many observers
thought the changes would fatally weaken the immigrant-based machine
that had dominated New Orleans politics during the last quarter of the
nineteenth century. But, in 1904, a remarkable politician, Martin
Behrman, reorganized the old machine, turned it into the Choctaw Club,
and, through it, maintained an effective alliance between the working-class
white ethnics and those conservative businessmen who wanted help and
stability from city hall. Behrman held together his coalition, also known
as the Regular Democrats, with great skill.[5]

The Choctaw Club, a veritable Southern Tammany Hall, also controlled
key levers of power in the state capital. Its loyalists held a majority of
seats on the state Democratic Central Committee, and their disciplined bloc
of votes in the state legislature made it difficult for any governor to ignore
them. In New Orleans, the Choctaw Club organized itself as a mirror of

the ward and precinct structure of the city. The club's executive committee was ruled by seventeen men each of whom came from one of the city's seventeen wards. Beneath them were more than a hundred lieutenants whose status depended on their ability to deliver votes from their own precincts.[6]

On the face of it, the Public School Alliance seemed no match for Behrman's city machine. The women were voteless and like the men in the PSA, came from a narrow social base drawn primarily from the Protestant uptown elite. Their first campaign in 1905 betrayed their cultural and social biases. In seeking revenues for teachers' raises, the Alliance attacked the Behrman machine at its very base. The PSA demanded that the city council establish a $1,000 license fee on all "retailers of malt and spiritous liquors." Many of the reformers paid high taxes on their uptown properties, which were often appraised unfairly by the city assessors. The PSA insisted that high liquor licenses on the city's almost 2,000 saloons would not only shift some of the burden of taxation but would also penalize the saloons for creating "illiteracy . . . crime, insanity, pauperism" and "the need of criminal courts."[7]

The city council quickly defeated the reformers' high license fee and turned a deaf ear to their school-improvement program. School reform on the local level looked like a dead issue. But, then quite suddenly, the reform movement gained an unexpected ally—the boss himself, Mayor Martin Behrman.

Behrman had his own reasons for supporting the schools. As a protégé of Ernest B. Kruttschnitt, he had inherited a natural interest in public education. From 1892 to 1896, he had served as a school board member from the Fifteenth Ward, on the west bank of the Mississippi River in Algiers. Later he won election as a delegate to the Constitutional Convention of 1898 and served on its education committee where he helped draft a provision that permitted New Orleans to distribute free textbooks to indigent children. At first, he had argued for free texts for all students but finally accepted changes that watered down the measure to an annual appropriation of $2,000, which limited textbooks to only the very poorest children.[8]

When he ran for mayor in 1904, Behrman had said he was going to be remembered as the "School Mayor of New Orleans," and he eventually delivered on that promise. He helped to defeat the reformers' "high license," but before his first term had ended, he got a compliant city council to approve a $200 liquor license and persuaded the city assessors to increase assessments on real estate throughout the city. The new revenue doubled the school allocation, from about a half million dollars to over a million.

To his delight, Behrman discovered that expansion of public schools was good politics. His machine could take credit for meeting public demands for new school buildings in every ward of the city, and at the same time, fill hundreds of patronage jobs in construction and maintenance.

During Behrman's first three terms in office, the city council provided additional funding, over and above the school board's operating budget, for more than twenty school buildings. The "unprecedented growth of school revenues" also allowed the school board to increase teacher salaries in 1906 and to hire several hundred more teachers. Warren Easton could crow that he no longer had "the most poorly paid teachers of any city system in the Untied States" and that the lowering of the student ratio in the white schools to thirty students per teacher compared "favorably with that of any other system in the country."[9]   In addition, Easton took advantage of the Behrman prosperity to expand evening schools from two to five, to launch an athletic and physical education program, and to set up a health department staffed by three doctors.[10]

In 1908, Behrman strengthened his grip over the public schools by persuading the state governor, Newton Blanchard, to relinquish almost all state control over the schools in New Orleans. Since 1888, the governor had appointed eight of the twenty members of the board, the city council appointed the other twelve. Behrman's new arrangement made seventeen members of the new school board elective. The scheme fit neatly into the structure of Behrman's Choctaw machine, for each school board member ran from one of the city's seventeen wards. As mayor, Behrman along with the city treasurer and the comptroller served as ex-officio members of the board. He was thus able to turn the school board into a virtual satrap of his city machine.

The reformers were furious. Not only had the boss out-reformed them, but he now ran the school board, personally intervening in school board decisions.[11]   To strike back at their nemesis, the Public School Alliance and the cooperative clubs, raised their demands.

Behrman's board had concentrated on expanding elementary education, which met the needs as well as the wishes of the largest number of the city's parents. Although immigration into New Orleans had dwindled, the children and grandchildren of its earlier flood of Irish and German families still made up a large part of the city's population. It was not without significance that men with German and Irish names dominated Behrman's school board.

54   Martin Behrman

Behrman's own life symbolized the self-conscious, immigrant background of the city's white working class. He was the son of German Jews who came to New Orleans during the 1850s. After a limited education, he worked his way up through municipal politics. Despite his own conversion to Catholicism, he made a point of sending his son not to the Catholic schools but to public schools.[12] His example in doing so added prestige to the public schools, particularly among his Catholic, immigrant following, and checked the rivalry that often existed between the public and parochial schools in the city. He was probably the last mayor to send his own children to the city's public schools.

Table IV
Public, Private, and Parochial Students in Orleans Parish, 1915.

Race	Age	Public	Private	Parochial	Employed	Jobless
White	6-18	32,548	4,824	10,654	6,333	7,387
(Percentages)		(52.7)	(7.8)	(17.3)	(10.2)	(12)
Black	6-18	8,428	3,377	1,992	2,282	4,538
(Percentages)		(40.9)	(16.4)	(9.7)	(11.1)	(22)
Both	6-18	41,076	8,201	12,646	8,615	11,925
(Percentages)		(49.8)	(10)	(15.3)	(10.4)	(14.5)
White	8					
Male		1,632	187	611	0	99
Female		1,684	163	648	0	91
Total		3,316	350	1,259	0	190
(Percentages)		(64.8)	(6.8)	(24.6)		(3.7)
Black	8					
Male		351	163	122	0	190
Female		409	186	146	0	188
Total		760	349	268	0	378
(Percentages)		(33.9)	(19.9)	(15.3)		(21.5)
White	12					
Male		1,622	190	608	4	53
Female		1,628	189	606	0	52
Total		3,250	379	1,214	4	105
(Percentages)		(65.6)	(7.6)	(24.5)		(2.1)
Black	12					
Male		546	126	97	11	88
Female		559	127	91	21	116
Total		1,105	253	188	32	204
(Percentages)		(62)	(14.2)	(10.5)	(1.8)	(11.4)

Race	Age	Public	Private	Parochial	Employed	Jobless
White	16					
Male		646	223	41	891	259
Female		806	209	113	510	582
Total		1,452	432	154	1,401	841
(Percentages)		(33.9)	(10.1)	(3.6)	(32.7)	(19.6)
Black	16					
Male		106	59	17	241	82
Female		123	120	19	216	161
Total		229	179	36	457	243
(Percentages)		(20)	(15.6)	(3.1)	(39.9)	(21.2)

(Source: Paul B. Habans, *The School Census* (New Orleans, 1915), pp. 13, 18-24.)

Despite Behrman's achievements, the reformers never seemed to understand or appreciate his commitment to public education. They dismissed him as uncouth and self-serving. At the same time, they often pushed for programs that reflected their own narrow self-interest. Their chief concern focused on the secondary school system, which had changed little since Civil War officials consolidated the eight antebellum high schools into one boys and two girls high schools. At the end of Reconstruction, the Redeemers had tried to close the high schools, but Superintendent William O. Rogers managed to salvage two of them, one for boys and another for girls. And, in 1889, a second high school opened for girls. That arrangement lasted for the next twenty years.[13]

As a result, New Orleans fell behind other Southern cities in the development of its high schools. The stunted development was particularly acute for young men. Since the 1860s, far more girls than boys had attended high schools, and by 1907 Warren Easton found that boys made up only twenty-seven percent of the enrollment. In other cities boys usually made up about forty to fifty percent of enrollment.[14]

If Easton had probed further, he would have found even greater sexual disparity in the number of high school graduates. In 1907 the fifty-five graduates of the boys high school made up less than twenty percent of the graduating seniors. This unusually low level of male attendance and graduation continued for about a quarter of a century. The similarity of sexual ratios in both the Catholic and public secondary schools suggests that the local pattern reflected some peculiar cultural and economic proclivities of New Orleans. Because older boys often left elementary schools after the fifth or sixth grades to take jobs in the city, girls finished elementary schools in greater numbers. True, many of the girls went to the high schools in order to gain entry to the normal school and the teaching profession. But in other cases, parents probably kept their daughters in schools because they viewed the public high schools much as they did convent schools, places where girls would be protected until they reached an appropriate age for marriage.

That interpretation is confirmed by the fact that the major pressure for new high schools came largely from the parents of students at the existing girls' high schools. They joined with the alumnae organizations and the leaders of the Presidents' Cooperative Club. By 1908, their petitions and pleas for new high schools so dominated school board meetings that they posed a threat to the Behrman board's priorities for school construction.

55 Committee from McDonogh High School No. 3 which first agitated for the building of new high schools.

Sensing the growing strength of the high school forces, Behrman once again stole their thunder by championing the cause himself. And he found the funds in a rather remarkable place. After he discovered that some of the silk-stocking members of the McDonogh Fund board and other quasi-public commissions had invested public funds in their own banks at less than usual interest rates, he forced them to return about $400,000 of their profits to build the high schools. He also forced the school board to sell the two girls high school buildings and pledge another $100,000 from their existing revenues for the new construction program. By the 1912-13 school year, three high schools emerged from his enterprising and imaginative handling of the situation: Boys Central High School (later Warren Easton), Sophie Wright High School, and the Esplanade High School (later John McDonogh).

Because each side laid claim to the triumph, Warren Easton had to write with great delicacy, in his official report, that credit for the "unexpected

56 Warren Easton High School. No more than one college preparatory public high school existed for white boys in New Orleans between the Civil War and the Great Depression. Until the opening of Easton in 1912, earlier boys' high schools used old, converted buildings.

57 Sophie B. Wright High School. The uptown girls' high school on Napoleon Avenue.

58 Esplanade High School. The downtown girls' high school on Esplanade Avenue. Its
name was later changed to the John McDonogh High School.

59 The facilities in the new high schools were a welcomed contrast
from the old and often decrepit facilities of the earlier high school
buildings. The art room (above) belonged to the Esplanade Girls High
School and the library (below) to the Sophie B. Wright Girls High
School.

culmination" of the campaign for the new high schools "cannot be definitely placed." He lauded the parent's organizations, the Public School Alliance, and the newspapers, but concluded that without Martin Behrman's "active and powerful influence, new high school buildings could not have been secured at this time."[15]

The contest over the high schools did not end Behrman's struggle with the reformers nor reconcile their interests. In 1910, when Warren Easton died, the boss and the reformers came to another showdown. Because Easton had been seriously ill for several months, his assistants, John R. Conniff and Nicholas Bauer, had begun to seek out support to become his replacement.

Three years older than Bauer, Conniff proved the more aggressive in building community support for his candidacy. Because he had taken a prominent role in both the New Orleans Education Association and the Public School Alliance, he had become the clear favorite of the school reformers. Local newspapers even took for granted that he would be the new superintendent.[16]

But Behrman had different ideas. Probably resentful of Conniff's close relationship with the reformers, Behrman let it be known that he wanted a "big man" to take over and that the two assistants did not fit his bill. His mayoral power was sufficient to force a postponement of the selection.[17] The delay gave Behrman two weeks to find his own candidate.

After a dissident board member complained of "outside or undue influence" and insisted that "the members of the Board had been elected by the people to operate and maintain the public schools," Behrman openly declared his rules for the political game in New Orleans:

> I have no apology to make for my attitude. I am the head of the administration, and the local Democratic organization. The members of the school board were nominated by that organization the same time I was, and I have a right to a voice in the policies of the board, to which the city under my administration and through my efforts has given hundreds of thousands of dollars, to the end that their execution shall reflect credit both on the organization and on my administration.[18]

Before the next regular meeting of the school board, Behrman found his "big man." He first made an overture to James H. Dillard, but the former dean of Tulane had just accepted a position as director of the Jeanes Education Fund which was trying to improve the miserable condition of black schools in the rural South. Dillard might have made an extraordinary leader of the New Orleans public schools and worked to improve black as well as white schools, but he reluctantly turned down the offer.[19] Behrman then turned to Joseph Marr Gwinn, an associate professor of education at Tulane and a graduate of the Columbia University's Teachers College. Before Gwinn had come to Tulane in 1907, he had played a prominent role in the public schools of Missouri.[20]

To secure Gwinn's election, Behrman had to force one of Conniff's supporters on the board to resign, and then persuade the governor, J. Y. Sanders, to appoint a New Orleans city hall employee in his place.[21] The

60 John R. Conniff. After he resigned from his position with the public schools, he became an assistant state superintendent of education (1912-1926), the president of Louisiana Polytechnic Institute in Ruston (1926-1928). In 1928, he returned to become an instructor at Warren Easton High School until Alcée Fortier High School was completed. He served as Fortier's first principal from 1931 to 1946.

raw display of power polarized both school and city politics. Educational reformers coalesced with Behrman's silk-stocking opponents in the Good Government League and stirred up an immense row in the city.[22] That coalition became possible purely by chance, because Behrman's loyalists on the school board had, just before Easton's death, already antagonized the women leaders of the Presidents' Cooperative Club.

Although the school board no longer hired teachers directly—after they agreed to take new candidates only from a list based on applicants' scores on a test administered by a teachers' committee—key board members still controlled the assignment of teachers and principals. When they transferred a prominent and respected teacher, Kate Eastman, from a highly desirable kindergarten post to a much less desirable one, they created a stir among the parent-activists. After hearing a series of protests from the group, the school board president issued an edict banning the troublesome mothers' clubs from meeting in the public schools. He made a serious mistake.

Mrs. Adolph Baumgartner, president of the Presidents' Cooperative Club, immediately called a public meeting and complained about "favoritism and politics" on the board. Like many of the key female school reformers, she was also a member of the feminist Era Club. Mrs. Jessie Goetz Skinner, the group's secretary, was even more outspoken. She issued a manifesto that displayed the frustrations of women locked out of public power: "If we want better directors, we'll ask our husbands to vote for better. Now are we to sit calmly by and thank them for incompetent teachers? That's my fight. We have shown the public what public spirited women can do. We are here in the interest of the child, and if we can't meet as a women's club, we'll exist as a women's league."[23] And the Cooperative Club endorsed Conniff. Even as they were acting, Behrman's loyalists elected Joseph Marr Gwinn superintendent.

Mrs. Baumgartner right away called another mass meeting to protest "against the methods used by the school board in the selection of Prof. Gwinn." Simultaneously the Good Government League appointed one of its leading progressive leaders, John M. Parker, to develop an organization in every ward of the city to overthrow "ring politics."[24]

With his usual bravado, Martin Behrman showed up at the mass meeting, and brought with him his own cheering squad of loyalists. But their actions only inflamed the ire of the crowd. In response, the 1200 or so women voted to send Joseph Gwinn a message that his election was

61 Mrs. Adolph (Fannie Ellen) Baumgartner. In winning a seat on the New Orleans School Board in 1920, she became not only the first woman on any school board in the state but also the first woman elected to public office in Louisiana.

62 Jessie Goetz Skinner. She was the president of the Washington Girls School Cooperative Club and a leading associate of Fannie Baumgartner in citywide activism for public school reform.

"tainted with political trickery and petty ward-heeler manipulations" and called upon him to resign. Within a few days, the Era Club followed with their own demand that the legislature initiate a constitutional amendment that would allow women to serve on school boards in Louisiana.[25]

A week later the Good Government League called its own mass meeting. A former president of the Public School Alliance, Samuel A. Montgomery, launched into an attack on Behrman and solicited his audience's response: "You are summoned by the distress cry of the mothers to the bar of duty. What is your remedy? What are you going to do about it?" A reporter carefully documented the response: "The crowd caught the old familiar ring of these words, and there were cries of 'Impeach him,' and it even sounded as though some over-enthusiastic individual said, 'Lynch him'."[26]

But Behrman withstood the onslaught. He had cleverly appointed a respected Tulane professor with far better credentials than Conniff. Gwinn

63 The Gordon Sisters. Kate (right) and Jean were founders of the Era Club, the city's chief feminist organization during the early twentieth century.

had also been a leader in the Public School Alliance, and his wife worked closely with the Era Club and the women school reformers. The reformers could hardly attack him personally. Meanwhile, Gwinn moved quickly to meet with the Presidents' Cooperative Club in order to applaud their efforts to remove the schools from politics.[27]   On that front, Behrman had them blocked.

Behrman's business allies also came forward to give him support. They showed up on the platform for his annual Civic Parade, which showed off every agency of city government, from the police to the health department in a long procession of his faithful city hall work force. With that show of force, the open battle stopped. The *Picayune*, the city's most powerful newspaper, had initially chided the mayor for his heavy-handed role, but now in the dispute with the women, its editors made it clear that they supported the boss.[28]

Despite Behrman's obvious victory, his actions produced a rift among the city's public school advocates that lasted for another fifteen years and shaped the course of the public schools until the Great Depression. His enemies were defeated and sullen, for sure, but they had coalesced. The Presidents' Cooperative Club quickly endorsed the call of the Era Club to put women on the school boards, and the Public School Alliance expanded its executive committee to give two positions to the women of the Presidents' Cooperative Club. The school reformers, in turn, joined hands with the Good Government League to support a reformer, Luther Hall, for governor in 1912. To round out the coalition, the wife of the head of the Good Government League, John M. Parker, became president of the Era Club.[29]

The reformers' agenda called for a package of legislative changes which they felt certain would destroy the hated political "ring" in New Orleans. They wanted the city council and mayor replaced with a nonpartisan commission form of government and a five-member school board which would be elected at large. Both were classic progressive-era reforms designed to counter city bosses.

Once again, however, the reformers underestimated Behrman. He had actually issued his own call for an elected five-member school board as soon as he entered the fray over the superintendent's election in 1910, and, by 1912, he offered his support to Governor Hall and endorsed the idea of a commission council form of government for New Orleans. Behrman realized that, since he controlled the citywide vote in New Orleans, he could just as easily elect his men to a five-member body as he could to a seventeen-member body. In fact, smaller boards strengthened his hand and made it easier for him to govern. Moreover, in a citywide vote, he faced no danger of silk-stocking wards electing any mavericks.

In the fall elections of 1912, Behrman made a clean sweep. Choctaw candidates won every seat on the commission council and the school board. Behrman easily won his own slot on the council and was accordingly selected as mayor. To rub salt in the wounds of the women activists, Behrman's cohorts, in a follow-up election, campaigned against the "suffragette amendment" that would have allowed women to serve on school boards as well as another amendment that would have taken tax assessment power away from the local machine. In the two elections, just a month apart, the count was uncannily similar. The Choctaws defeated both the reformers and their amendments by almost exactly a fifty-five to forty-five percent margin.[30]

Much to the chagrin of the reformers, Behrman's handpicked superintendent and school board retained effective control of the public schools in New Orleans for the next decade. And Behrman himself constantly drew praise from many public school parents. Indeed, until Behrman vetoed the idea, the grateful parents club at the new boys high school almost succeeded in naming it after him.[31]   The reformers were never willing to admit with similar grace that Behrman and his loyal team brought about some of the major achievements in the history of public education in New Orleans.

Behrman's superintendent, Joseph Marr Gwinn, brought exactly what the mayor thought was needed in the public schools: outside leadership and experience to shake up the system. To be sure, the system had grown during the twenty-two years that Easton had served as superintendent. New schools had been built, and more departments and personnel had been added. But New Orleans ranked last among large urban school systems in student achievement. Behrman wanted change.

In 1909, the Russell Sage Foundation released a study that had a profound impact on American public education. Its provocative title, *Laggards in Our Schools*, dramatized its message: that public schools had failed to educate many of their poorer urban students. With devastating statistics, Leonard P. Ayres, the director of the study, showed that less than half of big city school children finished elementary school and that many of the drop-outs had failed to win promotion several times before they finally abandoned the classrooms.

The New Orleans schools ranked at the bottom of most of Ayres' statistical tables. Only a quarter of the white public school children in New Orleans finished elementary school. Of more than sixty school systems surveyed, New Orleans had the third largest percentage of "repeaters" and some of the worst attendance levels. In the overall rating of "efficiency," New Orleans ranked fifty-ninth out of sixty-one urban school districts. Only Camden, New Jersey, and the black schools of Memphis fell below it.

It was embarrassing. Unlike Northern cities, New Orleans could not blame its failure on a recent deluge of non-English-speaking immigrant children. Almost all of the New Orleans school children (98.5%) were native born. Nor could authorities blame black students for the poor performance, because Ayres used only results from the New Orleans white schools in his study. Indeed, the black schools of Richmond and Nashville showed up better than the white schools of New Orleans.[32]

During that same year, the medical staff of Easton's new Department of Hygiene completed a local study that confirmed many of Ayres' findings. They examined every white student in the New Orleans public schools and

64 Joseph Marr Gwinn, Superintendent 1910-1923

discovered a shocking number of overage children in the lower elementary grades. Moreover, the doctors noted—much to their own surprise—that physical and mental defects accounted for only a small percentage of the lag or "retardation."[33] The conclusion had become quite obvious that the fault lay in the poor quality of the schools themselves.

Before Gwinn took over the direction of the New Orleans schools, Easton and the Public School Alliance had tried repeatedly, since 1906, to solve some of the problems by pushing for compulsory attendance laws. Most rural legislators as well as the powerful New Orleans *Picayune* scorned the idea of "forcing free education" upon all persons of school age. But in the spring of 1910, the New Orleans school reformers finally managed to convince the legislature to pass the measure.

Recent laws restricting child labor and setting up a juvenile court in New Orleans had made compulsory education seem a logical step. But the legislators confined the experiment to New Orleans and provided only weak enforcement measures. The law applied only to children between eight and fourteen years of age and required a minimum of only eighteen weeks of schooling during the year. It also excluded physically and mentally handicapped children, as well as those who had already finished a "primary school course" (the fourth grade), and those who lived more than twenty blocks from a school.[34]

White elementary enrollment spurted by about 2,500 students after the law went into effect in the fall of 1910, just as Gwinn became superintendent. He faced real problems in the schools. True, he had more financial resources at his disposal than any previous superintendent. In his first report, he noted that the "financial growth of the system has been marvelous" and happily gave his patron, Martin Behrman, full credit. But Gwinn also realized that Behrman had given him greatly increased responsibilities. The mayor had forced the board to give Gwinn complete control over the assignment of all teaching personnel as well as the selection of his own administrative staff. Behrman declared that he wanted Gwinn "entirely untrammeled in his efforts to raise the standard of the educational system."[35]

Gwinn concentrated his efforts on improving the elementary schools. He kept Nicholas Bauer as one of his assistants but shifted responsibility for the primary grades to Paul Habans, whom he hired to replace John Conniff, who resigned in a public huff after he lost his bid for the superintendency. Gwinn also drew the board's attention to the high dropout rate of the

65 Gwinn's management team. From right (above) P. B. Habans,
assistant superintendent; J. M. Gore, inspector (in charge of buildings
and maintenance); from right (below) J. M. Gwinn; Nicholas Bauer, first
assistant superintendent.

students in the lower grades, and vowed to make the New Orleans schools
more "efficient."[36]

Initially Gwinn tried to control dropouts by instituting manual training
classes in the upper elementary or so-called grammar grades from fifth to
eighth. He was convinced, as most educators of his day were, that classical
literary training could not hold the interest of working-class students.
Vocational training had already become fashionable in many Northern high

schools in order to diversify the curriculum for students who had no interest in going to college. But, since dropout rates were so high in the local elementary schools, Gwinn felt that manual training had to start earlier. These pre-vocational classes provided sewing and cooking for girls and simple craft training for boys.

Gwinn never introduced advanced vocational training for boys, because, in 1912, an unexpected donation disrupted his plans. In his will, Issac Delgado left money to establish a central trades school for white boys. Because the legacy provided only for land and buildings, the city council had to find funds to operate the school. In 1914, Gwinn's staff produced an elaborate survey of vocational training needs in the city, but it failed to generate much support among business and labor leaders. When, in 1921,

66 Isaac Delgado. His bequest paid for the first building at the Delgado Central Trades School across from City Park.

the school finally opened, supported by limited federal and state funds, it had its own separate board and seldom coordinated its meager programs with the public school system.[37]

The Delgado donation forced Gwinn to limit public school vocational training to girls. This accidental development added to the sexual imbalance in secondary training already evident in the high schools. The girls' vocational school, Francis T. Nicholls, tried to teach textile trades but never stimulated much development of the city's small clothing industry.

Gwinn had greater success in his efforts to improve the enforcement of the compulsory education act. In 1912, he got the state legislature to amend the law to enforce attendance for the entire school term and to require all students to finish at least the eighth grade.[38]

Gwinn realized that improvement of student learning required changes in the curriculum and the teaching staff. Like Leonard Ayres, he felt that teachers too often judged success by the severity of their standards rather than by the achievement of their students. To improve the quality of the teaching staff, he began removing all temporary teachers from the white elementary schools, and by 1911-12, was able to boast that all of his teachers were certified.

Overall, Gwinn's conception of efficiency called for greater central management and hierarchical authority. His rapid expansion of the school system's bureaucracy, however, soon led him into a frightful clash with his teaching staff. The erosion of teacher autonomy may not have caused such a stir by itself, but that issue became so intertwined with a simultaneous struggle over financial resources that Gwinn's drive for fundamental change eventually ended in failure.

Teachers and principals already had to keep some records on individual student performance, but Gwinn standardized the record keeping and required timely reports to the central office. In addition, supervisors of special subjects such as music, drawing, and manual education began regular inspections of classrooms and made evaluations of individual teachers.[39] Gwinn also began standardized testing to measure "the value and extent of each school study and activity." For him such innovations brought "scientific methods of measurement to education just as such matters have been applied to engineering."[40] And by 1913, he obtained authority to set up his Department of Educational Research to coordinate the vast flow of paperwork. Thereafter, he seldom visited individual schools or spoke directly to his teachers.[41]

In part, the growth of the central bureaucracy resulted from having a five-member school board. It was so small that the supervisory staff had to take over more and more of the work formerly done by the committees of the earlier, larger boards. The membership and outlook of the new board also contributed to the shift of authority. Made up of prominent businessmen, the board considered Gwinn to be implementing methods and structures familiar to them in their own corporate worlds. The first president of the new board, Sol Wexler, a vice-president of the Whitney Bank, was particularly insistent that teachers and principals follow the dictates of the central office.[42]

To counter the growing impersonality of the expanding bureaucracy, teachers, in 1914, formed the Associate Teachers' League. They excluded all supervisory personnel from their group, including principals, who had earlier formed the Principals Association. As a result of having two different organizations, teachers and principals also grew apart.[43]

The teachers became particularly assertive over salaries. They had been restive for some time because of the failure of the board to use its increased funds to improve their meager salaries. They had received no raises since 1907. At every point, the board and administration found more compelling uses for the money—school buildings, staff increases, and new program development. Finally, in the fall of 1913, when expenditures overran revenues, the board cut teachers' salaries in order to balance their budget.

The shock of the cuts led to the formation of the Associate Teachers League and a new militancy among teachers. They complained not only about their low pay but also grumbled about the "too constant supervision and too frequent markings by principals, superintendents and three supervisors of special subjects." The rebellion persuaded the board to drop evaluations by the special supervising teachers, but Gwinn and the board president, Sol Wexler, offered pay increases only if the restive teachers accepted a merit plan.[44] To set up such an "efficiency" plan, the assistant superintendents evaluated and ranked each teacher in one of five categories ranging from "very poor" to "superior." Additional raises would also be given for bachelors and advanced college degrees.

At first, the teachers accepted the plan, at least until the results of the evaluations and the pay schedules were announced. Only eighty-seven teachers in the whole system had been ranked "superior," and the salary schedule included a major differential between male and female salaries at every level. Moreover, almost all male teachers escaped any evaluation,

67 Sol Wexler. School board president, vice president of Whitney Bank, and close associate of Mayor Martin Behrman. He helped Behrman build close ties between the public schools and local businessmen.

68 Warren Easton High School Faculty. By the 1920s only this boys' high school had
male teachers for white students. It became the training ground of the system's supervising
staff. This group contained three future superintendents: L. J. Bourgeois, F. G. Eberle, and
A. J. Tête.

because not one white male worked any longer in the elementary grades and
none of the high school teachers fell under the merit program.

When women teachers and principals protested, Wexler insisted that the
sexual differential had to be maintained in order to recruit male teachers
and that "many of the women in our schools could not earn as much in any
other line of work."[45] Such attitudes eventually forced the women to turn
the Associate Teachers League into a local of the New Orleans Federation
of Labor and to make their cause a part of the reform opposition to
Behrman's administration.

The women's suffrage movement encouraged the women teachers in their
assertiveness. In fact, Wexler himself noted the logical connection between
the two when he insisted that the idea of "equal pay for equal work" would
come into existence "only when woman suffrage has been established."[46]

69 Summer Vacation Schools. Warren Easton began these summer programs for working-class students to provide them with some vocational training. The girls' program (above) taught millinery skills and the boys' program (below) taught shoe repair.

70 The White Waifs' Home. The public schools took charge of education in both white and black reform schools in the city. Here students were being taught basket making. In 1901, the school system began classes for the deaf; in 1911, for the blind; and in 1912, for the mentally retarded.

71 Francis T. Nicholls Industrial School. This school offered secondary vocational training just for girls. The public schools offered no similar training for boys until 1939.

152

72 Vocational classes began in the upper elementary grades under the administration of J. M. Gwinn to help keep white working-class students in school. The innovation required special teachers and facilities as seen in this picture of a sewing class at Davey School.

73 This shop class for boys was at Beauregard School.

74 Nicholls Industrial School classes. The training concentrated on apparel manufacturing to asssist a small industrial sector in New Orleans. Top, electric power sewing; below, millinery department.

75 Early hot lunch programs. In 1909, a social fraternity at Tulane University began
serving lunches to poor students at the Paulding School (above); later the program called
the "penny lunch" expanded to other schools under a new department. The photo (below)
shows new facilities at the Merrick School. Opposite page: The city government of Martin
Behrman contributed a special truck to expand the program in 1918.

155

76 Night schools.   Some adults (above) came back for high school
training; immigrant men (below) and women (opposite page) also came to
learn English and attend Americanization classes which became important
during World War I.

77 Public School Gymnasiums. Mayor Martin Behrman had the city buy the gym of the Southern Athletic Association (above) for the public schools. He offered no objection when the school board named it after him. Its pool was particularly popular and led to the construction of the Wiltz Public School Gymnasium for the downtown students (below). It had an outdoor pool.

78 Competitive athletics. The boys high school began interscholastic competition in the late nineteenth century in both baseball and football. In 1907, with the creation of the New Orleans Public School Athletic Association, competition began between elementary schools in track, gymnastics, and team sports. It also included girls teams. Administrators were convinced that sports would help stop the high dropout rate in the schools.

79 Teachers at Gayarré School set up a model store to help students learn arithmetic.

THE NEW ORLEANS BOOK

PUBLISHED BY

ORLEANS PARISH SCHOOL BOARD

New Orleans.
SEARCY & PFAFF, Ltd.
720-722 Perdido Street.
1919.

INTRODUCTION.

I F the opportunities within her reach are intelligently realized, New Orleans will become one of the great centers of the world. Love of country is a feeling inherent in every normal boy and girl. Community patriotism—an outgrowth of the modern conditions of life— takes the form of great pride in one's native city, or in the city one has adopted as one's home, and inevitably leads to good results.

We want to inculcate in the children of our city a keen, vivid interest in its past history, in its present, and in its future. Economy in government, good order, cleanliness, and honesty must be the outcome of the education of the children, if our city is to take and maintain its place in civilization. That the growth of a city is measured by the civic interest of its people is a recognized fact. New conditions demand that all children should be taught they are the coming responsible heads of the community.

There was a time when the national government was controlled principally by men from small towns or farms. Today, our Presidents are city men who are calling into their cabinets advisors from our great municipalities, thus proving, "He who makes the city makes the world."

80 J. M. Gwinn encouraged teachers to take part in planning the curriculum in the schools. In 1915, several teachers led by Caroline Pfaff prepared a history of New Orleans called *The New Orleans Book* to use as the text in a Louisiana history course. The book's cover, opposite page; the Introduction, above. Several other urban school systems adopted the idea.

The teachers soon began opening their journal, *The Teachers' Forum*, to the suffrage question. In its columns, one of the more outspoken teachers, Julia Powell, declared that affiliation with a labor union might check the "work of the insidious disease, which is sucking the life-blood and sapping the energies of the army of women teachers; but the ballot in the hands of teachers, would be a powerful weapon for its gradual but certain annihilation."[47]

In some ways, the teachers' rebellion was the least of Gwinn's worries. By 1916, his ambitious program to lower the dropout and failure rates in the elementary schools had overreached the system's financial resources.[48] Even the increased revenues under the Behrman administrations from 1904 to 1912 failed to bring the public schools of New Orleans to the funding levels of other large cities in the United States. In 1913, its receipts of about $24.00 per child placed New Orleans funding at levels ranging from thirty to fifty percent below those of Northern cities.[49]

Until World War I, the Behrman administration had always found ways to meet the ever-increasing demands of the schools. But in the fall of 1915 a devastating hurricane emptied Behrman's bag of fiscal solutions. His diversion of large sums from the city's treasury to repair heavily damaged schools not only left other areas of city government desperately short of funds, but also jeopardized the city's credit standing. By the end of the 1915-16 school year, the board of education added to the fiscal crisis by borrowing more than $600,000 from Chicago and New Orleans banks to cover its growing deficit.[50]

Alarmed business leaders forced Behrman to cut back on expenditures and to reorganize city finances. A series of state constitutional amendments, originally drafted by businessmen on the Board of City Debt and Liquidation, paid off the school debts and established for the school board its own dedicated property tax. The amendment package also forbade city government to use any of its funds for public education. To ensure the separation and independence of the schools, a state law in 1916 extended the terms of school board members to six years and staggered them on two-year intervals. The latter provision was designed to end any wholesale change during a mayoral election. The same law also renamed the school board the Orleans Parish School Board to make clear that the schools were now outside the official jurisdiction of city government.[51]

It became immediately clear that the school system would suffer under the new arrangements. The reduced funding that the changes produced forced Gwinn to curtail much of his educational program. The board ended his merit pay program along with his elaborate evaluation and testing procedures. Later they dismissed the social workers used to check on drop-outs and scrapped his "Stay in School" publicity campaign. Especially painful for Gwinn, the board also brought a halt to any more "scientific planning" by closing down his prized Division of Educational Research.[52] Of his unfinished program, the board passed only his recommendation for free textbooks, but they waited until 1919 to implement that measure. The school system, in short, returned to educational patchwork and emergency maintenance.

As usual during such cutbacks, teachers faced another round of salary cuts. This time, however, the unusual conditions produced by World War I favored their protests. As soon as large numbers of young men left their jobs to join the armed forces in 1918, teachers took advantage of the favorable labor market. Many either resigned or obtained leaves of absence in order to take new government jobs or vacant commercial positions in the busy port of embarkation. By the fall of 1918, local and national newspapers noted the exodus from the classrooms of New Orleans and other large cities and began calling for measures to check the teacher shortage. "Formerly," one paper noted, "nothing but marriage or death served to take a teacher from her desk."[53]

At first, the school board tried to remedy the situation by lowering admission standards to the normal school and by halting any further leaves of absence, but neither measure alleviated the severe classroom shortage. In the well-publicized and unprecedented crisis, teachers regrouped their old reform coalition and began to demand higher salaries. A procession of community groups bombarded the school board with petitions, memorials, and arguments in support of the teachers. After the Associate Teachers League became Local 26 of the Central Trades and Labor Council of New Orleans—the first teachers' union in the Deep South—local and national labor leaders also joined in advocating the teachers' cause.[54]

Within just two days during the summer of 1919, Augustine Aurianne, the head of the new union, gathered over 1,200 signatures of local citizens on a petition calling upon the board to postpone the introduction of free textbooks in order to increase teacher salaries.[55] Over fifty women's groups, represented by the city's Federation of Women's Clubs, pressed the issue by joining the teachers in open rallies.[56] Not to be outdone, the Association of Commerce and the Board of Trade joined labor leaders and the Public School Alliance in the demand for improved salaries. Recruitment of the business elite proved to be the key, because they ended their earlier resistance to new taxation and freed Behrman to propose a substantial tax increase.[57]

Although normally reluctant to endorse any new taxes just before an election, Behrman and his school board responded to the pressure. With the cooperation of Behrman's city attorney, the school board levied a legally questionable tax in January 1920 and raised salaries by one-third. The commission council greatly aided in the effort by raising the school tax base from seventy-five to ninety percent of the assessed value of property in the city. And the Board of Assessors, feeling the combined pressure of city hall and the business elite, increased assessments by thirty-five million dollars.[58]

Though he had helped them, the triumphant teachers and their reform coalition felt in no mood to applaud the mayor. His school board, with its majority of German-Americans, had been seriously wounded by the general anti-German sentiment that surged through the United States during the war. Uptown reformers had actually accused board president J. Zach Spearing and vice-president, Joseph Reuther, of pro-German loyalties in 1918, and had forced the board to drop all German courses from the schools and to fire any teachers who professed admiration for German culture or who retained "enemy" citizenship.[59]

Several women reformers also wildly accused Behrman of fostering prostitution among schoolgirls in the city's infamous Storyville district. Their groundless accusations, however, gained national publicity when the secretary of war closed down the city's legalized prostitution. Many women still resented Behrman's resistance to female suffrage, which he made evident as late as 1916 when his organization once again defeated the recurrent state constitutional amendment to allow women to serve on local school boards.

When, in 1920, women first used their newly gained right to vote, these resentments helped, first, to elect John Parker as governor of Louisiana and, later, with Parker's support to end the long reign of Behrman at city hall.[60] The reformers also elected two of their own candidates to the school board. One of them, Mrs. Adolph Baumgartner, was the former head of the Presidents' Cooperative Club. She became the first woman to win elective office in New Orleans or anywhere else in Louisiana.

The elections of 1920 marked the triumph of the school reformers in New Orleans. They defeated the boss, won both open school board seats, and passed constitutional amendments that raised property taxes to seven mills on both real and personal property in the city. During the next several

81 The five-man school board at the beginning of World War I. Some anti-Behrman leaders accused it of being pro-German and forced the end of German language classes and the dismissal of foreign-born teachers from enemy nations. From left: William Frantz, Joseph Reuther, P. A. Capdau, J. Zach Spearing, and A. C. Sharon.

82   John M. Parker, reform governor of Louisiana, 1920-1924.   He helped oust Behrman from the mayor's office in New Orleans in 1920 and elect an anti-machine board.

years, they extended these victories, first, by anchoring the taxes in the new state constitution of 1921 and, then, by taking control of the school board. In 1922 they elected a third reformer to the school board, James Fortier, and he became its president. When Joseph Gwinn resigned as superintendent in 1923 to head the schools of San Francisco, the reformers appeared to complete their triumph by selecting Nicholas Bauer the new superintendent.[61]

The reformers savored only some symbolic victories, because common foes unified them more than any shared vision for public education in the city. By 1924, when they had to face the responsibility of power, their coalition splintered badly. Mrs. Baumgartner proved unable to win equal pay for women teachers or to end the ban on married teachers. Nor could she open any top positions for women on the central office staff.

83 James Fortier, school board president from 1922 to 1926.

The new mayor, Andrew McShane, showed little interest in public education and, during the recession that followed the war, quickly responded to the call of businessmen to lower tax assessments on real estate. The new school board president, James Fortier, also showed his limitations as a progressive reformer. He brought fierce racial animosity to the discussion of black education and showed little interest in the concerns of women teachers. He reversed the move toward coeducation in the few junior high schools begun by Gwinn and showed virtually no interest in curriculum matters. To remedy the differences in salaries between men and women, he simply persuaded a majority of the board to lower men's salaries to those of women. His "solution" ended unity among male and female teachers, shattered their union local, and also set off a bitter struggle between women teachers and the school board that lasted for almost twenty years.

When the lower tax assessments cut school board revenues in 1923, the board refused to back away from its determination to build a number of new schools in the uptown area of the city—two high schools, Alcée Fortier for boys and Eleanor McMain for girls, as well as several large elementary schools in adjacent, newly developed neighborhoods. To obtain the money, they cut back teachers' salaries as well as support for vocational education. The end of the war had eliminated jobs temporarily opened to women and removed the major pressure to maintain higher teacher salaries.

The triumph of the reformers thus was very short-lived. In 1924, the Old Regulars regained control of city politics and reelected Martin Behrman as mayor, but after less than a year in office he died. If his successors shared little of his devotion to public education, they inherited most of his political animosities. They defeated Mrs. Baumgartner in 1926 and reclaimed control of the school board, making it into a bastion of party patronage.[62] As a result, the city's schools began to slip back into a long period of financial deprivation and educational mediocrity.

When Joseph Gwinn resigned in 1923 to head the schools of San Francisco, the board had, without any search for other candidates, chosen Nicholas Bauer as the new superintendent. Bauer had waited a long time for the superintendency. For almost three decades, he had patiently and dutifully served first as a high school teacher and then as an assistant superintendent. He managed to remain loyal both to Warren Easton and to Joseph Gwinn. He antagonized neither the Old Regulars nor the reformers. He was a survivor, a perfect bureaucrat. Fortier explained that Bauer was "entitled to it because of his long and efficient service."[63]

Unfortunately, by the time he became superintendent, whatever ideas he may have once had to improve the schools had long been forgotten. One New Orleans newspaper, commenting on the snap decision that led to his appointment, warned that Bauer was "a product of the local system, drilled and broken in its ways, skilled to its peculiar tactics, with no experience outside it," and predicted the public school system would "go along in the old rut, perpetuating its faults."[64]

From 1923 to 1941, Bauer's ever-growing central staff issued thousands of directives for teachers and principals, but the flurry of activity failed either to solve the fundamental weaknesses of the school system or to remedy the havoc caused by the Great Depression. The board quit publishing annual reports and, after 1923, conducted most of its deliberations in closed meetings.

Attendance patterns of white students, more than anything else, became Bauer's major concern. After 1923, the number of white children in the schools leveled off at about 31,000 for about a decade; then, during the 1930s, declined to about 21,000 on the eve of World War II. During that twenty-year period, however, white high school enrollment more than tripled, from 3,700 in 1923 to about 12,000 in 1940.[65]

In normal times, the slow growth and eventual decline of white elementary enrollment might have given Bauer's administration a rare opportunity to develop sound secondary schools. But the Great Depression precluded such an outcome. After the state legislature passed a small tobacco tax in 1927 to restore the teacher paycuts of the mid-1920s, the city's schools obtained no further increase of revenues for almost a decade. Instead, property taxes declined so precipitously during the depression that the dominant banking consortium of the city forced the school board to reduce teacher salaries in order to pay the school system's outstanding loans and bonded debt.[66]

The publicity about impending paycuts shocked the teachers and mobilized them once more. This time the national emergency made them fear not just for their salaries, but for their jobs. Their alarm became acute after members of the board openly discussed the need to weaken the tenure laws of 1922 which had given New Orleans teachers some sense of economic security. At first, the teachers accepted pay cuts as an inevitable consequence of the deepening depression. And despite losses of sixteen to twenty-six percent of their monthly salaries, almost all at least kept their jobs. Discouragement grew, however, for the board held back an additional portion of their pay checks near the end of the 1932-33 school year.[67]

Finally, in 1935, when the board made another round of general salary reductions, a large group of teachers followed the lead of Sarah Towles Reed and joined a new labor union, the New Orleans Federation of Classroom Teachers, local 353 of the American Federation of Teachers. The union and the teachers formed an assertive political coalition pledged to protect teachers' rights and to help find new resources for public education throughout Louisiana. But they had to go it alone. Neither the local political leaders nor most of the other women's groups of New Orleans helped them very much. The city's political machine, for example, had taken control of the local chapter of the League of Women Voters and kept if from speaking out. The only major support the union and the teachers gained came from the state Parent Teachers Association, headed by a remarkable woman, Mrs. Paul A. (Emily) Blanchard. She and the PTA helped shape an assertive educational lobby in Baton Rouge.[68]

Huey Long offered hardly any direct help. Most of his educational reforms benefited the rural and small town schools of the state. His famous free textbook law in 1928 meant little for New Orleans schools since a free textbook policy had been in operation there for almost a decade. Other reforms, such as the state equalization formulas of 1932 and 1934, likewise brought no benefit to New Orleans because the city's schools already had the highest level of funding in the state.[69]

Economic relief for the public schools of New Orleans began only after Long's assassination in 1935, when national economic conditions began to improve and the administration of Franklin D. Roosevelt made peace with the new pro-Long leader, Governor Richard Leche. With the help of Leche, the aggressive coalition forged by Sarah Towles Reed and Mrs. Paul Blanchard's PTA helped enact a series of state measures that raised funding for the beleaguered public schools in New Orleans and throughout Louisiana. In 1936, Reed also convinced the state legislature to pass laws that finally forced the reluctant officials in New Orleans to end their archaic policy of firing female teachers who married. The following year the teachers won a further victory, when the New Orleans board passed a new pay schedule that not only raised salaries substantially but also ended all discrimination between men and women and between elementary and high school teachers.[70]

Activist teachers and women activists also used the depression emergency to force the school system to confront its most serious problem—the failure to give an adequate education to the overwhelming majority of its students. As early as 1933, *Quartee*, a new teachers' journal begun by

84 Sarah Towles Reed. She taught at Fortier High School and helped found the first local of the American Federation of Teachers. Here she is surrounded by students after the board failed to dismiss her.

Sarah Towles Reed, suggested that the board commission a survey—an independent, outside evaluation of its operations. At first, Bauer and the Old Regular dominated board resisted the demand. In fact, in 1933, the board took away all control over the non-teaching staff from the superintendent and then larded it with so many patronage positions that New Orleans gained the distinction of having the largest number of maintenance workers per student in the United States.[71]

Encouraged by the support of Emily Blanchard and Issac Heller, a dissident member of the board, the activists marshaled so much community pressure that the board relented and gave approval for a massive outside study of the city's public schools. But the board refused to pay for it. The women's groups formed an independent Survey Committee and raised funds for the study.

In a fashion similar to the original founders of the system a century before, these new activists turned once more to New England. By 1938, renamed as the Citizens Planning Committee for the Improvement of New Orleans Public Schools, the promoters of the survey selected Alonzo G. Grace, commissioner of education in Connecticut, to direct the investigation. He quickly assembled a staff of prominent Northern educators, who spent almost two years probing the New Orleans public schools.

They found a school system which had not fundamentally changed since the early twentieth century. True, the system had almost doubled in enrollment since 1910 and had vastly increased its facilities, but it had not solved the weaknesses exposed in 1909 by Leonard Ayres in his book, *Laggards in Our Schools*.

The survey revealed that a third of the public high school graduates in New Orleans obtained as good an education as existed anywhere in America's public schools. In fact, the seniors of its five white academic high schools scored better on achievement tests administered by the survey team than most high school seniors in the rest of the United States. And, even more remarkable, these New Orleans seniors had attended only eleven grades of schooling. The Grace team noted that New Orleans had only seven elementary grades and four high school grades while the rest of the nation's school systems generally ran twelve-year programs. New Orleans was the only city of over 100,000 to have an eleven-year system.[72]

Principals, teachers, and patrons had usually measured the quality of the New Orleans system by the admirable accomplishments of the favored students from the Easton, Wright, John McDonogh, McMain, and Fortier high schools. But the Grace report exposed the high price that New Orleans paid for this limited achievement. Only twenty-seven percent of the boys and thirty-three percent of the girls got through the white elementary schools without failing at least once. Many failed several times before they simply dropped out.[73] To deal with many of these drop-outs, the school board expanded its expensive and usually unproductive evening program until it contained over ten schools and more than 5,000 students.

Most of the students who finished the seven elementary grades did not go to the college preparatory, academic high schools, because they knew that the terrible failure rate continued there, even more relentlessly. The Grace commission never obtained satisfactory records from the academic boys high schools, but it discovered that only fifty-four percent of the girls remained in the academic high schools after three and a half years. Most of the dropouts left after the first semester.[74]

85　Eleanor McMain High School

86　McMain Auditorium.　Little expense was spared in building this facility.

87 McMain chemistry laboratory. While planning these superb laboratories in the uptown girls high school, the board eliminated foreign languages and chemistry at the only black high school.

88 Alcée Fortier High School for boys. Until the 1950s, New Orleans maintained sexual segregation of it white high schools. The uptown pair, McMain and Fortier, remained for many years the pride of the school system.

89   Fortier High School graduating class, 1941.

During the depression, youngsters with only an elementary education had few prospects for even low-skilled employment. Indeed, earlier in the twentieth century, such economic reality had already encouraged a majority of teenagers in American cities to attend some form of secondary education. The depression led to a similar expansion of secondary education in New Orleans, particularly for white boys who had traditionally attended secondary schools in much lower proportions than girls.

The Grace commission found that Bauer's administration had made no long-term plans for secondary education. By 1932, Bauer had eliminated almost all of the one-sex elementary schools, but despite several critiques by teachers and parents, neither Bauer nor the board ever questioned sexual segregation in the high schools. As a result, New Orleans kept sexually segregated high schools until the early 1950s, well after virtually all other school systems had abandoned the practice.[75]

Traditionalism also affected the development of secondary teaching. Shortly after he became superintendent, Bauer ended Gwinn's experiment with white junior high schools and largely gave up on the idea of vocational training in the regular high schools. Instead, he reasserted the preeminence of the academic high school. In 1925, to find more space for the favored academic program, he recommended the removal of the clerical and secretarial training curricula from the white high schools. He placed all girls' commercial classes in the Joseph S. Kohn Girls High School of Commerce and all boys' programs in the S. J. Peters High School of Commerce.

The commercial high schools never provided any meaningful vocational training. Girls found the best vocational training in the Francis T. Nicholls Industrial School, which gained new facilities in 1936 and changed its name to the Rabouin Memorial School after the board received a private donation from Lewis E. Rabouin. White boys never had a similar school. Haphazard development of additional commercial high schools only managed to produce an inferior set of secondary schools, usually attended by less prepared, working-class students.

When pressures of college requirements forced the board to create four-year high schools, rather than create a twelve-year system, they simply removed the eighth grade from the elementary school to the high schools. Thereafter, elementary school teachers had only seven years to prepare their students for secondary education. The Grace commission discovered the unfortunate results: only a little more than a third of the boys or girls who entered the commercial high schools remained there until their senior year.[76]   On the eve of World War II, New Orleans had a far lower percentage of its youngsters in either public or private high schools than other large Southern cities.

The Grace report made its conclusions very clear. "It should be realized," the investigators emphasized, "that the educational program and philosophy rather than the nature of the children need changing." When, the report went on to say, many of the drop-outs during the first semester of high school are "superior or very superior" and most at least of "normal intelligence," the standards "may be questioned as too high for a present-day secondary school" and the teaching questioned "as to its adaptation to pupil needs and abilities." They urged the school board to end its "training-to-be-a-failure" for two thirds of its white children.[77]

The Grace report reserved even more severe criticism for the system's neglect of its black children. Issac Heller and Emily Blanchard had particularly wanted a survey to force leaders in the city to focus on the most obvious failing of the public schools. Accordingly the report pointed to the "wide gulf in educational opportunity dating far back into the history of the state and region." The survey's investigators found wretched conditions in the black schools and pointed out "overcrowded classes, poor building facilities, inadequate staff and a shortage of teachers."[78]

As impressive as the Citizens Committee survey was, it unfortunately produced few substantial reforms. The school board and administrative

90 Joseph Kohn Commercial High School for Girls. Because the McDonogh No. 6 school for black students was in a white neighborhood, the school board transferred it to white students after a thorough remodeling in 1926. Commercial and secretarial classes were removed from the academic girls schools to create this new type of business school in the 1920s.

91 Rabouin Vocational High School. A donation from Lewis E. Rabouin paid for the construction of another vocational program for girls.

staff failed to confront the profound challenges raised so clearly by the
Grace report. True, they made a few changes. They revamped some of the
bureaucracy of the system and returned to the superintendent's control the
non-teaching operations that the board had taken from him in 1933. They
also planned two comprehensive, coeducational high schools, Francis T.
Nicholls for white students and Booker T. Washington for black students.
But Bauer, who resigned in 1941, as well as his immediate successor,
Auguste Tête, ignored most of Grace's recommendations.[79] Indeed, despite
furious opposition, the school board appointed Tête without any search for
other candidates.[80]

World War II explained only part of the tragic neglect. The burden of the
city's racial past accounted for this ultimate civic failure. The Grace report
could identify the problems, but it could not produce among local leaders
the will to act. When a few key officials tried to take up some
recommendations from the report several years after the war, it was too
late. Civil-rights leaders in the city and nation had already abandoned any
hope of obtaining any fundamental reforms from the conservative leadership
of New Orleans and other Southern school districts. Instead, the new
activists turned to the federal courts in an attempt to find a way to seek the
long-neglected promise of equal justice enshrined in the Constitution of the
United States. In the new attempt, the schools remained at the center of
their civil-rights campaign.

V

Black Schools, 1900-1945

The decision made by the New Orleans school board in 1900 to limit all public black education to the first five grades reflected the era's determination to establish and maintain white supremacy at all costs. That decision not only eliminated all opportunities for black public high schooling but cast the remaining elementary black schools into a long period of deprivation. True, during the period, white as well as black schools suffered. But black schools suffered more because the board treated them with benign neglect.[1]

New Orleans black leaders, however, sought ways to improve black education, even within the framework of the segregated dual system. Their struggle to improve black education remained largely apart from the political battles surrounding similar attempts to upgrade white education, for the state constitution of 1898 had taken the vote away from most of Louisiana's black citizens. Devoid of political power, black leaders had to move along other avenues. For the most part they worked through black community, civic, religious, and educational organizations. Many of the organizations were small and addressed only the needs of a particular school or neighborhood. For example, each of the black schools, like the white schools of the time, had "mothers' clubs" or "parents' clubs." Such clubs conducted neighborhood fund-raising campaigns and brought some tangible benefits to their schools. Also several ward-based organizations, such as the Third Ward Educational Association and the Seventh Ward Educational League, did similar work in their wards. Other groups—the Colored Educational Alliance, the Federation of Civic Leagues, the Interdenominational Ministerial Alliance, and the New Orleans NAACP— extended beyond neighborhood and ward boundaries and worked for improvement in black education generally.

In addition to raising private funds, the organizations also continually attempted to get the school board to allocate to black schools a larger share of public funds. Their strategy consisted of drawing up petitions and submitting reports on the deficiencies that existed in black schools. They would visit individual schools, conduct interviews, gather statistics, and present the evidence to school officials. Led by such figures as Reverend Henderson Dunn, Dr. Joseph Hardin, O. C. W. Taylor during the early years, and Dr. Percy Cruezot, Alexander P. Tureaud, and Daniel Byrd in

92   Reverend Henderson Dunn.

93   Dr. Joseph Hardin.

later years, the Colored Educational Alliance and the New Orleans NAACP stood in the forefront of the fight.

The school board and school officials usually treated black petitioners cordially. While politeness and willingness to hear grievances did not, in themselves, indicate either an acceptance of the petitioners as equals or a willingness to significantly increase funding for black education, the cordial atmosphere of the meetings made possible a continuing dialogue that kept the white officials aware that the city's black leadership was greatly dissatisfied with the meager education the board was providing black children. The black petitioners, it should be noted, were not without some sympathizers and even supporters on the all-white board. Their most notable sympathizers were Mrs. Adolph Baumgartner and Isaac Heller. And after the death of Warren Easton in 1910, all subsequent superintendents of the New Orleans school system—Joseph Gwinn, Nicholas Bauer, August Tete, F. Gordon Eberle, and Lionel Bourgeois—made some effort to improve black education.

The chief concerns of the petitioners focused on poor facilities and overcrowding, on the lack of a high school, and on the need for night schools and vocational training programs. At the same time, they continually pushed for employment of more black teachers and for the equalization of black and white teachers' salary schedules. Though the progress was slow, the persistent doggedness of the city's black leaders gradually wrung from the board a number of significant improvements, even during this lowest of the many low ebbs in New Orleans education.

The petitioners never tired of pointing out the small number and poor condition of the city's black schools. In 1910 New Orleans had sixteen black public schools and sixty-eight white schools. The black schools were invariably frame structures in need of repairs or replacement. To be sure, a large number of white schools were in similar condition. But school officials were more apt to spend construction and maintenance dollars on white schools than on black ones. Even the school-building boom led by Mayor Martin Behrman had little impact on black schools. Between 1900 and 1909, school officials erected twenty-two schools, but only four of them for black students. The average cost of the black schools was $21,500. By contrast, the average cost of the eighteen white schools built during the period was $42,500.

The superintendent's report for the 1920-21 school session showed that the situation had changed hardly at all. Out of a total of eighty-six public schools in the city, less than twenty served black students. Between 1910 and 1920, the city had built seventeen new schools, only two, however, for black students. And few of the black schools compared favorably in size or design with schools built for whites. The black newspaper, the *Louisiana Weekly*, commented: "Why is it that every time a Negro school is built, we are forced to economize—conserve, et cetera—and build a make-shift structure inadequate for present needs and impossible for future necessities?"[2]

The editorial exaggerated neither the physical conditions of the schools nor the school board's attitude towards the problem. The response by school officials to the condition of Fisk Branch illustrated the general neglect. The school was in such poor condition in 1925 that one observer remarked that the building "has completely fallen down." School officials dealt with the crisis one year later by acquiring two double-cottages as a replacement for Fisk Branch. Even after some remodeling, the structures remained of questionable fitness. A school hygienist labeled the buildings "poorly lighted, poorly ventilated, poorly arranged and not large enough to accommodate the number of students who are to be in attendance."[3]

From time to time school board members made visitations to the black schools, as they did to white schools. After a tour of several black elementary schools in 1923, school board members Mrs. Adolph Baumgartner and Fred Zengel expressed shock at the deplorable conditions. Overcrowding in the schools had often necessitated assignment of two students to each desk. One of the schools visited, Valena C. Jones, had reached such a state of disrepair by 1928 that Dr. Joseph Hardin appealed to school officials to immediately build a replacement. Hardin received welcomed support from Superintendent Nicholas Bauer who promised quick relief.[4]

Several months later school officials accepted bids for construction of the building at Annette and Miro streets. And in October 1929 over two thousand people attended dedication ceremonies for the new Valena C. Jones, "considered one of the best equipped school buildings in this section of the country." The lengthy program included speeches by Superintendent Bauer, board member Isaac Heller, community leader Hardin, and Jones' principal Miss Fannie C. Williams. Heller gave the keynote address on "The New Negro." And Miss Williams invited the crowd to tour the school to see some of its modern equipment, such as the radio in the auditorium and up-to-date appliances in the home economics room.[5]

94   Valena C. Jones School, completed in 1929.

Besides the new Valena C. Jones School, the new Craig School, completed in 1927, was the only black school erected during the 1920s that compared favorably with those built for whites. The Great Depression virtually halted school construction at the opening of the 1930s, which meant that black children had to continue to attend the remaining old, substandard schools. By the time the school board acknowledged the need to improve black school facilities, it had no money.

Even if the schools had been kept in repair, shortage of classroom space would still have been a problem. The number of black students enrolled in school increased dramatically between 1900 and 1945. Except for fluctuations in enrollment between 1901 and 1906, black enrollment steadily increased. In 1900 blacks accounted for 17.5 percent of total enrollment, by 1920 the percentage had increased to 21.3 percent. [See Table I] The increase occurred despite the consequent overcrowding, which forced many students to attend school on a part-time basis. Moreover, increased enrollment strained an already critical teacher-pupil ratio. In his 1912-1913 superintendent's report, Joseph Gwinn noted that "practically all of the schools for Negroes are overcrowded," and he called for classroom expansions at McDonogh 32, Bienville, McDonogh 6, and Thomy Lafon.[6]

TABLE I

New Orleans Public School Enrollment, 1900-1940[7]

Year Ending	Black	White	Total
1901	5,509	26,038	31,547
1902	5,072	26,133	31,205
1903	4,856	26,228	31,144
1904	4,949	26,751	31,700
1905	4,558	27,331	31,889
1906	4,847	27,125	31,972
1907	5,659	28,605	34,265
1908	6,295	31,710	38,005
1909	6,717	33,687	40,404
1910	6,616	36,117	42,733
1911	7,674	38,151	45,825
1912	8,105	38,499	46,604
1913	8,367	40,080	48,447
1914	8,706	39,161	47,867
1915	8,736	40,244	48,980
1916	9,656	39,161	47,868
1917	9,404	40,244	48,990
1918	9,685	41,836	41,647
1919	9,362	40,182	49,544
1920	10,984	40,611	51,595
1921	12,996	49,923	53,920
1922	15,256	44,662	59,918
1923	16,103	47,325	63,428
1924	16,128	47,087	63,215
1925	17,052	47,401	64,453
1926	16,500	47,952	64,452
1927	19,625	48,732	68,356
1928	21,025	50,165	71,189
1929	21,911	52,927	74,839
1930	23,018	52,891	75,909
1931	22,572	56,834	79,406
1932	24,897	55,948	80,935
1933	25,130	57,364	82,494
1935	26,640	58,968	85,608
1936	29,256	59,587	88,843
1937	29,062	57,496	88,558
1938	27,537	54,797	82,334
1939	28,322	54,140	82,402
1940	27,787	53,657	81,444

Source: New Orleans Annual Reports, 1900-1920; New Orleans Statistical Reports, 1921-1940.

95 Grammar grade class at McDonogh No. 6 in 1904.

96 Thomy Lafon School. Located in the uptown area, Lafon experienced constant overcrowding in the 1920s and 1930s. Indeed, enrollment usually remained above 2,500.

Even the recently built schools often became overcrowded. The new Thomy Lafon School, erected in 1906, was so overfilled a year later that an annex had to be built. McDonogh 32, built in 1907, had to conduct some of its classes in a rented church building. Renting church buildings, though popular with school officials, worked hardships on teachers and students. School officials could not build partitions or even put desks in the rented churches, for the buildings had to be in condition for use by their congregations on Sundays.[8]

When the board lacked funds to construct annexes and failed to find suitable buildings to rent, it simply limited black pupils to attending school only part of the day. The idea of part-time classes developed slowly, but became widespread in the 1920s. Students at McDonogh 6, however, had

97 Sixth, seventh, and eighth grade classes at Leland University. Leland was one of several black colleges organized during Reconstruction. Nonetheless, because of the lack of educational exposure and attainment of most blacks in the city, Leland offered classes in primary, grammar, secondary, and higher education.

98 New Orleans University. Operated by the American Missionary Association, NOU also focused on grammar and secondary education. But from its inception NOU stressed higher education. Many members of the city's black leadership and professional class received college training at NOU.

99 Straight University. Located on historic Canal Street until 1935, Straight came closest to meeting the DuBoisian idea of training a talented tenth. The school offered degrees in medicine and law during its early years of existence. In 1935 Straight and New Orleans University merged to form Dillard University.

their school-day shortened as early as 1915. In the beginning of the 1922-23 school year, 5,396 black students attended school only part-time. By comparison, only 192 white students had less than full-day classes. School officials tried to limit part-time classes to the lower elementary grades, but that often proved impossible as the number of black students in upper grades increased. The length of the part-time school day varied from two-and-a-half to four hours. No official policy or regulation specified the length of the part-time school day. School administrators simply handled the overcrowding on a case by case basis.[9]

A far more fundamental problem was the total lack of secondary education. The school board's 1900 decision to limit black public schooling to the first five grades did more than eliminate the three bridge grades—the sixth, seventh, and eight—between elementary and high school. The absence of those grades meant two things. First, black public school students could not get the necessary preparation to enter the high school division of Southern University, then located in New Orleans. And second, it meant that before the New Orleans black leadership could begin to press the board to build a black high school, they had to press for restoration of the lost bridge grades. Hence the leaders concentrated their efforts, between 1900 and 1912, on getting the sixth, seventh, and eight grades restored. But they achieved only the restoration of the sixth grade in 1909.[10]

The closing of Southern University and its removal to Baton Rouge in 1913-14, however, led to a change of strategy. The move to change the location of Southern University stemmed from arguments that its location in an urban environment prevented it from fulfilling its mission of providing vocational and agricultural training for black students from throughout the state. Black leaders in the rest of the state also argued that the presence of three other black universities in New Orleans justified the removal of Southern. Joseph S. Clark, for example, a black educator who would later become president of Southern, actively worked for Southern's relocation. State officials including Governor Luther E. Hall, his predecessor Jared Sanders, and State Superintendent of Education Thomas H. Harris all supported the move. Most black New Orleanians, on the other hand, opposed the relocation. The New Orleans school board also passed several resolutions opposing the removal of Southern. The board realized that the removal would create an educational void that New Orleans black leadership would immediately pressure them to fill.[11]

100 Reflecting the desire of blacks for a comprehensive education, these students attend a music class at Southern University. Located in New Orleans until 1913, Southern helped fill the educational void created by the elimination of the grammar and high school grades by the school board.

101 Chemistry lab class at Southern University.

Indeed, in July 1913, as soon as it became clear that Southern would leave New Orleans, a coalition of black citizens petitioned the school board to "make arrangements for a colored high school, as the pupils formerly attending Southern University are now deprived of the State High School." About the same time a group of parents from McDonogh 6 demanded yet again that the missing bridge grades be added when school opened in the fall. Under such pressure, the board agreed to add the seventh grade to black schools in 1913 and the eighth in the following year but still refused to take any action on a high school.[12]

But black leaders and parents did not abandon their campaign. Between 1914 and 1917 blacks repeatedly petitioned the school board for a black high school. They considered public secondary schools crucial to the development of the black community. High schools, once only for the elite, were becoming a source of social mobility for the sons and daughters of the working class. But the white board refused to budge. Then in 1917 things changed. New Orleans' white leaders realized that if they were going to maintain a fully segregated society, the separate black community needed its own physicians, teachers, lawyers and clergymen; and to train such professionals, a black high school would be necessary. The school board decided to open a black high school that fall.

102 Sewing class at Southern University.

For the venture, school officials did not appropriate a large capital outlay as they had for the three recently built white high schools. Instead, they simply transferred white students from McDonogh 13 and converted the structure to black use. Though the black community would have preferred a new high school building in a less commercial part of the city, they readily accepted the arrangement, for it was a great deal better than no public high school at all. The school opened in 1917 as McDonogh 35 and would eventually win acclaim for academic excellence. John Hoffman, a native of Tougaloo, Mississippi, and a graduate of Wilberforce University and Michigan Agricultural College, became its first principal.[13]

The curriculum at McDonogh No. 35 featured traditional college preparatory courses. To graduate, students had to complete a mix of required and elected courses in English, Latin, history, science, music, mathematics, and physical education. "Credit for these subjects," according

103 McDonogh No. 35 opened in 1917 and remained the only four-year public high school for black students until the opening of Booker T. Washington in 1942. In 1965, Hurricane Betsy did what black leaders had attempted to force school officials to do for several decades—destroy the old deteriorating building.

to a school board resolution adopted in September 1917, was "to be given on same basis as in the white high schools." Except in general science, textbooks were the same as those used in the city's white high schools. Eighty-two students enrolled in the fall semester and an additional sixty-one in the spring.[14]

Assessing the first year of operation, Principal Hoffman noted that "from the beginning, both pupils and teachers have joined in their efforts to set a high standard of efficiency and promote a spirit of good will in the school." The staff and students, he went on to say, had worked effectively to smooth over some initial opposition from white residents of the area. "This wonderful spirit seems to have had its effect on the residents in the immediate vicinity," he reported, "and whatever opposition or uncertainty they may have expressed in the beginning has evidently been swept away." Hoffman realized that the growth and success of the city's first black public high school depended upon fostering good relations with neighboring whites.[15]

Meeting the educational needs of blacks, not improving race relations, however, was the school's mission. How well did it succeed? From the start the school faced a dilemma, or rather, a crisis of identity. Although it was established as a college preparatory school, Hoffman also wanted McDonogh 35 to "meet the larger needs of the community." He believed that as the only black public high school in the city it should offer a diverse curriculum. He therefore sought to expand the curriculum to include vocational education. He wanted to add courses in wood-working and home economics, and later, plumbing, printing, and automobile mechanics. Citing the opportunities available for employment in such fields, he concluded that "the majority of the boys will greatly benefit by such a change to fit themselves for practical service." He succeeded, and by 1927 vocational classes had become a regular part of the curriculum. A contemporary observed: "For a number of years the manual training department of the Negro high school made all the work desks for the whole system, [and] the cooking department takes care of the daily lunches."[16]

But the vocational program did not hinder the school's academic development. Hoffman stressed academic attainment as much if not more than vocational training. At the conclusion of the first year he called special attention to the "excellent showing made in the Department of Science." He credited its success to the teachers and students who "worked enthusiastically during the entire year to build up a first-class department."

The mathematics department drew praise for helping students develop "clear and concise reasoning" skills. The history classes "awaken in the pupils a high sense of duty and patriotism through a knowledge of the development of civilization and nations." Hoffman expressed great satisfaction with the student-formed debating society but less satisfaction with the English teacher. He wanted "a teacher of marked ability and special training in English."[17]

McDonogh 35's progress, however, was not without obstacles. For example, shortly before school opened in 1923, the school board inexplicably voted to suspend the teaching of Spanish, chemistry, and physics. That action jeopardized 35's standing as a college preparatory school and raised great concern in the black community. The resulting protestations to the board eventually got this decision reversed but not until the following year. The very popularity and success of the school also soon produced overcrowding. [See table II]

TABLE II
Black High School Enrollment, 1918-1940[18]

Year Ending	Total
1918	143
1919	235
1920	372
1921	565
1922	613
1923	766
1924	509
1925	454
1926	694
1927	869
1928	902
1929	1226
1930	1372
1931	2182
1932	2425
1933	2578
1934	2811
1935	3286
1936	3682
1937	4006
1938	4111
1939	4274
1940	4568

Source: New Orleans Annual Reports, 1920-1921; New Orleans Statistical Reports, 1924-1940.

In addition to a high school, black leaders had long argued the need for a black evening program. Many black children, like many white children, failed to attend school simply because they lacked the initiative. Large numbers of others, both black and white, worked at part- or full-time jobs such long hours that they could not attend regular day classes. In 1910, of the city's black youth aged seven to twenty, 45.7 percent attended school, compared to 54.2 percent for the total group, black and white. In 1920 approximately fifty-eight percent of blacks between seven and twenty years old attended school. Figures for the entire city remained slightly higher, at nearly sixty percent. Evening schools had already significantly expanded educational opportunities for the white youth of the city. School board members had voted to start an evening school at the Boys High School for the 1903-04 school year. School officials in the nineteenth century had discontinued a similiar program because of financial problems. The school opened with 142 students and enrollment reached 180 before the end of the session, five months later. In addition to classes in English, reading, mathematics, geography, and history, students received instruction in typing, bookkeeping, and stenography. Increased enrollment led Superintendent Easton to request additional evening schools. When the 1911-12 school year started, nine white evening schools operated in the city.[19]

From 1900 to 1918, securing evening schools remained a high priority of the black community. The frustration felt by many black leaders in their quest was echoed in an editorial in the *Southwestern Christian Advocate* that questioned "the right of a people to rule who are so nearsighted and thoroughly selfish as to refuse the petition of an element of the citizenship that is loyal, though poor and helpless."[20]

At the same time, the black leadership and press applauded the introduction of the new white evening program. They understood, as one scholar observed, that "the Southern educational revival widened the gap between the schooling of whites and blacks at the same time that it extended opportunity for both groups." Once a new program for whites became operational, black leaders and parents were in a position to increase their own demands for the same program.[21]

And the persistence paid off. After countless appeals and petitions, the school board, in November 1918, established an evening school for blacks. Despite its restrictive admission requirements and limitations—males had to be employed six hours a day and instruction could not extend beyond the fourth-grade level—the evening school made a profound impact. Enrollment reached 398 in the first year and increased dramatically in subsequent years. [See table III]

<table>
<tr><td colspan="2" align="center">Table III</td></tr>
<tr><td colspan="2" align="center">Black Evening School Enrollment, 1919-1940[22]</td></tr>
<tr><td align="center">Year Ending</td><td align="center">Total</td></tr>
<tr><td align="center">1919</td><td align="center">398</td></tr>
<tr><td align="center">1920</td><td align="center">922</td></tr>
<tr><td align="center">1921</td><td align="center">2321</td></tr>
<tr><td align="center">1922</td><td align="center">2824</td></tr>
<tr><td align="center">1923</td><td align="center">2277</td></tr>
<tr><td align="center">1924</td><td align="center">2021</td></tr>
<tr><td align="center">1925</td><td align="center">2527</td></tr>
<tr><td align="center">1926</td><td align="center">2023</td></tr>
<tr><td align="center">1927</td><td align="center">3890</td></tr>
<tr><td align="center">1928</td><td align="center">4203</td></tr>
<tr><td align="center">1929</td><td align="center">4402</td></tr>
<tr><td align="center">1930</td><td align="center">4754</td></tr>
<tr><td align="center">1931</td><td align="center">4710</td></tr>
<tr><td align="center">1932</td><td align="center">4702</td></tr>
<tr><td align="center">1933</td><td align="center">4754</td></tr>
<tr><td align="center">1934</td><td align="center">3581</td></tr>
<tr><td align="center">1935</td><td align="center">4780</td></tr>
<tr><td align="center">1936</td><td align="center">4808</td></tr>
<tr><td align="center">1937</td><td align="center">3282</td></tr>
<tr><td align="center">1938</td><td align="center">2413</td></tr>
<tr><td align="center">1939</td><td align="center">2764</td></tr>
<tr><td align="center">1940</td><td align="center">2166</td></tr>
</table>

Source: New Orleans Annual Reports, 1918-1921; New Orleans Statistical Reports, 1924-1940.

The success of the evening program prompted the black leadership to then take up the cause of vocational training, on which they already had a toehold in John Hoffman's work at McDonogh 35. Under pressure from black petitioners, the board, in 1916, considered building additional classrooms at the Thomy Lafon elementary school to accommodate instruction in vocational training. But a lack of funds forced school officials to abandon the plan; during the year they had spent $100,000 for vocational training in the white schools. Two years later the board finally appropriated funds for construction of a three-room annex at Lafon. Even that was possible only because Joseph Kohn, a civic-minded businessman and former president of the Chamber of Commerce, had pledged $1,200 to purchase industrial equipment for black vocational classes if the board would provide the facilities.

After that initial expansion, other black elementary schools gradually added manual and domestic training. Female students received instruction in sewing and cooking, and males in printing, carpentry, and bricklaying. The vocational programs in the various elementary schools and the one at McDonogh 35 High only partially filled the need. The school board agreed with the city's black leadership that what was needed was a trade school for graduates of the black elementary schools who would not be going on to high school. But money remained the problem.[23] Then into the void stepped representatives of the Julius Rosenwald Fund. School officials had been attempting to get money from the Rosenwald Fund since 1923, but the Fund administrators wanted the school board to show good faith by sharing part of the cost. Finally, when the New Orleans school board sold three million dollars in bonds for school construction in 1930 and allocated $275,000 towards construction of a black trade school, the Rosenwald Fund pledged $125,000 for the proposed $400,000 project.[24]

A few black intellectuals, notably John Guillaume, himself an educator, opposed the building of a black trade school. He had a philosophical commitment to an increase in academic high schools. When it appeared likely that the school would be built, Guillaume wrote Superintendent Bauer a letter of dissent, urging that the funds be used instead to build two new black high schools, one downtown and one uptown. Most black leaders, however, shared the view of the editor of the *Louisiana Weekly* who stressed that black youth needed both vocational and academic training, just as white youth.[25]

Members of the white community also divided over the school. They expressed concern that black trade school training might threaten white jobs. Speaking to a group in March 1930, school board member Isaac Heller stressed that the trade school would not heighten trade competition between the races. Black students, he pointed out, would receive training only in those occupations that they traditionally held. A special conference of black teachers and school board officials helped calm white fears with a public statement "that the trades to be taught at the school would be exclusively those which are largely occupied by colored labor at this time." Actually, the decision to so limit the training had almost certainly been made prior to the conference.[26]

But it really did not matter because it soon became bitterly clear that the school was not going to be built anyway. After purchasing a parcel of land bounded by Thalia, Derbigny, Roman, and Melpomene streets, the school board announced that it did not have the money to match the offer of the Rosenwald Fund to construct the building. In fact, the board had used part of the set-aside funds to purchase a former hospital on Carondelet Street to serve as its own central office. The black community was left only promises.[27]

In October 1934 the school board built, on the site that had been purchased for the trade school, a twenty-one-room, temporary, i.e., frame, black elementary school for $21,000. The school bore the name Sylvanie F. Williams in honor of a woman who had long labored for the cause of black education in New Orleans.

To be sure, additional elementary classroom space was badly needed, but black community leaders thought it more than a coincidence that school officials chose the proposed trade school site for the new school. And they loosed a thunder of protest. In an editorial the *Louisiana Weekly* wondered if school officials had chosen the trade school site to avoid building a vocational school at all. The realization that the loss of the trade school greatly exceeded the gain in additional elementary classrooms dampened enthusiasm for the Sylvanie Williams addition.[28]

Black leaders, however, did not give up hope but continued to press the board for a trade school. Throughout the rest of the 1930s, the Colored Educational Alliance, the New Orleans NAACP, and the Federation of Civic Leagues kept the issue alive. And when the trade school finally came, it came not from local but from federal funding. The Works Progress Administration made the trade school a reality, and it was built near the original site. The board named the school after Booker T. Washington, the man who had devoted his life's energies to industrial education, and appointed Lawrence Crocker its first principal.[29]

If the unusual persistence of its black leaders, which was a legacy left by the city's large and assertive antebellum free black population, set New Orleans apart from most other Southern cities, so did the frequency and high degree of violence of white protest that surrounded the building of virtually every new black school. The violence was, in part, a reaction to the very persistence that characterized New Orleans' black leadership: exceptional black assertiveness engendered exceptionally strong white

104 Lawrence Crocker.

resistance. The friction also stemmed in part from the unusual residential patterns of New Orleans. In most other Southern cities black populations tended to live in a few, huge, virtually exclusive black neighborhoods. But in New Orleans a very large number of quite small black and white neighborhoods were joined together in a checkerboard pattern. As a result, a black school built even in the middle of a black neighborhood was rarely more than a block or two from a white neighborhood.

A typical case in point involved the school board's 1922 plan to rebuild the old Bayou Road School, located in the city's heavily mixed Sixth Ward.

Plagued with numerous health code violations, school officials had made a commitment as early as 1914 to replace the old school building. And after many delays, usually explained in terms of lack of funds, the board acted because increased enrollment forced its hand. Following their almost standard practice of building replacements on or near the site of the school to be demolished, officials announced that they were going to build the new school on the same location, and rename it the Joseph Craig School.

Immediately white residents of the area raised a chorus of opposition. The first protest came in July 1922 when a white delegation appeared at a school board meeting and presented a petition asking the board to locate the school in another area. The proposed site, according to a spokesman for the group, "was not the logical place for a Negro school . . . the section was not a Negro neighborhood." Another member of the group said that property in the area would depreciate in value because more blacks would move into the neighborhood to take advantage of the new school. In addition, an increased number of blacks, according to the white protestor, "would prove obnoxious to the residents of that section." The protestors wanted the board to make the new school white and convert Parham School, located at Columbus and Robertson streets, into a black school. If that proved unacceptable, they recommended building the new school for blacks at St. Bernard and Roman streets.[30]

As the new school building neared completion, the opponents intensified their efforts. On January 12, 1923, a large delegation of white protestors attended the regularly scheduled school board meeting to voice their dissatisfaction. Some members of the group argued that the location of Craig School would inflict a hardship on blacks, for black students would have to walk a great distance to school or black parents would have to seek housing closer to the school site. Abandoning hypocrisy, a white woman in the delegation became more direct. She considered it wrong to make white children attend deteriorating and hazardous schools, while giving black students a modern structure that she considered "really a monument," simply too good for black children.[31]

James Fortier, school board president, took the side of the protestors and opposed the opening of Craig as a school for black students. He urged the board to erect black schools only in purely black areas. If school officials allowed blacks to enroll in the new school, Fortier reasoned, it would threaten white supremacy, and he proclaimed that he was, as the minutes reported, "unwilling to do anything that would affect the white man's supremacy." He was "ready to deny the Negro political equalities and if necessary to resort to force to do so." Since the proper role for blacks in an industrial society was manual labor, he continued, they did not need an education beyond the elementary grade level. And he labeled as absurd any educational plan for black students that provided more than learning how to read, write, and perform a semi-skilled trade. Moreover, blacks should not receive any kind of training that put them in competition with skilled whites.[32]

When Fortier finished, board member Percy Moise asked him if he had a plan to provide the eight hundred children scheduled to attend Craig School with other facilities. If not, Moise said, he thought the school should be opened as planned and suggested the board borrow money to erect another school for black students in a black neighborhood and later transfer them. Fortier refused to accept Moise's plan and asked the board to assure the protesting delegation that no blacks would ever attend the Craig School. By a vote of four to one, the board adopted as policy Moise's motion to proceed with the opening of Craig School. In addition, the motion stipulated that if anyone presented a workable plan to provide educational opportunities for the children scheduled to attend Craig School, school officials would transfer the students immediately. Fortier cast the lone dissenting vote.[33]

Still determined to keep black students out of Craig, Fortier immediately called another special meeting of the board to try to get the action reversed. Fortier urged the board to distribute the eight hundred students among the other black schools in the city and reduce them to part-time school days. Percy Moise objected, and, after a short debate, the meeting adjourned without a vote. At the next regularly scheduled meeting, Fortier brought up his proposal again. This time Fortier's motion, with the support of board members Fred Zengel and Mrs. Adolph Baumgartner, carried. Over the objections of Moise and Daniel Murphy, the school board voted to delay the opening of Craig School until Fortier could submit a more detailed plan to house the eight hundred students in other schools. In consultation with Superintendent Gwinn, Fortier proceeded to formulate a plan for assigning the Craig students to Bienville, Valena C. Jones, Marigny, and McDonogh 35 schools.[34]

105 Joseph Craig School. One of several schools transferred by the board from black to white use because of white protest.

When the New Orleans black community heard what had happened, they gathered at a mass meeting to devise their own plan of action. Among those in attendance were representatives of the NAACP, the Colored Educational Alliance, the National Progressive Association of Negroes, and various parents' clubs. The participants decided to draft a petition protesting the school board's decision and present it at the next board meeting. They elected Emile J. Labranche to be chairman and spokesman of the group.[35]

Two things happened during the days following the mass meeting that greatly strengthened the black community's hand. First, the *Times-Picayune*, which was not usually sympathetic to black causes, on January 27, printed an editorial critical of the school board's decision. And second, following the appearance of the newspaper piece, school board members Zengel and Baumgartner visited three of the schools to which Fortier's plan assigned a number of the eight hundred students. What they saw at those schools convinced both to rethink their position on Fortier's proposal.[36]

106 The "new" Joseph Craig School.

At the February 9 board meeting, Emile Labranche presented the blacks' case in calm, rational terms. He recalled that various black groups had come before the board numerous times during the last ten years asking for a new building to replace the Bayou Road School. And he recalled that for over forty years blacks had attended the school. "Last year," Labranche concluded, "the board again investigated, but this time they did build a new school, Joseph Craig. We now come to you and ask that you open to the colored children this school which has been built for them."[37]

The next two speakers, both white, stressed white supremacy and race segregation. Directing his comments to Fortier, one of the white protestors declared: "Mr. President, you and I, and all of us of the Southland who are of the white race are firm in one belief and that is the supremacy of the white race and the segregation of these races in all things political and social." In support of that view, another white delegate said he considered it unfair to force an "objectionable institution of this kind on the white race. Move this institution where . . . it will be for the good of the welfare of the city of New Orleans as a whole."[38]

The aging black political leader, Walter Cohen, rose. Reflecting the caution shaped from decades of participation in Republican politics, and probably hoping to mollify the hostile whites at the meeting, he said: "I just want to say that we agree with Dr. Sword. We recognize that this is a white man's country and we are at your mercy. We are not desirous of social equality."[39]

But Cohen's deferential plea had no effect on the raging James Fortier, who burst forth:

> It is with difficulty I maintain my patience; it is with difficulty that I can look upon this argument without seeing something more important than this discussion. I say this matter will not die. This is only the beginning of the problem. The fact that we have not denied them our counsel, that we have deferred in one fundamental detail, that they have dared to say to us that this School Board has done a grave injustice, the very fact that they are before it, the discussion is going to continue.[40]

When Fortier completed his diatribe, Mrs. Baumgartner asked if he had visited any of the schools where he wanted to place the eight hundred students. Fortier replied he had not visited the schools and that he relied on Superintendent Gwinn to furnish him with all necessary information. Mrs. Baumgartner then explained that she and Zengel had visited the schools and found them deplorable. Zengel agreed, labeled Fortier's plan impractical, and made a motion to open Craig School as scheduled. With Fortier's single acrimonious no-vote, the new motion passed. The motion, however, carried with it the understanding that the board would borrow money to build another school for black students and transfer them out of Craig as soon as possible. The transfer to a new building on Philip Street in fact occurred in January 1927.[41]

Fortier was right about one thing, black leaders would press their campaign for improved school facilities. They continually kept their needs before school officials. Black residents of less developed sections of the city, however, fared worst in the quest for schools. Residents in the Milneburg area, an outlying district near Lake Pontchartrain, for example, repeatedly petitioned the board for a school, but without success. In the main, the school board was a reactive body, seldom taking action until massive community pressure developed. In matters related to black education, this tendency was particularly pronounced. Activism, therefore, became a crucial element in the campaign for improved black schools.

107 Active parental support helped finance many extracurricular activities, like this youthful band group at Joseph Craig.

Black activism entailed more than efforts to secure expanded and improved facilities. It also involved quality of instruction and often focused on the quality of teachers. Despite Jim Crow legislation, white teachers continued to teach in black schools well into the twentieth century. Both blacks and whites opposed the practice and frequently petitioned the board to stop it.

In the face of such widespread opposition, why did it persist? Various factors operated at various times to perpetuate the practice. First, native white teachers steeped in the tradition of the region's racial mores could be counted on to support and reinforce the segregationist and white supremacy ideals. Second, the use of white teachers in black schools increased employment opportunities for white females, a significant consideration because of the small number of professional jobs for women. And third, the number of qualified black teachers lagged behind the demand.[42]

On at least two occasions board members considered expanding the practice rather than phasing it out. In 1906 two board members, Harry Knickerbocker and James Brennan, tried to win board support for replacing all black teachers with white ones. Neither Brennan nor Knickerbocker recorded reasons for their proposal and their motives remained unclear. In any event, the board voted them down. On another occasion, when school officials built an annex to Thomy Lafon in 1910, they proposed staffing the annex with white teachers. They justified their decision by claiming that the annex represented a new school. When black leaders learned of the plan, they quickly registered a protest led by Reverend Henderson Dunn. He successfully argued that the new building was not a new school but simply an annex to Lafon and should have black teachers. The board reversed itself and hired black teachers.[43]

Conversely, attempts by black leaders to have all white teachers removed from black schools proved just as elusive as Brennan and Knickerbocker's effort to remove all black teachers. Blacks residing in Algiers persistently, but unsuccessfully, tried to get only black teachers at McDonogh 32. But their brethren in the Second and Fourth districts did achieve that goal at Bayou Road and First Street schools. As late as the 1912-13 school year, four black schools still had white teachers—Lawton, McCarthy, McDonogh 6, and McDonogh 32.

At that point, increased white sentiment for residential segregation brought about a more concentrated insistence upon removing all white teachers from black schools. The board voted to make the change at McDonogh 6 and McDonogh 32 in August 1913. Two years later Lawton became an all-black-teacher school, and in 1916 McCarthy got an all black faculty. Reverend Elijah Jones and other black leaders supported the changes because they believed that the racial views of the white community made it virtually impossible for white teachers to provide quality instruction to black students.[44]

Also the increased numbers of qualified black teachers available during the early twentieth century made it possible for the board to remove white teachers from black schools. Fannie C. Williams, O. C. W. Taylor, Lucien Alexis, and John Hoffman were only a few of the young black teachers who joined the public school system at the time. Ironically, the lack of professional opportunities for blacks had actually helped the development of black education. Black college students had few options in most professions, and consequently, the majority of them went into teaching.

Despite the willingness of black students to pursue teaching as a career, several obstacles existed. The absence of an inexpensive or free teacher-training program posed the biggest problem. The school board sponsored a normal school for whites but not, until the establishment of Valena C. Jones Normal School in 1923, for blacks. In addition, the board, in cooperation with Tulane University, conducted a normal school in the summer for white teachers which afforded them an opportunity to improve their teaching skills. Black teachers recognized the importance of the summer normal programs and looked for ways to obtain those advantages for themselves. In 1915 the Reverend Mr. Dunn and the Reverend Mr. Jones led a successful campaign to establish a summer normal program for blacks. The school board contributed $250 to help defray expenses, and Straight University donated the use of its facilities. Superintendent Gwinn selected Alfred Lawless as the first director and named an advisory committee composed of Sylvanie Williams, Hattie Feger, and Thomas Sherrard. Lawless, along with the advisory committee, recommended the faculty, who were approved by the superintendent. Lawless conducted a successful program, and the next year Gwinn recommended its renewal. Registration for the 1919 session reached 230 and the board's contribution rose to $500.[45]

Another of the many inequities in educational policy during the era of Jim Crow was the widespread practice of paying black teachers less than white teachers. In 1920, a first-year white teacher earned eighty dollars a month; a black teacher with the same qualifications and experience earned seventy dollars. The discrepancy continued well into the twentieth century. For example, in 1938 a first-year white teacher with a B. A. degree earned $1,000 a year, while a black teacher with identical credentials earned $909 a year. The differential even grew larger as teachers moved into senior ranks. A white teacher with ten years of experience and a B. A. degree received a yearly salary of $2,200; a black teacher with the same training and

108 Sylvanie Williams served as principal of Thomy Lafon and worked with
the Colored Educational Alliance for
better black education.

experience only $1,440. And black teachers often had student loads fifty
percent higher than their white counterparts.[46]

After a 1938 black teachers' petition imploring the school board to
address the inequities in salaries went unheeded, black teachers realized the
court system represented their only hope. They had followed with keen
interest the various suits initiated throughout the country by Thurgood
Marshall and the NAACP calling for equalization of salaries, and they
enlisted his support. Marshall arrived in New Orleans in March 1939, and
advised the group that before filing suit they should form a committee to
raise funds and agree on a plaintiff. Marshall also arranged to work with
the local black attorney Alexander P. Tureaud, who would handle most of
the day-to-day work on the case. Marshall then returned to New York, and
local leaders began work. They organized the New Orleans Citizens
Committee for Equalizing Educational Opportunities and elected Donald
Jones chairman.[47]

But the determination of the teachers did not translate into quick action.
Some of them expressed understandable concern over possible reprisals by
school officials. Many remembered the dismissal of one of their

109 Valena C. Jones faculty. Located in the Seventh Ward, Jones School stressed academic excellence and garnered a reputation as one of the better public schools in the city. Under the skillful leadership of longtime principal Fannie C. Williams (seated, center), Jones also housed the black normal school.

colleagues, James F. Browne, who in 1923 had spoken out against white supremacy. A teacher at McDonogh 35 and a native of Iowa, Browne had incurred the wrath of Fortier and other board members by suggesting "that social equality is freeborn, recognizing no artificial distinction and lives whenever Christ is found." Browne's comments had appeared in the New Orleans *Bulletin*, a short-lived newspaper that he edited. Interpreting Browne's remarks as inflammatory, the board members, at Fortier's urging, gave Browne a suspension and summoned him before them to explain his remarks.

At the meeting, all of the board members, with the possible exception of Fortier, seem to have favored reinstatement if Browne publicly disavowed social equality of the races. Fortier, the self-appointed guardian of white supremacy, asked Browne to explain his statement concerning social equality. Although conscious of the sentiments of his accusers,

Browne held fast and insisted that "social equality takes care of itself . . . whenever men with like dispositions, tastes, and temperaments associate there is social equality with no preference to color . . . ." Browne went on to explain that during his years of travel in foreign countries, his race was never a factor, for "the fact of being white or black was merely an artificial distinction." As the interrogation continued, it became clear that Browne would not retreat from his position.

The board ordered Browne out of the room so they could discuss his fate in private. Agreeing with Fortier that "such utterances as Browne had made to persons easily led and deluded would foment trouble of a most serious nature," the board voted unanimously to fire him. His termination sent a clear signal to the black teaching corps that improved education was opened to discussion but white supremacy was not.[48]

Even with such memories in mind, New Orleans' black teachers remained determined to push their suit. The militant *Louisiana Weekly* reflected their mood: ". . . if the Negro teachers employed by the Orleans Parish School Board accept without protest this most recent [salary] discrimination, we fear for children who enter their classrooms, so humble and lacking independence will they doubtless be due to the attitude of their instructors." Joseph McKelpin, a non-tenured teacher at Ricard School, agreed to act as the plaintiff, and in May 1941 McKelpin, through his attorney, Alexander P. Tureaud, petitioned the school board to "abolish the present discriminatory schedule of teachers' salaries."[49]

School Board President Henry C. Schaumburg informed the petitioners that the board would consider their request. But when two weeks passed with no word from the board, Tureaud wrote Schaumburg urging the board not to delay in abolishing the differential salary scale. Assistant Superintendent Auguste J. Tête responded for the school board, stating that the petition would be considered at the June 10, 1941, school board meeting. When the board took no substantive action at that meeting, Tureaud filed suit on June 14, 1941.[50]

Assistant City Attorney Howard Lenfant, representing the school board, won court approval of a motion for extension of time, and in September filed a motion to have the suit dismissed. Tureaud quickly wrote Marshall informing him of the motion and asking his advice and to "indicate the time at which you would like to argue the motion to dismiss." Marshall, who was fast becoming an expert in civil-rights law, replied that the motion to dismiss was "completely without foundation," and that, in his opinion, any points that the board could raise had already been dismissed by courts in other cases.[51]

By January 1942, much to the dismay of Tureaud and Marshall, Judge Wayne Borah, who was hearing the case, still had not ruled on the school board's motion to dismiss. Marshall wrote to Tureaud expressing his disgust with the delay and suggested that it might be helpful if he and Tureaud talked with Judge Borah personally. Marshall's timely intervention appears to have hastened Borah's decision, for on February 3 Tureaud wrote Marshall advising him that Judge Borah had denied the motion to dismiss.[52]

Finally, in June 1942 the case began to move toward a conclusion. The school board had asked for a series of delays, but by June such delaying tactics had run their course, and the board made Tureaud an offer. They proposed to raise the salary of black teachers by twenty percent of the differential each year for five years, at which time the salaries of black and white teachers with the same training and education would be equal. The board also promised not to attempt any reprisals against the black teachers. Tureaud wrote Marshall detailing the proposal. Marshall was incredulous: "I think the plan submitted by the school board stinks. In the first place five years is too long. In the second place, there are too many catches. And in the third place, I am sure that our teachers are opposed to it." And Marshall added that he would be in New Orleans in late June.[53]

The school board again tried to settle the issue out of court by proposing a three-year plan of gradual salary increases and by having new school superintendent, Auguste Tête, promise that if funds became available he would attempt to equalize the salaries sooner. Tureaud asked Tête if the three-year proposition would date back to September 1941. Tête replied no. When Tureaud informed Marshall of the new plan, Marshall said he was "completely opposed to the three-year plan dating from the coming September; and as to a three-year plan dating from September, 1941, I think that should be submitted to the Committee."[54]

But apparently Tureaud thought a compromise was advisable, for he proposed an equalization plan to be completed in two years, beginning in September 1942. The plan called for the school board to immediately close the differential between white and black teachers' salaries to fifty percent of the current salary of white and black teachers. For example, if a white

110 George Longe. Active in the New Orleans Classroom Teachers' Association and the
Louisiana Federation of Teachers, Longe served as principal of several schools, including
Alfred Lawless.

teacher with a B. A. degree and ten years of experience earned $2,400 a year,
and a black teacher with the same credentials earned $1,400 a year, a
difference of $1,000, the school board had to close the difference to $500 in
1942. And by 1943 the salaries had to be equal. After working out the
wording of the proposal, both parties signed it on September 1, 1942.[55]

Almost simultaneous with the effort of black teachers to gain equal
salaries, but not related to that issue, was a decision by the school board to
commission a comprehensive study of the city's public schools. Black
leaders immediately voiced fears that Alonzo Grace and his staff, who were
to make the study, would minimize the problems in the city's black
schools, or worse, ignore black education altogether. But they worried
needlessly. Grace started the study in April 1938 and announced his
commitment to give black schools the same scrutiny as white schools.

111 Albert Wicker. An educator and community leader, Wicker served as principal of Bienville School from 1908 to 1928.

During the course of his investigation he met frequently with black teachers and community leaders to gather information for the report.

One of the seven volumes comprising the report focused on black education. Grace's findings confirmed what many blacks had contended throughout the century—that the school system had continuously failed to meet the needs of the black community. The content and conclusions of the report came as no revelation to blacks, but they hoped it might finally force school officials to address some of the more intolerable conditions.

The study publicly exposed many serious problems. Commenting on the twenty-five elementary schools for blacks, the report stated: "Four of the buildings are fairly new, but the others are quite poor, some of them serving as shelters in which children may be collected for a minimum of academic instruction." The study concluded that the Craig, Lockett, Jones, and Landry Schools were fairly good but that the "other schools are so poor that a general recommendation for a replacement program seems to be the only possible course."[56]

Indeed, three of the four "fairly good" black schools had major deficiencies. The Landry School building, completed in 1938, compared favorably with some of the other new structures erected by the school board. But Lockett School, completed in 1934, had small classrooms with insufficient light, and some of the floors were in bad condition. The researchers considered the facilities at Jones and Craig even worse than those found at Lockett. But with Craig's obvious inadequacies, the survey concluded it was "so much better than most of the other colored schools that, with all of its shortcomings, it seems good in comparison." The report characterized Jones, with its 2,800 students, as badly overcrowded and noted that its poor construction accounted for numerous cracks, leaky walls, and uneven floors.[57]

The Grace report showed that, like their white counterparts, black students performed below the national norm in most categories. Approximately sixty-five percent of the black students were "over age" for their grade. Normally, at the age of nine a student should have been in the fourth grade. Out of the 2,377 black children in the fourth grade, 1,727 were ten or over. And the "over age" problem became more pronounced in upper grades.[58]

An analysis of the promotion rates of 3,674 black elementary school students revealed that seventy-three percent of them had failed at least one semester, fifty-three percent at least two semesters, and an astonishing ten percent had failed five to fifteen semesters. Black high school students fared little better. Approximately seventy-five percent of the students who entered eighth grade in 1934 left school without graduating. The researchers viewed the problems of dropping out and failure to pass as an indication that the school system had not adapted to the needs of the students. As the Grace study bluntly put it, the whole approach defied common sense. The research team recommended, among other items, a thorough revision of the curriculum and promotional practices and the inclusion of a greatly expanded vocational training program.[59]

Although the survey steered clear of placing blame for the low educational achievement level of the black students they tested, it offered an interesting observation on the relationship of the students' performance and the training they had received. The researchers declared that "without question, these pupils have not been given practice in taking objective tests or in working at top speed for periods as long as forty minutes."[60]

The Grace report's recommendations were clear:

1. Kindergartens should be inaugurated as fast as facilities and finances permit.
2. Playground and recreational facilities are needed and pay dividends.

3. Overcrowded conditions obtain in practically all of the schools.
4. The teacher load is excessively high; additional teachers are required.
5. A twelve year school program should be developed.
6. At least three groups should be formed after comprehensive testing results are available, each with a curricula program adjusted to its special needs.
7. The compulsory attendance law should be enforced to an increasing degree as rapidly as building and teaching facilities permit.
8. The possibility of a vocational school with state and federal or philanthropic support.
9. The program of secondary education needs a complete reorganization.[61]

But the recommendations of the Grace report, at least for New Orleans' black schools, remained just that and nothing more. The report became a source of reference rather than a blueprint for action. The failure of school officials to respond to the report and to the educational needs of the city's black community, convinced many black leaders that eventually they would have to abandon the strategy of petitioning school officials for improvements. The success of the teachers' equalization suit and various NAACP suits against inequality in higher education demonstrated the potential of the federal courts as a means of relief. And after the end of World War II a more aggressive group of black leaders emerged, determined to take that route.

VI

The Challenge of Growth and the
Ordeal of Desegregation

In 1945, New Orleanians, like most Americans, looked forward to a postwar period of normalcy and prosperity. Teachers and school officials had supported the war effort by adapting the school curriculum to train workers in defense-related industries. And many school employees had volunteered for the armed services, secure in the knowledge that their jobs awaited them when they returned. With the war won, patriotism high, and prosperity on the horizon, few New Orleanians realized peace abroad did not necessarily mean tranquility at home. Demands by the black community for equality soon dispelled the postwar euphoria, forcing Americans to face anew the troubling question of the meaning of democracy in America. And the Orleans Parish School Board became the first official body in the state to have to grapple with the changing spectrum of race relations.

Other problems, however, unrelated to race, also pressed for solution. Most were not new, only larger and more urgent. School officials had long faced them—inadequate revenue, low teacher salaries, the need for more schools, rising student enrollment, and demands by the community for increased efficiency.

At the end of the war the school board still had the structure given it in the reorganization of 1912: a five member board, all elected at large. To be sure, that arrangement remained a marked improvement over the earlier, larger boards with seventeen or more members. And arguably, the smaller board attracted more qualified candidates. The reorganization had also assured the board's independence by giving it taxing authority. The school system was no longer hostage to a parsimonious mayor and city council.

Nonetheless, several storm clouds still hung low. Since the mayor and city council no longer controlled the school budget or contributed to school maintenance and construction, they withdrew from the educational arena altogether. Consequently, a number of school-related problems that often could have benefited from political solutions had to be handled by the school board alone. Until the mid-1940s the system worked fairly well, but at that point some urgent problems began to surface.

112 Lionel J. Bourgeois.

113 Jacqueline T. Leonhard. First woman to serve as president of the Orleans Parish
School Board.

In July of 1946 Superintendent F. Gordon Eberle, who had succeeded Auguste J. Tête, resigned, and the board—Robert Haas (president), Louis Pilie (vice-president), William Fletcher, Emmett Mahoney, and Salvatore Roccaforte—followed a practice that had become the norm. They filled the position from within the system. By unanimous vote the board selected Lionel J. Bourgeois. At the time, Bourgeois was assistant superintendent in charge of instruction, a position that had been created as a result of the administrative reorganization recommended in the 1938-1939 Grace report.[1]

Most interested New Orleanians thought Bourgeois' selection marked the dawn of a new day in the city's school history. Bourgeois' training and professional experience appeared to justify high expectations. Born in the small town of Convent, Louisiana, Bourgeois came from a Catholic family that stressed education and professional careers. After graduating from college he taught school in his home parish, St. James. In 1920 he went to New Orleans to study law at Loyola University, where he took a bachelor of law degree in 1921.

For the next two decades Bourgeois was a man on the move. He continued his formal education, earning a master's degree from Tulane in 1925, and, on and off, taught classes at Loyola and Tulane while holding a regular, full-time job at Warren Easton High School. He became principal of McDonogh 18 in 1936, the next year moved to Edward White School as principal, and less than a year later was made district superintendent of high schools. In 1940 he became assistant superintendent in charge of instruction.[2]

When the board appointed Bourgeois system superintendent in 1946, he immediately launched a series of studies on the various aspects of the school system. Instead of commissioning a single individual or group to study the entire system, as had been done in 1938-1939 with the Grace report, Bourgeois had several agencies, some public, some private, examine different aspects of the public schools. For his first report he had the school board commission the Louisiana State Department of Education to evaluate the procedure the board used for financing and constructing schools.

While that study was underway, Bourgeois sought to broaden public support for the school system by forming a citizens' committee to advise his office on education-related issues. The citizens' advisory committee later used the findings of the Department of Education study, along with recommendations from the superintendent himself, to push for adoption of a comprehensive forty million dollar school construction program. In the meantime, Bourgeois, acting through the board, had commissioned several other studies. In 1948 the Bureau of Governmental Research reported on the system's administrative structure and recommended changes. During the same year, the board hired a firm to assess the financial needs of the schools and in 1950 contracted with the accounting firm of Denis Barry to conduct a complete audit of school finances.[3]

Bourgeois had several reasons for his incessant calls for studies. He believed community involvement in the various studies would bolster public support for schools generally, but more importantly, he believed the reports would increase public confidence in the board and in the superintendent. No elected officials in the city were more subject to public wrath or whim than school board members, and Bourgeois wanted to try to ensure stability and continuity of his board. Bourgeois also saw his reports as a means to increase efficiency in the system and ensure progress in education, both cardinal principles of his administration.

His program, however, had only mixed success. While he frequently gained a community consensus on problems, he often had less success in gaining agreement or support on solutions. The difficulties Bourgeois and the board encountered in their attempts to build additional schools furnish a case in point.

When Bourgeois took office in 1946 most of the inadequacies of school plant facilities documented in the Grace report remained. Many schools built during Reconstruction and not a few built before the Civil War remained in use. In addition, shifts in residential patterns in the older parts of town and the development of new neighborhoods in outlying parts of the city added to the crisis. The massive building program proposed by Bourgeois and his citizens' committee would begin to solve some of the problems.

School officials sought to finance the school construction project through a millage increase. The increase depended first on legislative and then on voter approval. Bourgeois and board members immediately launched into speaking to any civic group that they could get to hear them. Their efforts succeeded, and the legislature approved the increase and put the measure on the ballot. The referendum, because it involved a constitutional amendment, needed a favorable vote throughout the state. As it turned out, winning approval from voters outside the city proved easier than convincing local citizens to support the tax increase.

Local opposition to the millage originated in several sources. The New Orleans newspapers and Mayor DeLesseps Morrison, always nervous about property tax increases, opposed the millage, and it became an issue in the 1948 school board election. One of the incumbent board members, Salvadore Roccaforte, faced challenge from Mrs. Jacqueline McCullough, a former news reporter and public relations officer for the Congress of Industrial Organizations. During the campaign Mrs. McCullough, supported by the Independent Women's Organization, emerged as a staunch opponent of the millage increase. She contended that the school board had yet to fully account for the millions of dollars appropriated for school construction over the past twenty years.[4]

On election day the millage hike passed statewide, though voters in New Orleans had rejected it. It was thus possible for the board to levy the increase, but newly elected board member Mrs. McCullough and two incumbents, William Fletcher and Emmett Mahoney, vowed to vote against any such attempt. Their stance drew the hearty endorsement of the New Orleans *Times-Picayune*. The editor contended: "The propriety of the position of the board majority is obvious. Public sentiment is against the tax and doubtless just as emphatically against having a new property tax imposed by a vote of the state exclusively on the city."[5]

When the new board reorganized in December 1948, Superintendent Bourgeois turned his attention to persuading the board to increase the millage. Bourgeois, realizing that Mrs. McCullough would remain opposed, rested his hopes on persuading the other four members to vote for the increase. Robert Haas and Louis Pilie were both inclined to support the hike, and despite the public pronouncements of Fletcher and Mahoney, Bourgeois thought he could convert at least one of them to his position. It took him the better part of a year, but he finally succeeded. In October 1949 Bourgeois got the three votes he needed to levy the remaining two mills of the authorized millage increase.[6]

From the beginning Bourgeois knew that the building program would prove adequate for white enrollment but would not provide enough classrooms for black students. He hoped to close the gap by consolidating some underutilized white schools and converting the leftover buildings to black use. The superintendent established a dialogue with black leaders such as Daniel Byrd and Alexander P. Tureaud in order to win their support for his plan. They made it clear that although they would support the plan,

114   Alexander P. Tureaud.

115 Daniel Byrd.

they wanted to make sure that buildings assigned for black use were fit and sound, not throwaways.

Bourgeois had much less success, however, in gaining backing from white leaders and parents. Comments by a parents' group concerning the conversion of McDonogh 16 typified the reaction of the white community. In March 1948 the group presented school officials with a petition signed by 1,782 citizens opposed to the conversion. The spokesperson for the group argued that the proposed conversion would force white students to cross too many busy streets. If school officials continued to pursue the conversion, the group said it would sue. Superintendent Bourgeois told the petitioners that black leaders had placed increased pressure on the board to equalize facilities and were also threatening to sue. He emphasized that if the board failed to equalize school facilities, the courts could very well compel the board to admit black students into white schools. The spokesperson for the delegation responded that the group "certainly did not intend that Negroes should be housed" at white schools. Bourgeois reiterated his belief that federal courts would mandate a solution and that his plan of consolidation and conversion would prove much less offensive.[7]

Despite Bourgeois' urgings, board members assured the delegation that they would consider the petition. That action encouraged other groups to attempt to prevent the consolidation and conversion of schools. For example, on March 18, 1948 a large number of white parents attended a special meeting of the board to protest the rumored conversion of several schools, including two vacant ones, Zachary Taylor and Edward White. Under the escalating pressure from the white community and with less than enthusiastic support from his board, Bourgeois offered to scale down his plan if white leaders would campaign for money for additional school construction. But he insisted that he needed to proceed with the immediate conversion of the two vacant white schools.[8]

While he won over a few white leaders, many remained opposed to any conversions and turned to the courts and their legislators for help. State Senator Arthur O'Keefe of New Orleans sponsored a bill to prohibit the conversion of a school from white to black use without the consent of seventy percent of the property owners in the area where the school was located. The bill, Act 463, passed the legislature and Governor Earl K. Long signed it into law in July 1948.[9]

Despite the law, the school board voted on November 30, 1948, to convert the Edward White school. White parents reacted swiftly. Their attorneys filed suit to halt the conversion. But the court ruled Act 463 unconstitutional in February 1949, and school officials proceeded with the conversion. Another suit filed by patrons of Kruttschnitt school suffered a similar fate, and it was converted. These two conversions, however, were exceptions rather than the rule. On several other occasions the board caved in to white pressure and cancelled planned conversions.[10]

Such concessions invariably brought angry protests from black leaders. Alexander P. Tureaud appeared before the school board in May 1948 to argue that black students were entitled to additional facilities and pointed to a case in another state in which the court had forced a local school board to equalize black and white schools. A year later NAACP leader Daniel Byrd was more direct. He demanded to know "if the school board reacts to pressure and antagonism," and said that if so, "then we are ready, and ready now, to start our antagonism and pressure." Byrd went on to remind the board members that talking with representatives of the NAACP was "not the same as talking to groups of black principals and teachers." But the board still declined to endorse the full conversion plan.[11]

The consolidation and conversion program advanced by Bourgeois differed significantly from earlier conversions. School officials had, in times past, changed the racial designation of schools solely in response to changing residential patterns; conversions were not part of a larger plan. Bourgeois' plan, on the other hand, was part of his overall strategy to equalize educational facilities between blacks and whites. He acted in part because of mounting pressure from the black community and in part because he perceived something of the legal battle that was likely to come. Indeed, as early as 1945, a group of black parents had asked the local NAACP branch to file a suit in support of equal facilities. The branch's leadership decided against filing suit immediately but opted to present a list of grievances to the board. The petitioners pointedly informed the board in 1946 that the policy of black educational neglect violated the equal protection clause of the Fourteenth Amendment. In subsequent communications Byrd and Tureaud indicated they would file suit if the board refused to remedy the deficiencies raised in the petition. For his part, Bourgeois pledged his unstinting support of black-white educational parity and begged black patience to give him time to undo a century of educational inequality.[12]

But patience within the black community had its limits. The strong white opposition to the millage and the school conversion plan convinced black leaders that they could wait no longer. In June 1948, the NAACP, on behalf of Wilfred Aubert, a community activist from the Ninth Ward, filed a suit to equalize school facilities in New Orleans. When the board met on June 11, the members responded to the suit by declaring their commitment to educational equality, promising to ask the legislature for increased funds, and endorsing several proposals to improve black schools. The difficulty of transforming that sentiment into practice, however, was evidenced, at the very same meeting, by their decision to delay Bourgeois' recommendation for immediate conversion of several schools; they decided instead to rely on new school construction to achieve parity.[13]

In August 1949 Daniel Byrd, in an appearance before the board, stated what would become the black educational argument for the next decade. "If a parent of a colored pupil living in the district of an overcrowded school took a child to a white school and asked for admission," he said, "in accordance with the Fourteenth Amendment of the Constitution local discriminatory statues would not apply, and there would be no legal arguments that would show that such school should be reserved for whites." But the board could not see the future and continued its slow and halting efforts at equalization.[14]

In the meantime, the optimism and enthusiasm that greeted Bourgeois when he became superintendent in 1946 had begun to wane. He had faced several storms. One of the worse centered around a highly publicized incident at Samuel Peters High School. A number of Peters faculty members accused their principal, Joseph Kluchin, of failing to perform his duties, which, they said, contributed to low morale and discord at the school. Kluchin denied the charges and accused the faculty members with refusing to cooperate with him. In the fall of 1948 the longstanding dissension came to a head. The board conducted a full investigation and heard testimony from Kluchin and several teachers—Haze Bergeron, Alfred Firment, Albert Henry, William Hickey, and Adrian Martinez. In the course of the hearings it became clear that Bourgeois had known of the problems but had done little to solve them, and board members and the public voiced sharp criticism of his failure to act.

The hearings occurred in the midst of the heated millage controversy, and the board members wanted to contain the negative publicity, so they took quick and decisive action themselves. They transferred Kluchin and several teachers to other schools. The board's preemptory action returned Peters to a state of normalcy but left Bourgeois looking silly.[15]

At almost the same time, Bourgeois got into a politically embarrassing situation. During the 1948 school board election he exercised questionable judgement by publicly supporting the candidacy of Salvatore Roccaforte. But the November returns elevated Mrs. Jacqueline McCullough to the seat in question. Over the next few years Mrs. McCullough emerged as a consistent critic of the superintendent and would eventually spearhead the movement to oust him.[16]

By 1950 the superintendent had generated considerable ill-will. Almost any incident, no matter how small, had the potential of bringing about his fall. The "wiener case," as it came to be called, nearly proved to be the one. The controversy started when a local meat processor sought to raise the price of wieners sold to the school lunch program. When the head of the board's accounting department refused the higher price, the vendor reduced the meat content of the wieners. Bourgeois brought the matter before the board and recommended referring the case to the district attorney.[17]

At a series of meetings held in April 1950, the board discussed the matter but decided not to send the case to the district attorney. Bourgeois, however, insisted that they should. Annoyed, two members, Fletcher and McCullough, said that if the superintendent thought it was a criminal matter he should take it to the D.A. himself; he did not need the board's approval, for he already had the authority and the responsibility to confer with law enforcement officials on all criminal matters. But Bourgeois still insisted that the board, not he, should make the case. In a subsequent meeting the board's majority supported Bourgeois' position and issued a statement saying that neither Bourgeois nor his staff were guilty of any impropriety.[18]

But the local newspapers delighted in reporting the incident. An editorial lambasted both the board and Bourgeois: "Superintendent Bourgeois is displaying the agility of a mountain goat in escaping from the wiener fraud. If the School Board continues to accept without question his version of what happened, he may emerge as the hero he deems himself to be." Many citizens agreed that the wiener incident was symptomatic of a lack of leadership by either the superintendent or the board. Eventually the *New Orleans Item* called for a complete change in school board leadership. "New Orleans needs a new Superintendent of Schools," an *Item* editorial pronounced, and "New Orleans needs a house cleaning in the school board." And, the editorial went on:

> The controversy growing out of the wiener fraud has destroyed what public
> confidence there was in the men administering our school system. The details of
> the dispute are of secondary importance. It is now apparent that progress within
> the school system depends upon acquiring the services of a new superintendent
> and a better board.[19]

Board members Fletcher and McCullough had insisted all along that Bourgeois should have been more diligent in his handling of the wiener case. They needed no prodding from the editors of the *Item* to seek Bourgeois' termination. At a special meeting of the board, Fletcher brought formal charges against the superintendent and recommended his suspension pending a full investigation. Bourgeois countered by demanding a hearing immediately. Fletcher and McCullough said that was agreeable to them, but the other board members, Haas, Mahoney, and Pilie, voted to sidetrack the whole issue, and Bourgeois was safe, at least for the moment.[20]

During the next school board election in 1950 Bourgeois again involved himself in the campaign. On several occasions he voiced public support for the reelection of Emmett Mahoney. One of Mahoney's opponents in the race, Dr. Clarence Scheps, an administrator at Tulane University and an avowed "need for a change" candidate, chided Bourgeois for his involvement in the campaign. It was ironic, he said, that a superintendent who repeatedly expressed a desire to remove politics from school affairs would actively participate in the election.[21]

Scheps, along with another anti-Bourgeois candidate, Celestine Besse, won the election, both with support from some of the same groups that had previously supported McCullough. When the board installed the new members in December and elevated Mrs. McCullough to the presidency, the anti-Bourgeois forces took control of public school policy.[22]

Immediately Mrs. McCullough (now re-married and known as Mrs. Leonhard), Scheps, and Besse initiated a move to get rid of Bourgeois. They at first tried to get him to resign. He refused, declaring that "not a million dollars could bribe" him into leaving. At a special meeting on December 21, 1950, the group issued a statement that "the majority of the Board did not have the confidence in the present superintendent that a Board should have to properly function and carry on its responsibilities," and lodged official charges of malfeasance and incompetency against Bourgeois.[23]

116 Celestine Besse.

The charges held that Bourgeois had intimidated members of the former board in connection with the adulterated wieners, had made allegations against former board member William Fletcher, had endorsed a candidate in the last school board election, had forced various school employees to contribute money to his campaign to publicly refute charges of incompetency, and had refused to give school records and information to two board members. In addition, Bourgeois was said to have submitted an erroneous budget for 1949-1950 and to have attempted to usurp the powers of the board. Bourgeois protested the allegations and submitted a hundred or so letters and telegrams from individuals and community groups attesting to his competency and character. The board formally noted the communications, voted four to one to accept the charges against Bourgeois, and scheduled a hearing for January 9, 1951.[24]

Although Louis Pilie voted with the majority, he explained that he had done so not because he considered Bourgeois incompetent or unfit for his position, but because of the no confidence vote of the board. "It was going to be impossible," Pilie said, "for the Board to maintain a proper equilibrium in the future if the majority of the members of the Board have to go along with Mr. Bourgeois in a manner that might be compared to a forced marriage between two incompatible people."[25]

On January 9, 1951, the board met to consider the superintendent's fate. Through his counsel—Paul Habans, Albert Koorie, and Charles Rivet—Bourgeois maintained that the charges were "frivolous, base, insubstantial, and untrue." He also questioned the "right and authority of the School Board to hear and pass upon the charges," for he considered it unfair that his accusers would also serve as his judge and jury. Fairness and justice, he contended, demanded a trial in civil court. The board noted his objections but proceeded to hear testimony from witnesses. Late that afternoon the board recessed until the following morning, with the issue undecided.[26]

The recess gave the members an opportunity to ponder the exceptions raised by Bourgeois' counsel. When they reconvened on January 10, they decided to shift their course of action and place the burden of proof on the superintendent. They informed Bourgeois that the board had no legal obligation to give him a hearing and that if he wanted such he would have to have it in civil court. The board then voted unanimously to fire him for incompetency, inefficiency, and unworthiness.[27]

Bourgeois immediately took his case to civil court where he won a restraining order prohibiting the board from removing him from office without a fair hearing. The board appealed the decision to the state supreme court which, in May 1951, sustained the lower court's ruling. But the decision was hardly a victory for Bourgeois; it merely ordered the board to do what the board members had initially agreed to do, hold a hearing on the charges. Bourgeois realized as much, and knowing that his effectiveness as superintendent was lost, stepped down. The board accepted his resignation effective January 1, 1952, with a leave of absence until that date, named O. Perry Walker acting superintendent, and began a search for a permanent replacement. Walker served for nearly two years before the board selected Dr. James Redmond for the new post.[28]

117 O. Perry Walker.

By the time Redmond assumed office, the long-dreaded issue of desegregation had surfaced. During the close of Bourgeois' sometimes turbulent administration, New Orleans black leaders had made a decision to push for desegregation. In November 1951 Alexander P. Tureaud presented a petition to the board detailing the substantial inequalities in educational opportunities available to black students. Declaring that his position "represented the sentiments of the entire Negro citizenry," Tureaud demanded the immediate integration of the New Orleans public schools. The board responded that it would "study the petition and prepare an answer in due time" to this "very grave question."[29]

Two weeks later the board unanimously approved and issued its response. "After careful study of the petition," the board resolution began, "the board is of the firm opinion that such a radical change of policy could not, at this time, serve the best interests of the system. The board believes, rather, that such a departure from tradition and custom, quite apart from the fact that such action by the board would be illegal, could result in chaos and confusion and further, quite possibly cause a very serious worsening of race relationships in the community as a whole." The content of the board's resolution did not come as a surprise to Tureaud; by the time he submitted the petition, he was already formulating desegregation strategy with Robert Carter and Thurgood Marshall of the NAACP.[30]

Nearly a year later, on September 5, 1952, attorney Tureaud, on behalf of Earl Benjamin Bush, filed suit to force the desegregation of the schools. At its next meeting, the board ordered Superintendent Walker to forward the suit to the state attorney general. The board members also approved a recommendation for additional platooning at several black schools in order to reduce the pupil-teacher ratio to forty-five or below, in hopes of remedying the situation that had caused the black community to file the suit.[31]

The Bush suit was one of several filed nationwide by the NAACP. Three months earlier, the United State Supreme Court had agreed to hear two similar cases originating in Kansas and South Carolina. In October and November of 1952, the justices added to their docket three more such cases, from Virginia, Washington, D.C., and Delaware, and consolidated the five as *Brown v. Board of Education of Topeka, Kansas.* [32]

The filing of the Bush suit made little impression on the New Orleans white community, and the school board continued business as usual. School officials continued to operate eighty-seven schools for white

118 James Redmond.

119 Members of the board and superintendent in 1954. Top row: Theodore Shephard, Jr., James Redmond, Matthew Sutherland. Bottom row: Celestine Besse, Clarence Scheps, Emile Wagner, Jr.

children and only thirty-four for black children, though black and white enrollment was just about equal.[33]

But for the city's black community the commitment to desegregation created a dilemma. They had to decide what actions to take in the interim between the filing of the suit and a court ruling. Should they press for improvements under the segregated system? To do so might undermine their position on desegregation. On the other hand, to take no action in the face of persistent inequalities seemed unconscionable. To people like Daniel Byrd, immediate improvements in black education had to be sacrificed to the ultimate and more important goal of integration. Other black leaders, however, wanted to see an immediate increase in school facilities, even under the segregated system. The outcome of the school desegregation case was unclear, they reasoned, and black students still needed an education.[34]

The dilemma was partly resolved in 1954. On May 17 of that year, in a unanimous decision, the Supreme Court ruled that "in the field of public education the doctrine of 'separate but equal' has no place. Separate educational facilities are inherently unequal." Black New Orleanians realized the importance of the decision. Tureaud called it a "momentous decision and one which will go down in the annals of our jurisprudence." But those who believed the Brown decision would bring about quick school desegregation in New Orleans were mistaken. The guardians of racial separation remained determined to keep the intent of the Brown decree in the city.[35]

Within days of the Brown decision, the intransigency that would characterize the white South's massive resistance to *Brown* surfaced. Governor Robert F. Kennon vowed to maintain segregated schools and weakly added that "Louisiana has done a great deal in the past few years to develop a good parallel school system." Louisiana congressman F. Edward Hebert assailed the ruling and joined the resistance forces. Members of Louisiana's all-white house of representatives voted eighty-four to three that "the abolition of segregation would be intolerable to both the white and Negro citizens of Louisiana." In a letter to a New Orleans newspaper a white writer condemned the Supreme Court's action as "vicious despotism" and called for non-compliance.[36]

The Louisiana legislature assumed the dominant role in the fight against desegregation of schools. The newly created Joint Legislative Committee on Segregation, chaired by Senator William Rainach of Summerfield, coordinated the resistance. By the end of 1954, the legislature had passed a raft of bills designed to keep the schools segregated. Acts 555 and 556 formed the centerpiece of the collection. Act 555 prohibited local school systems from establishing desegregated schools, a violation of which would result in the loss of accreditation and funding. And Act 556 established a pupil placement law which prohibited cross-race assignments.[37]

The New Orleans school board applauded the legislature's actions. Superintendent Redmond insisted that segregation was strictly a state and local issue and questioned the right of federal intervention. After the Brown decision he asked the board members to provide "some further direction on how to proceed in preparing the budget." Board member Celestine Besse noted that the recent decision failed to provide guidelines for implementation and in fact gave the parties in the case until November 1954 to present recommendations on how to implement the decision. Given that schedule, Besse argued that no specific demands would be made by the court until the next spring or summer. Therefore, he moved "that the board instruct the Superintendent and the staff to prepare all preliminary budgets and plans for organization of the 1954-1955 school year on the basis of the same kind of organization and programs as the board was currently operating." Theodore Shephard seconded the motion and it passed without opposition, but not before the board made its intention doubly clear by adding that "by this action the Superintendent would be directed to operate schools on a segregated basis."[38]

The Supreme Court's May 1955 decision on implementation led to another flurry of activity. The ruling that desegregation should proceed "with all deliberate speed" gave the school board and the legislature reason for optimism. Extreme segregationists saw it as a sign of judicial retreat, and moderates interpreted it as an order to desegregate the schools only gradually. John Garrett, a leading segregationist in the state house of representatives, thought "the justices realized that they had made a mistake . . . and this was their easiest way out, putting it back on the local level." The more moderate Robert Ainsworth, president pro tempore of the senate, said he welcomed "the new order's mild tone which furnishes us an opportunity to get our house in order."[39]

The black community saw the decision quite differently. Tureaud expressed disappointment because he "expected the Supreme Court to put a time schedule beyond which local school boards may not delay in carrying out the decree." Tureaud's concerns were well placed, for over the next several years black leaders had to counter many tactics designed to prevent desegregation. In the process they pursued three objectives. First and foremost, they continued to litigate. The vague language of the decree on implementation, coupled with the state's legislative resistance, led to a long and costly legal battle. Since the school board refused to initiate any desegregation plan, black leaders had to sue for compliance.

Second, black leaders believed they had to display enough aggressiveness to keep the desegregation effort moving forward. Black leaders repeatedly submitted petitions, and black parents continually filed applications for admission of their children to white schools. Both groups also constantly worked to raise money to pay for the litigation. And third, black leaders attempted to win support from within the white community. That proved difficult because almost immediately staunch segregationists had gained the ascendancy. Except for the small interracial Southern Conference Education Fund, a handful of civic groups, and a few officials in the Catholic Church, notably Archbishop Francis Rummel, large-scale white support proved impossible to find.[40]

On June 27, 1955, Tureaud filed another petition with the school board seeking desegregation. In part, it stated that "the May 31 ruling means that the time for delay, evasion, or procrastination is passed, and it is the duty of the school board to seek a solution in accordance with the law of the land." The board refused to act, claiming in the words of their vice-presi-dent, Celestine Besse, that they were "responsible to the state government, and our state laws do not allow integration." Tureaud had no choice but to continue litigation of the Bush suit, which was scheduled for a hearing in September. He had to amend the suit to include arguments against Acts 555 and 556. Shortly before the scheduled hearing, Judge J. Skelly Wright requested that a three judge panel hear the suit because he thought the case involved the constitutionality of state law. Herbert Christenberry and Wayne Borah joined Wright on the bench.[41]

In the meantime, the legislature, under the growing influence of William Rainach and the Joint Committee on Segregation, received a $100,000 dollar appropriation to hire special counsel to help prevent the implementation of Brown. Rainach argued that "the state should step in and assist local school boards everywhere in defending themselves against suits by the National Association for the Advancement of Colored People seeking to destroy our policy of separation of the races." The Orleans Parish School Board used its share of the appropriation to pay part of the salary of its special counsel, Gerard Rault.[42]

Meeting in New Orleans, the three federal judges heard arguments on the constitutional issues in the case from Robert Carter and Tureaud for the plaintiff and Gerard Rault and W. Scott Wilkinson for the board. Tureaud and Carter pursued the original argument in the Bush suit, that school segregation by race was unconstitutional. They also charged that the Brown decision rendered Acts 555 and 556 unconstitutional as well. Rault and Wilkinson countered that the entire matter rested outside federal jurisdiction and that the state had acted within its "police power" to maintain health, safety, and educational standards. And they produced witnesses who supported their claim that health and educational problems would result from integrated schools. After hearing both sides, the judges took the case under advisement and issued their ruling in February 1956.[43]

After the court ruled Acts 555 and 556 unconstitutional, Judges Borah and Christenberry removed themselves from the case. Judge Wright alone issued the opinion on the specific issue of desegregation. In his ruling he recounted the facts of the case and referred to the several petitions black parents and leaders had submitted asking the board to desegregate the schools. He acknowledged the difficulties associated with desegregation and noted that the problems were "considerably more serious than generally appreciated in some sections of our country." Indeed, solution of the problems, he went on to say, "will require the utmost patience, understanding, generosity, and forbearance from all of us, of whatever race." Nonetheless, he maintained in his ruling that, "the magnitude of the problem may not nullify the principle. And that principle is that we are, all of us, freeborn Americans, with a right to make our way, unfettered by sanctions imposed by man because of the work of God." Citing the Brown decision, Judge Wright ruled the board's practice of assigning children to schools according to race unconstitutional.[44]

Reaction in New Orleans and around the state varied, but generally the forces of resistance were the most outspoken. Celestine Besse, the school board president, vowed to appeal the ruling and reiterated the board's commitment "to use every legal and honorable means to preserve segregation." Governor Earl K. Long, though refusing to reaffirm his campaign pledge to close the schools rather than integrate them, asserted that the South needed racial separation. For his part, Senator Rainach announced a new two-pronged strategy: the doctrine of interposition and the placing of all local school systems under the jurisdiction of the state. With tacit approval from Governor Long, Rainach easily and quickly guided an interposition resolution through the legislature. The house voted 82 to 0 for approval and the senate 37 to 0.[45]

The interposition doctrine simply revived the old idea that states had sovereignty in areas "not specifically enumerated to the federal government" in the Constitution. The legislative resolution maintained that Louisiana retained its sovereign right to administer its public schools; hence all desegregation court rulings violated both the state and federal constitutions. Interposition was at best a delaying tactic, but delay, no matter how brief, seemed more palatable to most whites than integration.[46]

The rapid rise of White Citizens' councils indicated the depth of Louisiana segregationist sentiment. The first White Citizens' Council appeared in Claiborne Parish in April 1955. A second formed in New Orleans in September, under the leadership of Louis Porterie, Jackson Ricau, and Dr. Emmett Lee Irvin.[47]

Spokesmen for the council quickly made their presence and ideology known. Appearing at a school board meeting within days after the New Orleans council formed, Porterie produced a petition with nearly 15,000 signatures "requesting that the board not abandon segregation in the schools." Porterie assured the board that if necessary the council could secure even more signatures. Several months later, over 8,000 white New Orleanians attended a council-sponsored rally to protest Archbishop Rummel's call for acceptance of school desegregation. And the council followed that with a parade and another rally in May 1956 attended by over 4,000 sympathizers.[48]

The rise of the citizens' councils coincided with state efforts in 1956 to undermine or eliminate the NAACP. Senator Rainach had earlier lashed out at the organization, accusing it of trying to "destroy the friendly relations now existing between our races." He said he deeply resented "the carpetbag NAACP so cynically exploiting our colored people only as an instrument to an end to be discarded when their ignoble purpose is served." Others shared Rainach's sentiments. Governor Long insisted that "our colored people will get a square deal without the NAACP." And the state, in 1956, invoked a 1924 law, originally enacted to curtail the activities of the Ku Klux Klan. The law required virtually all organizations except churches and the National Guard to file their membership lists with the state. When the NAACP refused to submit its list, the attorney general filed suit against the organization, and a state court prohibited the NAACP from operating. The ban lasted until February 1960 when a federal court overturned the earlier decision.[49]

The few proponents of desegregation who did exist in the white community increased their numbers somewhat as the state exhausted its legislative and legal options. It is significant, however, that throughout most of the period, no political figure in the city advocated compliance with the Brown decision. The few courageous white integrationists such as James Dombrowski of the SCEF had little influence of any kind, and moderates, to the extent that they mobilized, had to rely on businessmen and professionals rather than politicians for leadership and consequently were able to do little to influence the desegregation struggle. And the number of moderates always remained small. For example, when a group organized by SCEF presented the school board a petition supporting desegregation with 179 signatures, the segregationists countered with a petition signed by thousands. Until the summer of 1960 school board policy reflected the fears of the segregationists, not the hopes of the moderates.[50]

After unsuccessful attempts to get Judge Wright's ruling reversed by the Fifth Circuit Court of Appeals and by the United States Supreme Court, the school board still refused to desegregate the schools. On June 18, 1959, Tureaud again asked Judge Wright to compel the board to devise a desegregation plan consistent with his February 1956 ruling. Wright scheduled arguments on the issue for the following month. In his decision, handed down in July, he abandoned the vagueness of "with all deliberate speed" and ordered the board "to prepare, present and file in the record of this case by March 1, 1960, an overall plan covering the complete desegregation of the public schools in this city." He suggested that the "board consider a plan under which the first grade would be desegregated the first year, the first and second grades the second year, and so on until all grades have been covered by this plan."[51]

Judge Wright hoped that the "responsible influences on our community life will take their places, as they have in the past, on the side of law and order." But the board ignored Wright's plan as well as his plea. Board president Matthew Sutherland took refuge in the myriad state laws designed to create a buffer between the board and federal judicial authority. Another board member, Emile Wagner, a member of the White Citizens' Council, a Catholic and a virulent critic of Archbishop Rummel's stance on desegregation, bitterly denounced Wright's proposed grade-a-year plan. Wagner preferred to see the public schools closed rather than allow any type of integration, and he pledged his support for the creation of private schools financed by the state.[52]

Following Judge Wright's ruling, school officials mailed a questionnaire to parents in an attempt to determine attitudes on keeping schools open or closing them in the event of court-mandated desegregation.

Parents returned slightly more than 27,000 of the 70,000 forms and voted 14,114 to 12,978 to keep the schools open. Less than a week after making public the results, school board president Lloyd Rittiner announced that he would disregard the survey because 11,407 of the 14,114 parents who voted to keep the schools open were black, and "whites are the people who support the system," Rittiner stated.[53]

Having given the board sufficient time to devise a desegregation plan and receiving none from them, Judge Wright in May 1960 issued his own. He ordered the gradual desegregation of the schools starting with the first grade when schools opened in the fall. School board members met his modest order with defiance. They again vowed to resist desegregation and declared their intention "to fight this order in the courts of the land and . . . use every legal means known to it to preserve a segregated school system." They also met with Governor Jimmie Davis and got his commitment to help maintain segregation in the city's schools. When the 1959-1960 school year came to an end students faced the possibility that their vacation might be exceedingly long.[54]

When higher courts confirmed Judge Wright's order, the board voted four to one to "call upon the Governor of Louisiana to interpose himself between the federal court and the School Board and keep the public schools of New Orleans open on their present segregated basis." Wagner voted against the resolution because he said he believed the board still had some legal options and thought the board should use interposition only as a last measure. Matthew Sutherland disagreed, pointing out that six years of litigation had produced delays but no victories. He warned the community that if interposition failed, they should prepare for either desegregated schools or no public schools at all.[55]

The NAACP, operating again after the federal court lifted the ban on it, immediately attacked the board's position. In a letter to the board, NAACP branch president Arthur Chapital denounced the board's actions and questioned the propriety of elected officials openly advocating disrespect for the law. During the summer the NAACP also held meetings designed to keep the black community informed about the integration effort. In addition, it coordinated the efforts of black parents who were planning to send their children to previously all white schools.[56]

During the summer recess, four board members—Louis Riecke, Lloyd Rittiner, Theodore Shephard, Jr., and Matthew Sutherland—started a slow retreat from their previous refusal even to consider desegregation. The other

120 Louis Riecke (above). Riecke won
election to the board in 1956 and served
until 1968.

121 Lloyd Rittner (above right).
President of the board when
desegregation started in November 1960.
Rittner, along with many of his board
colleagues during the long desegregation
ordeal, saw his business suffer and often
experienced the wrath of the white
community.

122 Emile Wagner (right).

member, Emile Wagner, Jr., continued to champion segregation at all cost. What caused the four board members to change their position was the increased visibility and number of white moderates and the repeated losses in court. They also began to fear the prospect of closing schools. And they reasoned that Judge Wright's grade-a-year plan would require only a gradual increase in the number of black students in white schools.[57]

Faced with the possibility of closed schools, white integrationists and moderates finally acted. Moderates such as Rabbi Julian Feibleman, John P. Nelson, Jr., Mrs. Fred B. Wright, and Mrs. Paul Morrison provided some leadership at this critical stage of school desegregation. They put together a group called Save Our Schools, but because the moderates greatly outnumbered the integrationists, S. O. S. refused to endorse desegregation on its merits. They made it clear they only wanted to keep the schools open, even at the cost of limited desegregation. Another group, the Committee of Public Education, adopted a similiar position. In May 1960 S. O. S. leaders opened their public campaign by painting a bleak picture of consequences of school closure. "The closing of public schools inevitably means an increase in juvenile delinquency," they stressed. At the same time they also warned that the economy would suffer because "new industries refuse to move into an area in which the public schools have been closed."[58]

Although more visible and increasing in number, the moderates had to share center stage with the segregationists. The segregationist forces still controlled the state legislature and had a strong ally in Governor Jimmie Davis. In a last desperate attempt to prevent racially mixed schools in New Orleans, the legislature passed a series of segregation bills in 1960. The most important of these, Act 496, gave the governor the power to assume administrative control of any school district under court order to deseg- regate. On August 17 Governor Davis exercised that power and took charge of the New Orleans schools. The governor directed Redmond to open the schools as scheduled on September 7 and on a segregated basis.[59]

The NAACP and a group of white parents immediately filed suits in federal court to block Governor Davis. A three judge panel acted quickly and on August 27 ruled that "all Louisiana statutes which would directly or indirectly require segregation of the races in the public schools for the Parish of Orleans, or authorize the closure of such schools, or deny them public funds because they are desegregated, are unconstitutional." The ruling returned the schools to the authority of the school board and kept in place Judge Wright's desegregation order requiring the opening of school in September. Redmond, seeking "to eliminate as much confusion [as possible] for everyone concerned," met with board members to assess and respond to the most recent court order.[60]

At a special meeting on August 29 attended by Redmond, special counsel Rault, and all of the board members except Emile Wagner, discussed various options. State Attorney General Jack Gremillion had already indicated that the state planned to appeal directly to the United States Supreme Court. Rault said he believed that the board could join in the appeal. He admitted, however, that he doubted the success of such an effort. The board members postponed a decision on whether to appeal and authorized Rittiner to ask Judge Wright to meet with them or their attorney. "If the conference is granted," Riecke stated, "the board should attend in good faith without any mental reservations." Despite the discussion of an appeal, the board had finally accepted the inevitability of school desegregation; Rittiner and the rest of the board now sought only to minimize its effect.[61]

The board members wanted to meet with Wright in order to try to get him to delay his ruling for a year. With schools scheduled to open in less than two weeks, they believed they needed more time. They pursued their new strategy without Emile Wagner who remained "so convinced that integration as required by the court's order would be an evil far worse than closing the schools," that he announced he was "going to advocate shutting down the public school system." Wagner refused to attend the meeting held on August 30 between the board and Judge Wright. The board asked for a year, expected to receive four or five months, but would gladly accept any respite. Over the protest of Tureaud, Wright granted them two months, until November 14.[62]

The delay enabled the board to institute a pupil-placement plan that reduced the number of black students who would have to be admitted to white schools. In 1960 the legislature had approved Act 492, which gave local school boards the authority to assign students to district schools. The board's pupil-placement plan conformed both to state law and to the guidelines in Judge Wright's order. Under the plan, students wishing to attend a school outside of their district had to request a transfer. Moreover, all students had to start school in their school districts and could apply for a transfer only during a brief period between September 27 and October 7, 1960.[63]

During the transfer-application period, school officials received 208 requests for transfers. They automatically rejected nine of the applications, eight because they arrived after the deadline and the other because it was incomplete. The remaining 199 applications included 137 from black students requesting transfer to white schools, 15 from black students asking to change to another black school, 46 from white students seeking a different white school, and one from a white student wishing to go to a black school. The board established a four-step procedure to screen the 199 applications. It also prepared guidelines for each step showing who would make the decision and on what basis. To protect the safety of the students and their parents, school officials withheld the names of the students applying for transfers.

Four of the parents—three black and one white—withdrew their applications. Two of the withdrawals came from black students seeking admission to white schools, which reduced the number of black students applying for white schools to 135. After an exhaustive administrative review, school officials approved only five of that 135. The five black students approved for transfer to white schools were all girls, one of whom then withdrew her application. Thus, in the end, four little girls stood poised to do what no black New Orleanian had legally done since the end of Reconstruction—attend a desegregated school.[64]

Despite last minute maneuvers by the governor, the attorney general, and the legislature, the four black girls entered the previously all white William Frantz and McDonogh 19 schools on November 14, 1960. They entered accompanied by their parents and escorted by armed federal marshalls. Local police also stood guard. Even so mobs of white adults and children gathered and shouted obscenities and racial slurs as the girls passed. Many white parents hurried to the schools to remove their children, much to the delight of the onlookers who now applauded. The large crowds remained at the two schools most of the day, at times shouting "the south will rise again," and "two, four, six, eight, we don't want to integrate" and in the late afternoon dispersed without violence.[65]

On the second day, however, a group of white teenagers attempted to force their way past police into McDonogh 19, and Chief of Police Joseph Giarrusso had to send reinforcements to keep order. Over the next several days police made several arrests at the two schools and at other spots in the city where racial attacks were sparked. New Orleans at last reaped the bitter fruit that six years of court defiance and racist rhetoric had sown.[66]

123 Black first grader prepares to enter McDonogh 19 for her second day of class. The presence of United States marshals, like the one shown here, and the support of black community groups, such as the NAACP, helped lessen her fears of hostile white protestors.

124 Uniformed and plain clothes detectives provide protection and crowd control for the few white students who still attended Frantz School. The black student (below), as did her three counterparts at McDonogh 19, relied on United States marshals for protection.

125 Not all of the white clergy remained silent during the desegregation crisis. Here a Catholic priest engages in a "discussion" on the merits of desegregation with several protestors.

126 Police often used barricades to keep demonstrators from gathering too close to Frantz and McDonogh 19.

249

127 A crowd protesting New Orleans school desegregation took their complaints to the Louisiana legislature.

128 The specter of violence sometimes hung heavy in the air.

Once the four black students entered class, the New Orleans NAACP concentrated on ensuring that the students were not harmed physically or psychologically. Arthur Chapital coordinated a massive campaign to give moral support to the students. Chapital suggested that anyone wishing to write to the children should do so in care of the NAACP office. The response was overwhelming. Cards, letters, gifts, and small donations began arriving immediately. A typical letter came from Mrs. A. J. Shaw of Brookline, Massachusetts, who sent five dollars for "candy for the children." A parent-teacher association in New York City sent a resolution congratulating the children and indicating its support of integrated schools in New Orleans. Chester W. Hartman of Cambridge, Massachusetts, wrote that the girl's "daily anguish must be so great that it was very important to try to offset this with some expression of friendliness." He had collected several thousand signatures, including that of noted economist John Kenneth Galbraith, on a huge greeting card for the four girls.[67]

That only four black students attended mixed schools in November 1960 portended how slow the pace of desegregation would be in New Orleans. The school board continued its cautious and deliberate approach, determined to minimize the effect of the Brown decision. Black parents and leaders tried, with limited success, to force the board to accelerate the process. As late as the 1962-63 school year, however, only 107 black children attended formally all-white schools. Still, a start had been made, and the board as well the community began to adjust to the new reality. The board and the community knew that a racially unified system had the potential for both promise and peril. Determining which of the two would triumph became the responsibility of the educational guardian of the rising generation—the Orleans Parish School Board.

VII

A New and Uncertain Era

Desegregation failed to produce immediate widespread change within the New Orleans public school system, but the presence, during the 1960-61 school year, of four black students at two formerly all-white schools contained the seeds of change. By the close of the decade of the sixties—a decade as momentous in the nation's history as the twenties or the thirties—desegregation of the schools neared completion. And in the following decade, school officials completed the equally thorny task of faculty desegregation. To be sure, the men and women who guided school policy after 1960 addressed other issues as well—pressure from teacher groups for more pay, increased benefits, and improved working conditions, escalating costs and a declining tax base, and public criticism because of low student performance.

Uncertain of the future and buffeted by winds they could not control, school board members continued their policy of protecting the status quo and of resisting rapid change advocated by external forces. They did so without the services of Superintendent Redmond, for he was one of several casualties of the desegregation crisis. It was somewhat ironic that the second person chosen as superintendent from outside the school system, or the New Orleans area, would find his administration almost totally absorbed in school desegregation. But his fate was inexorably tied to that issue even before he assumed his new position. Shortly before Redmond's arrival, NAACP leader Daniel Byrd had thought it "best to start out rough on him so that when he takes over he will have some respect for the [NAACP] Education Committee."[1]

The incessant debate and focus on desegregation stalled Redmond's hopes of producing educational improvement and reform. He did manage, however, to ensure the success of two reforms initiated the year before his arrival—the complete abandonment of the antiquated practice of sexual segregation in the high schools and the adoption of the 6-3-3 grade plan. In addition, his leadership proved instrumental in the opening of Benjamin Franklin in 1957, a high school for intellectually gifted students.

Unlike one of his predecessors, Lionel Bourgeois, Redmond refrained from direct involvement in school board elections. But he probably watched with dismay the replacing of avowed reform board members who secured his appointment with those concerned only with preventing desegregation. After the Brown decision an aggressive legislature and governor as well as segregationist board members usurped his leadership. Although Redmond remained at his post through the 1960-61 school year, he was a powerless lame-duck superintendent. In January 1961, just a few months after desegregation began in New Orleans schools, he submitted his resignation. Before the opening of schools for the next term, he accepted an offer to head the Chicago public schools and left New Orleans. In the midst of the desegregation crisis the task of leading the school system again fell to O. Perry Walker.

After the beginning of desegregation on November 14, 1960, Judge J. Skelly Wright, acutely cognizant of the effects his court orders had on race relations in the community, continued to pursue his policy of gradual desegregation. Thus, when the school year opened in 1961, Wright's grade-a-year desegregation plan remained in force. Eight black first-graders, along with the four black students admitted in November 1960, now attended desegregated schools. Four additional elementary schools—Benjamin, Lusher, Wilson and McDonogh 11—joined Frantz and McDonogh 19 as desegregated institutions. The twelve black students attending racially mixed schools in the fall of 1961 were spared the hostility and anger that had greeted Tessie, Leona, Gail, and Ruby in November 1960. And the almost total white boycott of classes at McDonogh 19 and Frantz that had remained in effect during the 1960-1961 school year was not replicated at Benjamin, Lusher, McDonogh 11, and Wilson. Nonetheless, enrollment at the four schools suffered a decline, for the school board allowed white students to transfer from any school affected by

Nearly ten years after the filing of the Bush suit and eight years after the Brown decision, only twelve black students were attending desegregated schools in New Orleans. That was not what Judge Wright had in mind when he had sanctioned a grade-a-year plan. Consequently, on April 3, 1962, he issued his most sweeping order to date:

> Beginning with the opening of school in September, 1962, all children entering, or presently enrolled in the public elementary schools of New Orleans, grades 1

129 Dr. Carl J. Dolce. A former principal of Capdau Junior High and Gregory Junior High, Dolce became superintendent in 1965.

254

130 Dr. Alton W. Cowan. Served as superintendent from 1969 to 1971.

through 6, may attend either the formerly all white public schools nearest their homes or the formerly all Negro public schools nearest their homes, at their option.[3]

Judge Wright took the additional step of forbidding the board to issue transfers based on race. He also prohibited the board from any longer using the pupil placement tests which effectively blocked most black admissions to formerly white schools.

The fire storm that Judge Wright anticipated broke immediately. Board president Theodore Shepard, away from the city on school business, returned to New Orleans intent on calling a special meeting of the board to consider appealing the court order. Three of the other four members—Matthew Sutherland, Lloyd Rittiner, and Louis Riecke—voiced support for the appeal. The lone other member, Emile Wagner, Jr., expressed disgust with the way his board colleagues, along with the board's attorney Samuel Rosenberg, had handled the desegregation crisis and refused to support the idea of an appeal. On the other hand, Wagner thought Wright's newest ruling would hasten the abandonment by whites of the public school system.[4]

Many white citizens in the community shared Wagner's view, and successful boycotts of classes at McDonogh 19 and Frantz appeared to justify their predictions. But surprisingly, the anticipated white exodus from the public schools did not occur. To be sure, schools in neighboring St. Bernard Parish absorbed some of the former Frantz and McDonogh 19 students, and a private school, with assistance from the state and the local school board, opened in the Frantz and McDonogh 19 school district. Even so, however, white school enrollment in the elementary schools declined by less than twelve hundred between 1960-61 and 1961-62. And overall white enrollment decreased by less than three hundred. But total white enrollment mattered very little to most white parents and leaders—what mattered was the effect of desegregation on specific schools. White parents in school districts not affected by desegregation generally sympathized with parents opposing desegregation, but they kept their own children in public schools. Enrollment figures for the first several years of desegregated schools show that whites adjusted to or at least tolerated limited racial mixing in the schools.[5]

After his 1956 ruling ordering the desegregation of the New Orleans public schools, Judge Wright suffered verbal abuse, threats of violence, and

131 Despite the lingering boycott of several schools, these white parents prepare to enter Frantz to register their children before the opening of the 1961-1962 school year.

132 Black student prepares to endure the ordeal of desegregation at the start of the 1961-1962 school year.

133 This group of black and white youngsters play at recess, seemingly unaffected by the newly desegregated status of Lusher Elementary.

134 Looking, as if to say, what is the controversy all about, this student prepares to enter McDonogh 19 for the second year of school desegregation.

social ostracism. His April 1962 order to accelerate the desegregation process only added to his personal woes. Obviously such feelings did not extend to Washington D. C., for in 1962 he was offered appointment as judge in the Court of Appeals for the District of Columbia. He accepted the position, though the decision was not an easy one, for he knew successful school desegregation in New Orleans, even if attainable, remained several years in the future. In a section of his last local decision, in *Bush* v. *OPSB*, though referring to the responsibility and travails of the school board, Wright might as well have been talking about himself. "The school board here," he stated:

> occupies an unenviable position. It's members, elected to serve without pay, have sought conscientiously, albeit reluctantly, to comply with the law on order of this court. Their reward for this service has been economic reprisal and personal recrimination from many of their constituents who have allowed hate to overcome their better judgement. But the plight of the Board cannot affect the rights of school children whose skin color is no choice of their own.[6]

With the departure of Judge Wright, Frank B. Ellis became the presiding judge and would hear the board's appeal for a stay order and a new trial. Before the 1961-1962 school year came to a close, Judge Ellis had made two significant rulings. He first granted the board a stay order effectively suspending Judge Wright's decision until he considered the board's request for a new trial. Obviously pleased with the order, board members tempered their elation with caution. Louis Riecke, for example, expressed satisfaction with the order but did not "think it's something . . . we can form a circle and clap hands about." And Rittiner viewed Ellis's ruling as a vindication of the board's efforts to desegregate the schools "with all deliberate speed."

Counsel for the plaintiffs, in the long-running Bush suit, immediately filed a motion with the U. S. Fifth Circuit Court of Appeals to vacate Judge Ellis's order. Chief Judge Elbert P. Tuttle, acting for the court, denied the request on the grounds that the plaintiffs rights "are not in serious jeopardy." Judge Tuttle made it clear, however, that "in denying the motion at this time I do so without prejudice to the rights of the movants to present the matter to the next panel of the court of appeals. . . ." Tuttle thought it best for the appeals court not to intervene until Judge Ellis ruled on the motion for a new trial, scheduled for May 8, 1962.[7]

On Tuesday morning, May 8, attorneys for the plaintiffs and the defendants arrived in court to present their arguments. A move by the city, the state, and the local police department to join the case as defendants created additional drama in the trial that many citizens believed just as important as the judicial proceeding that had led to the May 1960 court order to desegregate. City attorney Alvin J. Liska maintained that widespread desegregation of the elementary schools would cause social unrest, worsen race relations, and place strain on a police department already undermanned and underfinanced. Ellis expressed sympathy with the city's plight and invited Liska to submit amicus curiae briefs, but he refused the city's request to join the case as a defendant.[8]

In support of the board's motion for a new trial, Rosenberg argued that Judge Wright had greatly exceeded the intent of the Supreme Court decision in the Brown case. According to Rosenberg, local school officials had made a good faith effort to desegregate the schools and they were in the best position to assess the impact of desegregation on the public school system. Rosenberg's statements reflected the posture taken by the board since it had agreed to accept the grade-a-year desegregation plan: impress upon the court its willingness to comply with the order to desegregate but stress that community hostility and the maintenance of a good public school system necessitated the gradual, go-slow approach in place since 1960. Aware that part of the push for desegregation had originally stemmed from inadequate and overcrowded school facilities for black students, Rosenberg attempted to argue that the overcrowding in black schools had occurred because of a rising birth rate and migration to the city, not because of discrimination. Studies since the Grace report, however, had repeatedly demonstrated that the allocation of educational dollars and classrooms on a discriminatory basis had, in fact, caused the overcrowding. Rosenberg also knew, as did his local legal counterparts, Alexander P. Tureaud and Ernest Morial, that the issue of overcrowding had long since ceased to be central. Integration itself was now the issue. Although new to the case, Ellis also recognized the new central issue. Two weeks later he issued his decision.[9]

In the meantime, the board held a regular meeting on May 14 at which it departed from past desegregation policy. Throughout the desegregation crisis the board had refused, even when directed by the court, to formulate a plan to eliminate the dual system of education. By 1962, it was obvious that the courts might tolerate a gradual approach but only within the context of active compliance. In other words, courts throughout the country wanted local school boards to initiate specific timetables to comply with Brown. On May 14 the Orleans Parish School Board took the first step in that direction. The board passed a resolution allowing students entering the first grade in the 1962-63 school year to attend the school of their choice, though the board still maintained dual school districts. And a motion by Matthew Sutherland directed Superintendent Walker to eliminate race-specific attendance districts for the first grade, beginning in September 1963. Board members hoped their resolutions would conform to the court's desire for active compliance.[10]

The resolutions emerged as sound strategy, for in his ruling on May 23, Judge Ellis made a reference to the resolutions as a apparent attempt by the board to comply with Brown. Without those resolutions, his statement that it is "an irresistible conclusion that the Board has never actually complied with any order of this court . . . , nor had it ever entered into compliance with the Brown mandate as originally conceived," probably would have resulted in an affirmation of Wright's order for immediate desegregation of grades one through six. In the end, however, although he denied the board's request for a new trial, Ellis modified the previous ruling and withdrew the order to desegregate all elementary grades. In addition to the tentative steps taken by the board to comply, Ellis's belief that accelerated desegregation would create administrative and community problems also influenced his decision to scale back desegregation to the grade-a-year plan. Judge Ellis, to a greater degree than his predecessor, would weigh community sentiment in making all his rulings. The pace of school desegregation envisioned by Ellis matched that of school officials and, by then, many members of the city's white leadership.[11]

The court ruling gave school officials the time they claimed was needed to implement desegregation while maintaining educational standards. The board's task, over the next few years, involved convincing Ellis that its desegregation policy complied with the all deliberate speed test. Nonetheless, Tureaud and the other lawyers for the plaintiffs continued their court fight, for they believed the board's all deliberate speed policy represented nothing but delay and evasion. And student desegregation figures between 1962 and 1964 justified their skepticism. For example, in the school year following Ellis's decision (1962-63), only 107 black students attended desegregated schools. And again the board continued the practice of dispersing them among several schools to keep low the number of blacks attending any one formerly all-white school: the 107 black students attended twenty different schools. During the next school year the number of black students reached only 392 and the following year only 873.[12]

Such figures kept the case in court. But it was a slow fight. Several months or a year often elapsed between court appearances. The routine fell into a pattern. Tureaud and his people sued to speed up desegregation; Rosenberg and his people attempted to demonstrate the insurmountable problems that would result.

In August 1964, still displeased with the slow pace of desegregation as well as with the board's redrawing of school district boundaries, NAACP attorneys again went to court. Tureaud, along with James Nabritt from the NAACP Legal Defense Fund, wanted the court to order the school board to accelerate desegregation, stop gerrymandering the school districts, and adopt a long-range desegregation plan. During the proceedings, attorneys for the NAACP once again started attacking the board's few and slow desegregation efforts. But Judge Ellis wanted more than the customary attacks. He suggested that Nabritt and Tureaud produce specific alternate plans of their own, ideally plans drawn with assistance from recognized educational experts.

The task of securing the services of experts progressed slowly, but eventually Dr. Roger Bardwell, superintendent of School District 59 in Illinois and Dr. David Salten, superintendent of schools in New Rochelle, New York, agreed to work with the plaintiffs.[13]

"Any new matters, any new materials that may give the court a clearer insight, a clearer vision into what ought to be done," Ellis stated at the opening of additional hearings in April 1965, "the court is willing to listen to and accept. . . ." He envisioned three or four days of testimony, at the most, and warned the attorneys not to introduce points already contained in the trial record. Dr. Bardwell took the stand first and answered a series of questions designed to determine if the court would accept him as an expert witness. His training and professional experience won his acceptance as an expert in school administration but not in matters related to school desegregation. Considering Bardwell's background, superintendent of a virtual all-white suburban school district, the court's rejection of him as an expert in school desegregation could not have come as much of a surprise to Nabritt and Tureaud. Nonetheless, he proved to be a good witness for the plaintiffs and frequently, in response to questions by Nabritt, challenged the board's desegregation plan.[14]

Nabritt wanted Bardwell's testimony to support the plaintiffs' contention that overcrowding in the black schools, a lower average per-pupil cost, and a higher pupil-to-teacher ratio resulted from the continuation of a racially dual system of education. In response to a question from Nabritt, Bardwell, referring to charts and graphs he had compiled, answered that a significant imbalance existed in pupil-to-teacher ratios at black and white schools. Judge Ellis asked: "But you cannot discount the fact that the problem is aggravated by the fact that there is a material difference in number, can you?" Bardwell answered: "I can't, but I would add that there is a material difference in the allocation of the resources that are available to education in this parish." Bardwell also contended, later challenged by Rosenberg, that since 1954 the board had enough money for construction to prevent overcrowding. He suggested that overcrowding existed in black schools and underutilization in white schools because the board continued to build race-specific schools.[15]

Bardwell next ventured into an area that would later loom large in school desegregation—busing. Bardwell maintained that busing students to achieve a balanced pupil-to-teacher ratio and reduced class size represented sound administrative strategy that the board should pursue. Ellis asked if busing was practical, and Bardwell answered affirmatively, pointing out that thirty percent of his students were bused. Bardwell noted that the board already used busing, but to promote segregation. Using official school board figures, he pointed out, for example, that every school day hundreds of blacks rode buses to Benjamin School while passing two underutilized white schools, Wilson and Lafayette. School facilities, he stated, responding to a question from Nabritt, "are not being used as efficiently as they could be if there were more integration between the schools."[16]

At that point, Judge Ellis felt compelled to intervene. He then went into an extended summary of the court's previous efforts at desegregation. In his estimation, he said, he thought the court had done a splendid job in advancing school desegregation and noted that "serious problems" would occur from plans to accelerate desegregation. Ellis completed his summary assessment and asked Bardwell, in Ellis's words "a man of integrity," what he would do to accelerate desegregation? Bardwell, a resident of Illinois and aware of his "alien" status, began his response cautiously by acknowledging the sensitive problem of race relations in New Orleans. But he thought it would be best, he forcefully stated, "to fully integrate all of the schools in one year." "All of them?" Ellis asked in apparent disbelief.

"All, right through the high schools," Bardwell insisted. "Well," Ellis added, "the court would like to appoint you as a special master to come down here and do that, and I think that you would end up in an institution for the insane."[17]

Judge Ellis's comments were more than an angry flourish. They represented his belief that school desegregation, if successful, had to proceed slowly. He had a pessimistic view of the long-range effects of desegregation and noted that desegregation of schools in Washington, D. C. had resulted in whites abandoning the system. He feared plans to accelerate desegregation would produce the same results in New Orleans. The entire struggle, he went on to say, would have been futile if, after several years of school integration, the system became resegregated because of parental choice. Ellis knew the law, as expressed in Brown and subsequent decisions, but he also knew white New Orleanians, as dramatically demonstrated in the boycott and eventual white abandonment of McDonogh 19.[18]

After Bardwell concluded his testimony, the other expert witness, Dr. Salten, took the stand. Dr. Salten was even more emphatic about immediate and total desegregation of all grades. He thought such a step would help the board in planning for future construction. Pleased with that response, Nabritt hoped for more. He asked Salten to express his views on faculty desegregation. Even Nabritt was unprepared for Salten's response. "I would think," he stated, "that this is a step which could be taken tomorrow morning . . . the fact that white children are exposed only to white teachers, and Negro children are exposed only to Negro teachers, is to me educationally unsound, and actually damaging to the future of not only the Negro children, but of the white children as well."[19]

When court reconvened the next day, Salten sought to moderate his position on total desegregation beginning in the 1965-66 school year. Although he still preferred immediate desegregation, he suggested a two-year plan. He recommended abolishing the dual system in the first, fifth, seventh and tenth grades the first year and the remaining grades the second year. Ellis asked Salten to comment on how well desegregation had worked in his own city of New Rochelle. Salten conceded, as he had done earlier, that problems had occurred. "And don't you recognize that the problem here is ten times, or twenty times more serious than the problems you had in New Rochelle, as far as public acceptance or reaction is concerned," Ellis wanted to know. Salten answered yes, and Ellis continued, "well, why don't you bring this out when you are indulging in all of your philosophical concepts as to the planning, and everything of that sort? Do you completely ignore the practicalities of the situation?"[20]

Salten remained convinced that rapid desegregation would prove less traumatic than the gradual, grade-a-year plan in use. Neither Rosenberg's cross-examination nor Ellis's pointed queries caused him to deviate from that position, and he continued to insist that complete faculty and student desegregation should start immediately. Unable to sway Salten, Rosenberg attempted to attack his credibility by mentioning the lack of time Salten had to study the problem of school desegregation in New Orleans. Therefore, Rosenberg charged, Salten could not make informed recommendations concerning increased student and teacher desegregation. Judge Ellis agreed with that assessment, and Salten's testimony had little, if any, influence on his ruling.[21]

Nonetheless, at the conclusion of the two-day hearing, Ellis substantially altered the pace of school desegregation. He ordered the board to establish single school districts for the fourth and fifth grades in 1965, the sixth and seventh in 1966, eighth and ninth in 1967, tenth and eleventh in 1968, and twelfth in 1969. Thus, beginning in the 1969-70 school year, New Orleans would have a totally desegregated public school system. Under the previous grade-a-year plan such would not have occurred until four years later, in 1973. The decision left neither the board nor the plaintiffs totally satisfied—it was more than the board had wanted to give and less than the plaintiffs had hoped to receive. Both sides, however, realized it could have been worse. And student desegregation, with slight alterations, followed that time schedule.[22]

When Judge Ellis made his April 1965 decision, 873 blacks attended thirty formerly all-white schools, the overwhelming majority of them in grades kindergarten through third. Only forty-seven of the total attended grades four or above. In addition, only one secondary school, Benjamin Franklin, had black students. Moreover, desegregation had been one way— blacks to formerly all-white schools. Only one white child, a student at Moton Elementary, had elected to attend a formerly all-black school. Despite the fears of white flight, white enrollment actually increased, at least for a time, after the start of desegregation. In the 1960-61 school year, white enrollment stood at 38,112 and by the 1964-65 school year had climbed to 39,314, after a decline in 1961-62 following desegregation. But the 39,314 white students in the public schools in 1964-65 represented the high point before the anticipated decline set in. Even the decline, however, proved not as rapid as many of the doomsayers had predicted.[23]

At the start of the 1966-67 school year, the junior high schools came under the desegregation plan. All eleven of the formerly all-white schools admitted black seventh grade students that first year. McMain, located on South Claiborne Avenue in the uptown section of the city, had the largest black enrollment, 229. Gregory, located on Pratt Drive in the downtown part of the city, had the lowest black enrollment with thirty-nine. In the following year, eight former exclusively white high schools, joined Franklin in admitting black students.[24]

In the 1969-70 school year, public school enrollment reached an all-time high of 111,939: 76,079 black students and 35,860 white students. Black enrollment had increased by slightly more than fifty percent during the past decade, while in the same period white enrollment had declined by

Table I[26]

Total Public School Enrollment, 1960-1961 to 1980-1981

Year	Black Students	White Students	Total
60-61	52,581	38,112	90,693
61-62	55,820	37,845	93,665
62-63	59,223	38,728	97,951
63-64	62,598	38,645	101,243
64-65	64,893	39,314	104,207
65-66	67,059	38,657	105,716
66-67	70,225	37,609	107,834
67-68	72,028	36,773	108,801
68-69	74,435	36,411	110,846
69-70	76,079	35,860	111,939
70-71	76,502	33,349	109,851
71-72	77,289	30,453	107,742
72-73	77,660	26,379	104,039
73-74	76,929	22,614	99,543
74-75	75,986	19,773	95,719
75-76	75,400	18,688	94,088
76-77	75,431	17,933	93,364
77-78	74,646	16,788	91,434
78-79	73,855	15,155	89,010
79-80	73,008	14,079	87,087
80-81	72,367	13,293	85,660

Source: Facts and Finances, 1960-1981.

approximately thirteen percent. Black enrollment continued to surge, peaking at 77,660 in 1972-73. But rising black enrollment after 1969 could not offset the rapid decrease in white enrollment. The long-feared white flight finally occurred during the second decade of desegregation, 1970-79. In the 1979-80 school year, only 14,079 whites attended the public schools. Within ten years the system had lost over twenty thousand white students. Looked at another way, in the 1960-61 school year blacks comprised 58 percent and whites 42 percent of total school enrollment. By the 1980-81 school session, black enrollment had reached 84.48 percent and white enrollment had declined to 15.52 percent. Thus twenty years after desegregation, the majority of black public school students were attending predominantly black schools.[25]

Overall public school enrollment figures for the ten years after the start of student desegregation show a steady but not drastic decline. So, it would appear that student desegregation alone did not account for eventual white abandonment of the public school system. True, the quickened pace of student desegregation after 1970 probably led to an increase in white flight, but the real answer probably lies in the start of faculty desegregation.

Faculty desegregation first started in the 1966-67 school year when the board assigned three black teachers to formerly all-white Kennedy High School and eleven whites to four formerly black schools, McDonogh 35, Bell, Clark, and Booker T. Washington. Meaningful faculty deseg-regation, however, occurred later, as the schedule for court-mandated school desegregation came to an end. By the 1969-70 school year the board still had not gone very far in desegregating the faculty. It appeared that faculty desegregation was destined to share the same go-slow, court-intervention fate of student desegregation. But in the early 1970s, the board began to display the good faith effort that Judge Wright had so courageously sought between 1956 and 1962. As a result, by the mid-1970s desegregated fac-ulties existed at all schools.

But that progress was not without problems. The board attempted to desegregate the faculty by transferring experienced and newly hired teachers to other-race schools. A look at staffing of eighteen randomly selected schools for the years 1969 through 1972 illustrates the point. Eleven of the schools were elementary schools, five formerly white and six formerly black. The racial mix at the six formerly black schools in 1969 was 209 black teachers and no white teachers. In the five formerly white schools in 1969, the racial composition was 106 white teachers and nine black teachers. Through voluntary transfers, the numbers improved slightly during the next two school sessions. Twenty-eight blacks taught at the five formerly white schools in 1970-71 and thirty-one in 1971-72. In the formerly black schools the number of white teachers stood at eight in 1970-71 and twenty-seven in 1971-72.[27]

Similar faculty desegregation patterns prevailed at the secondary schools, as shown by analyzing seven of them: formerly all-white Abramson, Easton, Karr, and McMain; formerly all-black Bell, Clark, and Green. At the latter group of schools, the board employed 170 black and 13 white teachers in 1969-70, 152 black and 31 white in 1970-71, and 142 black and 30 white in 1971-72. The same racial imbalance existed at the formerly all-white group of schools for the same three years: 285 whites and 20 blacks, 250 whites and 55 blacks, and 235 whites and 67 blacks. Though the board had full discretion in the assignment of teachers, it had wisely chosen to give voluntary transfer a chance to succeed, for school officials realized that the teacher corps usually resented transfers. But the policy of voluntarism had failed to achieve faculty desegregation.[28]

Table II[29]

Faculty Desegregation at Selected Schools, 1969-1972

School	1969-1970				1970-1971				1971-1972			
	T	B	W	%	T	B	W	%	T	B	W	%
Abrams	24	1	23	4	23	5	18	22	21	5	16	24
Bore	24	22	22	9	25	7	18	28	22	8	14	35
Crossman	23	2	21	9	23	6	17	26	21	5	16	24
Edwards	46	46	0	0	37	34	4	8	32	31	1	2
Guste	39	39	0	0	36	36	0	0	31	27	4	3
Lawless	54	54	0	0	42	41	1	2	37	32	5	14
McDon 7	16	4	12	25	15	4	11	28	14	6	8	41
McDon 32	24	24	0	0	23	19	4	18	27	20	7	25
Moton	36	36	0	0	35	35	0	0	35	27	8	23
Schaumburg	28	0	28	0	29	6	23	21	26	7	19	30
Wicker	10	10	0	0	9	9	0	0	8	6	2	25
Abramson	96	4	92	4	107	16	91	5	102	22	80	22
Bell	80	75	5	6	83	69	14	17	76	62	14	18
Clark	50	44	6	12	57	45	12	21	55	43	12	22
Easton	58	6	52	10	62	14	48	23	59	14	45	24
Karr	92	2	90	2	80	11	69	14	88	16	72	18
McMain	59	8	51	14	56	14	42	25	53	15	38	28

Source: "Information Report on Staff Desegregation."

During the voluntary phase of faculty desegregation, the board had several opportunities to staff entire schools because five new schools opened in 1970 and in 1971. Three were elementary schools and their students would reflect the racial composition of their location. Crocker and Edison, located in predominantly black areas, had staffs of 73.7 percent black teachers and 26.3 percent white teachers and 66.7 percent black teachers and 33.3 percent white teachers when they opened in 1970. In that same year, Eisenhower Elementary School started operation in a white subdivision in Algiers with a faculty 80 percent white and 20 percent black. One of the two secondary schools, Livingston, located in the rapidly developing eastern section of the city, the area of choice for many young black and white professionals, had 39 white teachers and 20 black ones when it opened in 1971, a percentage of 66.1 to 33.9. The other secondary school, Walker, also located in Algiers, replaced Behrman, a previously all-white high school, and had a white to black faculty percentage of 77.7 to 22.3. Additionally, the board appointed a black educator, Dr. Alvin J. Aubry, as principal.[30]

The board's appointments at the five new schools revealed several things. The most important of which was some commitment to advance faculty desegregation, especially at previously all-black schools. For example, using the same six randomly selected black elementary schools, only eight (4.4 percent) of the 182 teachers in the 1970-71 school year were white. But the two newly opened schools in black neighborhoods—Crocker and Edison—had thirty percent white faculty. And at the other three new schools, the board selected blacks to staff 25.7 of the teaching positions.

Although the board's efforts pushed the number of integrated faculties above that achieved through voluntary transfers, black leaders and the federal court insisted on greater and quicker faculty desegregation. Accordingly, on July 10, 1972, the board voted to use administrative transfers to achieve a ratio of sixty to forty black to white teachers in elementary schools and fifty-five to forty-five in secondary schools. The board also appointed a committee—the Advisory Committee on Implementation of Further Staff Desegregation—to make recommendations on implementation of the new policy.[31]

In August, school officials transferred over eight hundred teachers, nearly nineteen percent of the entire teaching staff. Opposition to the new transfer policy materialized almost immediately. Some of the affected teachers brought a class action suit against the board on August 17, 1972. In the suit—*Harry G. Caire, et al.* v. *Orleans Parish School Board*—the plaintiffs charged that "the orderly planning and operation and more particularly the effective teaching capacity in the Orleans Parish School System for the coming year had been severely impaired" because of the board's transfer of hundreds of teachers. They sought judicial relief to prevent "permanent damage to the education of the children involved." The attorney for the plaintiffs, Lawrence Smith, failed to win a restraining order, and a trial was scheduled for August 25.[32]

Attorneys for the board, including Franklin V. Endom, thought the case lacked merit and that the board possessed the authority and, in this instance, the legal obligation, because of court mandated orders, to transfer teachers. Endom, in his motion to have the suit dismissed, placed the suit in its proper context by arguing that "it is clear from reading the complaint that petitioners are really asking the court to delay the implementation of the Board's program to further desegregate the faculties for one school year." District Court Judge Herbert W. Christenberry, who had taken over the Bush case, ruled that the federal court lacked jurisdiction and dismissed the suit on August 28, 1972, without commenting on the merits of the case. Before he remanded the case to state court, however, he made it known that "if the state court grants any relief, particularly of an injunctive nature, which the court finds frustrates or is in derogation of the orders entered by this court in the case of *Bush v OPSB*, No. 3630, this court shall . . . stay such court action."[33]

After Christenberry's ruling, disposition of the suit became the responsibility of the Civil District Court for the Parish of Orleans. Judge Gerald P. Fedoroff scheduled a special hearing for September 15. In his brief to the court, Lawrence Smith tried to convince the court that the point of the "suit was not and is not to substantially delay or block integration of the faculties." The plaintiffs, Smith contended, wanted the board to "reverse its arbitrary and capricious decision to act in such haste and to plan properly before integrating the faculties on a massive basis." When the trial started, however, attorneys for both sides requested an indefinite delay in the trial, for they had agreed to implement a plan by which school officials would consider specific transfer cases with power to grant relief. Judge Federoff granted the request.[34]

The decision to review transfer cases individually led to charges of administrative bias, and the board established a grievance committee to resolve such cases. Lawrence Smith continued to act as an intervenor in transfer disputes and worked with Rosenberg and Alfred Hebeisen, assistant superintendent for personnel, in setting the claims. Most of the teachers who formally objected to the transfers cited personal reasons or charged that the board had acted unfairly. Charges of unfairness usually centered around seniority status in the system or within a particular school. The board eventually made several changes in assignment, but such changes did not substantially alter the faculty desegregation plan.[35]

School officials took several steps to help ensure successful faculty desegregation. They accepted several of the recommendations of the advisory committee, which included specific guidelines for transferring teachers, the formation of a bi-racial advisory committee, and enactment of a training program for teachers, principals, and administrators. Moreover, school officials elicited comments from teachers who had already served on desegregated faculties.[36]

How successful was the board's effort? In terms of producing a greater racial balance of faculty in the schools, the plan was a success. But progress towards improved race relations and an increase in meaningful contact between the races was more limited. Perhaps it was best summarized by Henry M. Williams, associate superintendent for human relations. Reflecting on the fact that black and white students tended to sit apart in classrooms and segregate themselves in the cafeteria and on the playground, Williams commented: "Polarization seldom disappears of its own accord. Unattended, it is more likely to increase than abate. There must be a genuine desire to overcome this divisive phenomenon and a willingness on the part of schools to work consistently with methods and procedures that unite students and faculty on bases other than race."[37]

By 1973 the membership of the school board had changed several times since the start of desegregation in November 1960. Emile Wagner, Jr., who had opposed even limited student desegregation, finally resigned in August 1962. And several months later Governor Davis appointed Daniel Ellis to serve the remainder of his unexpired term. Two years later, in 1964, Victor Hess and Andrew Rinker won board seats, replacing Ellis and Theodore Shephard. With the election of Robert C. Smith in 1966, Louis Riecke and Lloyd Rittiner were the only board members remaining who had been on the board in November 1960. When Mack J. Spears replaced Riecke in 1968 Rittiner became the lone survivor of the early desegregation crises. But Spears' election signaled more than the passing of another veteran board member, for he was the first black elected to the Orleans Parish School Board. And his election symbolized the already perceptible shift occurring in politics and power in the city, a shift towards increased black political power.[38]

Almost contemporaneous with Spears' election, although not related to it, was the start of federal monetary assistance to the local school board. The national efforts to gain federal dollars for education dated back to the 1870s. But positive action had to await President Lyndon Johnson's Great Society program of the 1960s. Before 1965 the school board received a minuscule amount of money from federal sources. From then on, however, the percentage of the budget derived from federal funds rose steadily. With federal money, of course, came federal regulations. Thus, the combination of increased revenues from the federal government and increased local black political power modified, and eventually altered, the board's stance on race-related issues.[39]

But neither the infusion of federal money nor the election of black board members solved another long-simmering problem in the public school system—low teacher salaries. Throughout the history of the school system, superintendents, board members, community leaders, and teachers themselves had lamented the low salaries and had persistently sought ways to increase them. Although salaries increased during the twentieth century, they still lagged behind those of most Southern cities. And to the chagrin of many New Orleanians, teachers' pay even in other Louisiana cities, such as Shreveport, surpassed teachers' pay in New Orleans. For example, in 1963 the $3,725 a year minimum salary in New Orleans placed Crescent City teachers behind those in Shreveport, who made a minimum of $3,900 a year.[40]

TABLE III[41]

Teacher Salaries in Selected Southern Cities

Baltimore	$4,800	Corpus Christi	4,550
Miami	4,750	San Antonio	4,500
St. Petersburg	4,750	Houston	4,500
Beaumont	4,700	Atlanta	4,440
Lubbock	4,600	Tampa	4,400
El Paso	4,600	Austin	4,400
Dallas	4,600	Jacksonville	4,400
Amarillo	4,600	New Orleans	3,725

Source: New Orleans Annual Report, 1963-1964.

272

135 Dr. Henry Williams.

136 Mildred Blomberg. A community activist for improved schools,
Blomberg served on the board from 1969 to 1974.

137 Dr. Mack Spears. A career educator and former principal of McDonogh 35, Spears won election to three terms on the board.

274

138 The infusion of federal money beginning in the 1960s made new
programs, like this head start class at Craig Elementary, possible.

139 Responding to the cultural diversity of New Orleans, the board
offered bilingual education.

140 A metric workshop held at McDonogh 19 in 1975 reflected the growing emphasis on continual teacher training. Indeed, in the 1980s many New Orleans teachers participated in a state-sponsored project, the Professional Improvement Program [PIP], that linked increased pay to additional classroom training.

141 Board members also stressed the need for additional planning sessions for its members and administrative team. A bit of levity interrupted an otherwise serious discussion of important school-related issues. Left to right: Samuel Scarnato, Gene Geisert, William Reeves, Edward Knight, Lloyd Rittiner, Freda DePolitte, Harwood Koppel, Mack Spears.

142 In 1976 the board moved to this more modern and spacious facility at 4100 Touro Street.

143 In the first school strike in the South, New Orleans public school teachers, members of the American Federation of Teachers (AFT), picketed schools and the administrative offices for three days in April 1966. Here the teachers are shown picketing in front of Carter G. Woodson Junior High.

277

144 Unfazed by their unsuccessful 1966 strike, hundreds of New Orleans public school teachers conducted an eleven-day strike in 1969. In a show of solidarity and attempting to garner public support and awareness, striking teachers staged a march down Canal Street.

145 Dr. Gene Geisert. Superintendent from 1971 to 1980, Geisert served as chief negotiator for the board during the 1978 teacher strike.

146 Rose Loving. With her election to the board in 1976, Loving became the first black woman elected to citywide office.

Teachers knew that the board needed increased revenues to administer a growing urban school system. They also realized that the board had the unenviable task of trying to reconcile salary needs with other financial obligations. Their sympathy with the board's plight, however, did not prevent them from becoming increasingly vocal on the issue of salaries. Indeed, in 1966 and 1969 teachers used the ultimate employee weapon, a strike, in an attempt to win improved pay. The two strikes, though unsuccessful because of poor community support and a lack of teacher solidarity, indicated a growing militancy within teacher ranks.[42]

The new militancy eventually led, in 1972, to the formation of the United Teachers of New Orleans. UTNO resulted from a rare merger of the local units of two major and rival teacher organizations, the predominantly black Local 527 of the American Federation of Teachers and the predominantly white Orleans Educators Association, a unit of the National Education Association. In its first year of existence, approximately seventeen hundred teachers joined the new union, a number which represented about thirty-eight percent of the teaching staff. UTNO members selected Nat LaCour, a former science teacher and head of Local 527, as president. Cheryl Epling, the former head of the Orleans Educators Association, became vice president of the new organization. LaCour and Epling, both energetic and skilled organizers, became an effective team as they slowly recruited new members and garnered community support for the new organization. Prior to 1978 their biggest victory was winning board approval of UTNO's right to bargain collectively for teachers. By 1978 UTNO was the third largest union in the city. Only the Communication Workers of America and the International Longshoremen's Association had more members.[43]

In April 1978, school officials and UTNO representatives started tentative discussions on the "wage-reopener" provision of the existing contract between teachers and the board. LaCour and his negotiating team asked for a nine percent pay increase and wanted the board to pay the entire cost of employee health insurance. School officials, led by Superintendent Gene Geisert, pleaded lack of funds but later promised to seek legislative approval to allow citizens to vote on a proposed half-cent sales tax increase. Despite some prior support in the legislature and massive lobbying by teacher groups as well as school officials, the legislators adjourned without passing the tax bill. With that revenue option closed, school board president Mack Spears and the other four members—Mrs. Rose Loving, Lloyd Rittiner, Harwood Koppel, and William Reeves—considered a push to gain support for a property tax increase. Predictably, that idea fizzled, largely because of the historical aversion of New Orleanians to property taxes.[44]

As the city endured its usual hot summer days, little change occurred in the wage and benefit impasse between the board and UTNO. Finally, in August, the board made the union an offer of $800,000, which union leaders rejected. The board raised its offer to one million dollars, which the union called an "insult." Throughout the summer it had become clear that sentiment was growing among the teachers to strike if the board failed to meet their demands.[45]

On August 28, the board issued a letter to all its employees warning them of the possibility of "serious adverse effects resulting from community based opposition to a strike and serious implications for each employee who participates." The letter, signed by Spears, went on to describe in graphic detail the possible consequences teachers faced if they went on strike. He stressed the loss of tenure, salary, fringe benefits, and sabbatical leave. Spears also warned that possibly "teachers and other employees could be held liable for damages in the event that state support for schools in this parish is withdrawn."[46]

Board members sensed, however, that it would take more than threats to avert a strike. After consulting with other board members, Spears authorized Superintendent Geisert to increase the board's offer to $2.5 million. But union leaders rejected it, too. Geisert and Jerry Hart, assistant superintendent for human resources management and a member of the board's negotiating team, indicated the board had made its best and final offer. Faced with accepting the $2.5 million or striking, thousands of

147 William Reeves.

teachers and teacher-aides gathered on the morning of August 30 and voted not to return to work until the board met their full demands. That same morning thousands of the city's children started their first day of school without their regular teachers.[47]

Once the strike started, battle lines and strategy became clear. UTNO wanted to disrupt the normal school routine by keeping as many teachers and teachers-aides out of the classrooms as possible. Through meetings and letters, LaCour and his staff kept the union members informed. LaCour refrained from publicly disclosing the percentage of teacher participation in the strike the union needed for it to be successful, but the union probably needed a minimum of sixty-five percent participation.

The board's strategy called for keeping the schools open at all cost and conducting them on a business-as-usual basis. Both sides wanted and cultivated public support. In order to keep the schools open, the board had to, one, keep some teachers in the schools and, two, keep student attendance low enough for the small staff to handle. On August 29, in anticipation of the strike, Deputy Superintendent Samuel Scarnato gave school principals the authority to hire substitute teachers immediately upon need, without securing central administration approval first. And to entice substitutes to take the jobs, the board announced a $49.00 a day pay-rate for them, nearly double the normal salary. To keep student attendance low,

148 Harwood Koppel. Elected to the board for a six-year term beginning in 1975, Koppel wanted to link salary increases for teachers to performance evaluations.

school officials informed parents and students that absences during the strike would not be counted.[48]

On the first day of the strike, sixty-seven percent of the teaching staff was absent from the classrooms. LaCour, Epling, and the rest of UTNO's leadership had reason for cautious optimism. And things looked better the second day, when some seventy-three percent of the teachers failed to report to work. For the duration of the strike, teacher participation remained above seventy-three percent, despite a concerted effort by school officials to force the striking teachers back to work.[49]

The conscious effort by union representatives to keep morale high with rallies, picnics, and financial support for teachers proved a wise course because the school board decided to toughen its policy on September 5. Geisert issued an announcement informing striking teachers that they could return to their school on or before September 6 without any disciplinary measures by the board. After that date, however, teachers would have to report to the administrative office to receive an assignment and face possible disciplinary action. The board also reduced its previous offer of $2.5 million to $1.5 million and said it was considering hiring teachers to replace those on strike. But the tactic failed. On the day following Geisert's announcement, seventy-five percent of the teachers still stayed out.[50]

149 A striking teacher at Fortier Senior High walks the picket line during the 1978 strike.

150 Superintendent Geisert conducts a press briefing.

As the strike continued, both the union and the board faced mounting community pressure to settle it. Students, parents, business leaders, city officials, and the news media urged the two sides to reach an agreement. On September 7, a local editorial declared that "the continuing school strike is clearly developing into a harmful—even dangerous—confrontation in which everyone will lose." The Young Men's Business Club sent telegrams to board members and union officials demanding that they resume negotiations. Mayor Ernest Morial did what he could to help the two sides reach a settlement. Many parents voiced their concerns through various school-based parent-teachers organizations. One group, calling itself the Parent-Community Coalition, demanded greater accountability from the board. The group charged that "the board has not fulfilled its obligation as evidenced by the present state of affairs." Some support also developed for a campaign to recall board members. And not surprisingly, because of their close contact with teachers, students supported the strike. "We are behind our teachers 100 percent," one student leader proclaimed and proceeded to help organize a student boycott of classes.[51]

It was clear by September 7 that Geisert's earlier prediction that teachers would return to work after the Labor Day holiday because their display of union solidarity would crumble as they "begin to consider their economic well-being" was wide of the mark. Teacher absenteeism climbed to seventy-four percent and above. On September 8 negotiations resumed, and three days later the two sides reached a tentative agreement, albeit one that caused almost as much controversy as the strike. The agreement called for seven percent raises for teachers and an increased contribution by the board for employee health insurance. Teachers-aides, maintenance workers, and bus drivers also received pay and benefit increases. What incensed many New Orleanians was that money to pay for the approximately $6.2 million agreement would have to come from cuts elsewhere in the school budget. In the end, the board voted to trim $1.95 million from the budget, $2.8 million from unallocated funds, and $1.5 million from payroll monies saved during the strike.[52]

"School Board Collapsed," headlined a *Times-Picayune* editorial two days following the settlement. "Unless the majority that authorized the settlement can explain its failure satisfactorily," the editor warned, "the board as a forceful policy-making body risks losing what credibility it had." Board member William Reeves, who along with Harwood Koppel had voted against the settlement, bitterly assailed the board's decision and

151 Elizabeth Rack. Board member from 1978 to 1984.

harshly criticized Spears' leadership during the strike. In a "Guest Comment" in the *Times-Picayune*, Reeves branded Spears a pawn in an alledged plan by Mayor Morial to gain control of the school board. He charged that Spears refused to call board meetings to discuss important issues and accused him of not relying on the professional advice of Geisert and Hart. He also criticized Rittiner and Mrs. Loving for their support of the agreement.[53]

Spears answered Reeves and his critics through another local newspaper, *Figaro*. He termed the allegation that he was a Morial pawn "the most preposterous, asinine thing anybody could have conceived." Spears said he supported the settlement because he "became convinced that the alternative was a community without schools for three months and the probability of violence." Increased student involvement and growing parental support, he went on, had convinced him to change his earlier position. And he acknowledged the skill with which union leaders had conducted the strike. To the charge that the settlement cost more in the end than it would have if the board had made it earlier, Spears answered that such was not the case, for conditions had changed as the strike continued.[54]

Despite the *Times-Picayune's* admonition that "it would be a mistake for anyone, including the teachers union, to view this settlement as a victory," and that "the whole tragic episode could well be just one more nail in the coffin of public education here," the teachers were jubilant. They saw the strike as more than a fight for more money. "I think that teachers can work together outside the classroom. We have a new unity and we will continue working together as one through the union," said one teacher after the strike. Another remarked on the new solidarity discernible among teachers.[55]

During the decade following the strike, school officials spent much of their time searching for ways to efficiently administer an urban school system hampered by community apathy, eroding public support, and dwindling revenues. In 1980, almost as if to start afresh in the new decade, board members decided to replace Superintendent Geisert. They chose Charles Martin, dean of education at the University of New Orleans. Though many black leaders thought the time ripe for naming a black educator to head the school system, few openly criticized Martin's selection. They eventually applauded him for his choice of deputy superintendent. He named to the system's second highest post Maxine Copelin, a black principal who had won praise for her leadership at Carver Middle School, an inner-city school in the city's Ninth Ward.

During Martin's tenure he sought to improve school board financial administration, which had been problem-ridden for a long time. City business and civic groups such as the Young Men's Business Club and the Bureau of Governmental Research had long called for such reform. Stagnant revenues and rising costs made Martin's emphasis on efficiency both sound business practice as well as good public relations. Although city leaders often criticized board policy and low student performance, school officials began to gain increased respect and support from the local business community, which entered cooperative ventures with various schools. Indeed, one of the more important developments in the 1980s was the success of the board's adopt-a-school program.

By the time Everett J. Williams, a veteran teacher and administrator, became the system's first black school superintendent in 1985, the main issue of the preceeding three decades—desegregation—had been replaced by the problem of operating an urban school system amid the many societal ills that plagued New Orleans. When Dr. Williams accepted the challenge of operating one of the South's oldest school systems he realized, as did the

152 Charles Martin. Superintendent from 1980-1985.

153 Maxine Copelin Pijeaux. With her selection as deputy superintendent, Pijeaux became the highest ranking female administrator in the system's history.

154 Matthew Proctor. Served as deputy superintendent from 1985 to 1990.

board and the community, that urban schools, if they were to succeed or even survive, had to find ways of solving many non-educational problems. Violence, drugs, and teenage pregancy constituted some of the new challenges to the future of education in New Orleans.

Is there hope for the children in our large cities who depend upon public schools for their education? The long travail of the New Orleans schools offers no easy answer. Its one hundred and fifty years of history demonstrate, however, that a large urban public school system never secures an ultimate triumph. The schools either improve or they deteriorate.

Despite some notable achievements, New Orleans public schools have never met the needs of the poorest children of the city, especially the black poor. Individual teachers and schools often demonstrated models of achievement and success, but those isolated efforts could not break the unremitting cycle of poverty and ignorance. From the beginning, issues of race stymied the public will to make any fundamental change. During the 1960s, public and private leaders failed the test of desegregation. For years afterward, most elected officials—particularly mayors and governors—ignored the schools and left them largely adrift, strapped for both human and financial resources. The New Orleans experience shows that, without the crucial leadership of mayors and governors, school officials and parents have not been able to mobilize voters for fundamental and long-term reform.

Yet somehow hope remains. Although federal court orders failed to integrate most classrooms, they redistributed funding for the poor. A greater percentage of black students in New Orleans and in other areas of the South are now graduating from high school and college. Expanded electorates have lessened the worst expressions of racial hatred and oppression. Those electorates have also encouraged public officials to give greater support to public education. In 1989, the nation's governors met in Charlottesville, Virginia, to set some common goals for public schools in the United States. The governors of Louisiana, Mississippi, and Arkansas came not as symbols of neglect and defiance, but as champions of educational reform. Each had made the improvement of public education a key goal of his administration.

Never has the nation reached such a consensus about the objectives of public education. By the year 2000, the governors envisioned that all children would start drug-free schools prepared to learn and that almost all would graduate from high school competent in basic subjects, including math and science.

Some model teachers and schools have always existed in New Orleans and other cities. They show us how to get youngsters ready for school and how to teach them to read, write, and compute. But the challenge still remains for federal and state authorities to help local governments deliver such care and schooling to all children and particularly to the urban poor. In truth, the challenge requires more than just change in public schools. America must rebuild its cities and bring hope to those who reside in them. In New Orleans and in the nation's other major cities lie the destiny of the United States and the quality of its civilization. Whatever is done, urban schools will shape prospects for America's rising generations. Like liberty and democracy, the education of a community requires from its citizens eternal vigilance.

Everett J. Williams

EPILOGUE

Some Personal Reflections on a Public Institution

by
Everett J. Williams, Ph. D.,
Superintendent, New Orleans Public Schools

In a thesis written more than fifty years ago, Margaret Williams observed that "public schools partake of the nature of the government under which they operate."[1]   In other words, the history of the New Orleans public schools is the history of New Orleans. Through this story of public education we can learn—and appreciate—the individuals and organizations that have waged courageous political and legal battles to educate the children at great personal cost.

The sesquicentennial of public education in New Orleans offers a vantage point from which to look back on the dreams and the defeats of those who came before us. It is important that we read about both the visionaries and the villains because their policies and plans comprise our past and shape our present. We have inherited both the benefits and the consequences of their actions. Through reading about them, we understand our responsibility to maintain this precious institution, improve it and pass it on to those who come after us.

We can feel pride in our past, and our story is filled with examples of persistence, unselfishness, dedication and love. In these pages there is no shortage of role models whose example would be beneficial to the children of today.

Many of the events in this book's later chapters shaped my career. In turn, I hope that in some way I helped shape the outcome of some of those events. I stepped into the role of superintendent when I was appointed in August of 1985 by a unanimous vote of the Orleans Parish School Board.

As I continue my work, new chapters of public school history are being written, and I realize that I play but a small part in a much larger narrative. Many of my joys and frustrations in operating a school system are but echoes of the experiences of the superintendents who came before me. More than a hundred years ago, Superintendent William O. Rogers talked about the difficulties of administering a public school system. In 1884, Rogers noted that public schools are faced with "the impossibility of satisfying all of the personal opinions and educational theories of many thousands who are interested in the results."[2] He went on to make a statement that is as true now as it was then: "Public education is an anvil upon which a good many hammers have been worn out." I can state with confidence that future superintendents and educational policymakers will find this to be true as long as there are public schools in New Orleans.

It is, however, my unique experience that fate has made me New Orleans' first black superintendent. In a city where racial problems have dogged the schools since 1841, it still comes as a surprise—even in 1991—that the melanin in one's skin is a factor in one's career. This is a very real part of the legacy of racial attitudes that is still being played out in New Orleans. I look forward to the time when the various professions will be filled with men and women of all races, so that sex and race will no longer matter. I also look forward to a time when there will be no more racial "firsts," so that we can be free to focus on the many concerns we share as members of a common community, rather than on superficialities such as skin hue.

There is no issue in our country more complex and more fervently debated than public education, and there is no shortage of opinions on how to educate a child. The difficulty arises in gaining a consensus in a community that is divided by differences in socioeconomic standing, political ideologies, racial attitudes, and educational attainment. Against this background of diverse and conflicting factors, it is no wonder that many charge that political pressures sometimes play a larger role in public education than the welfare of the children.

Despite educators' best efforts, it is a fact of life that public schools do operate in a political arena. Public education involves a huge infrastructure which controls a sizeable expenditure of money and, in the case of New Orleans, thousands of jobs. Public education provides construction contracts worth millions of dollars. Public education also provides millions of dollars of purchasing contracts to supply the schools with everything from desks, chalkboards, and chalk to food for school lunches and lawn mowers to cut the grass. There is a tremendous amount of political pressure exerted on school administrations and on school board members to favor certain vendors over others, to award contracts to one architect or contractor rather than to another. History has shown that sometimes educational leaders have been able to withstand such pressures and make proper decisions, and at other times they have sold the trust of their office to the highest bidder.

The thought of public education brings to people's minds an image of a child at a desk and a teacher at a chalkboard, and taxpayers wonder why that is so expensive. First, we must educate the more than 84,000 students entrusted to our care. We must also maintain the buses in which our students ride and the buildings in which they attend classes. We must pay and provide health insurance and other benefits to our employees. We must defend our actions in court against a growing number of legal challenges, and rid our school buildings of asbestos and termites—just to name a few of the many responsibilities that fall under the aegis of public education. And all of this is done on revenue sources over which we have no control and amidst political pressures that are unrelenting.

Superintendents must contend with community groups that are often interested in a single issue, a single program, or a single school. These groups are adept at using the headlines to their advantage, and they use the blunt pressure of bull horns, pickets, and shouting in an attempt to bring about change.

And then there are unions. I firmly believe that teachers and support personnel need the strength of unions to make their voices heard. This book has chronicled some of the abuses teachers have experienced when they have not been organized. But I would be less than honest if I did not also say that the demands of the unions often outrun the resources of the community, and this leads to a fierce struggle for money.

Public education is at the mercy of myriad special interest groups, and this gives rise to intense political pressure. This always has been the case, and it always will. To think otherwise is naive. Public school superintendents must be prepared to face the pressures connected with the job. It is important to listen carefully to the concerns of various special interest groups and carefully weigh their suggestions. It is just as important not to lose sight of the fact that, whereas this or that group addresses one aspect of a problem, a superintendent is responsible for solving the whole problem. Decision makers in public education stand on shifting political sand, and from this unstable foundation they must preserve and improve the school system.

Our history has shown an ebb and flow in the recognition of basic human rights. Gains have been made and gains have been lost. It is an interesting mirror of our own times and struggles that we read a report issued in 1870 by State Superintendent Thomas Conway. He wrote that in accordance with

> section five of the act of eighteen hundred and seventy, the State Board of Education, at its first meeting, adopted a rule for the government of the public schools of the State, by which they were all opened to children of educable age, *without distinction of color or race.*[3]

It was not long after that report that the state's and city's political leadership changed, and subsequent political pressure destroyed the racial gains and reestablished a segregated system of schools.

At the same time that the state was being pressured to achieve racial equality in the schools, there was a corresponding push to end discriminatory practices against women teachers. Conway also reported that the State Board of Education made the dramatic move of equalizing the pay between men and women teachers:

> This equitable rule, abolishing that relic of barbarism which underestimates a service because rendered by women, has received an approval from the people of the State which is practically unanimous; the few dissenting voices coming from men whose prejudices obscure their perceptions of justice, have been lost amidst the general and cordial assent given by the community at large, and this measure of justice to the feebler sex may be regarded as now permanently established in our state.[4]

Somehow, over time, that spirit and those gains were lost, and women were again paid less for the same services. It took years to regain that lost ground. I write this to remind the succession of leaders whose job it will be to guide the public schools in the future that social gains must not be merely fought for and won, they must also be safeguarded. It is the nature of public institutions to change; it is the responsibility of leaders to ensure that the schools do not lose ground as they change.

New Orleans has experimented repeatedly to find the magic formula that combines adequate representation with effective leadership. It has been a process of trial and error and politics. In the early days of the New Orleans Public School District, the majority of the school board members were appointed by the mayor or the city council. They knew that money appropriated to the schools was money taken away from the city budget; therefore, they withheld money from the schools—much to the detriment of the children's education.[5] In 1864, there were sixteen appointed members of the school board. In 1867, the city council passed an ordinance providing for the terms of twenty-four appointed board members. In 1888, the General Assembly of the State of Louisiana put the New Orleans schools under the direction of twenty board members, eight appointed by the governor and twelve appointed by the city council. Historians have noted that this change was "an open invitation to political meddling in the schools."[6]

The twenty-member board continued until 1908, when it was replaced by a seventeen-member board whose members were elected, one from each ward. This "reform" was later described as "a splendid opportunity for the ward leaders to exercise political control of the school system."[7]

Act 214, passed by the legislature in 1912, abolished the ward system and replaced it with a five-member at-large board serving six-year terms. This board survived seventy-seven years, when it was replaced in 1989 by a board composed of five single-district members and two members elected at large.

I submit this synopsis of the makeup of the Orleans Parish School Board to illustrate the fact that, as educators, we must be cautious when we hear the word "reform." Sometimes reform means improvement, but at other times it can mean change for the sake of change, and it can even signal that change is being touted as a means to favor one group over another or to fulfill someone's hidden agenda.

A reader might argue that in an essay such as this a superintendent should write more about "the children" and spend less time on politics and money. I would counter that by saying the first step to educating the children is understanding the political and social environment in which they must be educated. Understanding the social environment, first, means understanding the children and the strengths and weaknesses which they bring to the classroom. Understanding the political environment also means understanding the fluid equation between power and resources. Knowing who has the power and the influence is the first step in directing the needed resources to the children where they will do the most good.

Public education is a service, and it takes many people to provide that service. For the 1990-91 school year, salaries and benefits for employees accounted for more than 82 percent of the total expenditure of $288 million. When the average person sees the size of the budget for public education, it often comes as a surprise. Comparing it to his or her own salary, the millions of dollars appear to be an enormous amount. But when the price tag of the many urgent educational needs is compared to the money available to fulfill those needs, it becomes clear that education is not a priority in this city.

New Orleans is an interesting city, and I love it dearly. I was born here, and I grew up here, and I can appreciate its charm and beauty. Yet I am angered by its preference for merriment rather than education. Public education has grown despite a tradition of neglect. The schools have not lost financial support so much as they have never been able to rally the city around its schools. When it comes to community responsibility for the public schools, there are no nostalgic days of abundant and generous financial support.

Money, however, is not the only problem that has plagued public education since its inception. In 1845, at the dedication of the Franklin School House, Rev. W. A. Scott cautioned parents about neglecting their responsibilities and expecting teachers to handle the job of rearing their children:

> Be assured the ablest faculties are not parents to your children. Teachers may have the meekness of Moses, the patience of Job, the wisdom of Solomon, the courage of David and Daniel, the zeal of Peter and the fidelity of Paul, with the strength of Samson, and they may stand *in loco parentis*, but they are not the parents of your children. Your children may be their *pupils*, but that is all.[8]

Rev. Scott concluded with the admonition: "The father and mother must not cast all the responsibility upon the public school."[9] It has been my experience, and it has been the experience of the educational leaders who have come before me, that there is a noticeable positive attitude and improved student achievement in a school when the parents are united in their support of the school. Sadly, it seems as if the forces of society are making it more and more difficult for parents to find the time to get involved with their children's lives.

That I hold the position of superintendent today is a result of the intervention of my own mother more than forty years ago. I was a young man, away from home, and fresh out of the seminary in a small town in Illinois. I had realized that I did not have a vocation to the priesthood and found a job working for the post office in Chicago. I returned to New Orleans at Christmas to see my family, at which time I was going to inform them of my decision to return to Chicago to work full-time for the post office. I felt pretty lucky to be a high school graduate making $100 a week in 1949.

When it was time to depart I could not find my tickets. With only thirty minutes remaining until the train pulled out, I was frantically searching the house. My mother volunteered to help me and even went through the charade of searching under pillows and in drawers. I suddenly looked up and saw my mother staring at me, big tears rolling down her cheeks. "You're not going back to Chicago," she said hesitantly. "You're going to stay home and go to college."

I don't know whether it was the passion in her voice or the tears in her eyes, but I accepted her decision, and the very next day she cashed in the train tickets and gave the money to my older sister, who registered me at Xavier University.

I was lucky. Many of our students are not. We have children who are on their own at an early age, abandoned, neglected, and oftentimes abused by their parents. As many superintendents before me have done, I have accepted these students as our responsibility. They belong in our schools. Furthermore, I know that, for many of these children, their future depends upon someone reaching them now.

There are some public schools in New Orleans where children are isolated from many of the grim realities of life in the city. They come from quiet neighborhoods, and their schools are quiet, sheltered places of learning. There are other neighborhoods where the school is an oasis in the midst of an urban battlefield. Too many New Orleans children see death on a daily basis. They see the slow death of drug abuse, and they know all too well the sudden burst of gunfire that brings a tragic end to the precious lives of neighbors and friends. Even some of our students' lives have been claimed by stray bullets exchanged by warring drug dealers. Instead of children singing and playing jump rope, all that remains is a stark chalk outline on the blood-stained pavement.

Education has always been viewed as the pathway to success and the good life. For many of our children, that pathway seems closed. Life on the streets has taught them that they can make more money selling street drugs than they can by staying in school. How do teachers encourage students to stay in school and study and learn when easy money from street corner drug sales gives them designer clothes and expensive cars? What the youngsters do not understand is that such a lifestyle will likely result in their violent death before they reach the age of twenty-five.

The public schools must also deal with the reality of babies having babies. Young children, without education, without jobs, and without hope, are producing more and more babies. The social systems are straining to the bursting point to feed, house, and clothe these youngsters. The infants are beginning their lives with tremendous handicaps. Many of the young mothers do not have proper pre-natal care, and many have medical problems that would remain undetected were it not for a school nurse.

Born into poverty in an environment that is chillingly brutal, the youngsters would face lives of hunger and hopelessness were it not for the schools. There, at least they are fed, sheltered, and kept safe from the terror of their neighborhoods. Yet, people point fingers at these children in alarm and ask "Why aren't their test scores higher?"

How much time in a classroom will compensate those children whose families are torn asunder by the problems of poverty, ignorance, and unemployment, so that they can compete with children from middle class backgrounds? This is not a rhetorical question. It sums up the difficulties the schools—and particularly the teachers—face as they try to fulfill the responsibilities of their profession. The public schools will never give up on those children, but the city must not give up on its schools.

While more and more students are dropping out of school, the demands of the technological age have escalated, placing greater educational demands upon the population. The demand for unskilled laborers will shrink dramatically this decade. The economic survival of individuals in the 1990s and well on into the next century will depend upon their education more so than in any previous era. Unfortunately, despite this grim fact, many of our young people are turning their backs on education.

Other superintendents have grappled with this problem. Although the solution has eluded them, at least they have left their perseverance as an example to those of us who carry on in the search for solutions. I find it disheartening that, particularly in New Orleans, the *"public"* in "public education" no longer means *"of or concerning the public as a whole."* Instead, it has come to mean something apart from the community. It has come to have a stigma attached to it. What is even worse, many members of the community ignore the public schools as if they did not exist.

I am reminded of the time fifteen years ago when I was the only black man on Superintendent Alton Cowan's leadership team. While walking in the narrow halls of the Bauer Building at 703 Carondelet Street, many of my colleagues would pass me without even looking at me—as if I were invisible. I suppose they thought I would go away if they pretended not to see me. Some members of our community seem to think of our schools in the same way.

Crime, a by-product of a lack of education, threatens this community. Yet voters seem more eager to build prisons than schools. In 1876, State Superintendent William G. Brown, who was the first and only black man ever to be named state superintendent of education, complained that New Orleans was spending five times as much for prisons and police as it was for education. "The cost of public education throughout the state, including the purchase money for school houses, rent and repairs of the same school apparatus and furniture, does not equal the cost or the expenses of the city of New Orleans alone for criminal justice," he wrote.[10]

Brown further argued that "every dollar which is expended for education will inevitably cause a reduction of the cost of criminal justice."[11] New Orleans has heard this argument many times since, but has yet to heed it.

I have written candidly in this epilogue because I believe that the first step toward solving problems is to admit to having them. This book is a major step in giving back to our community its history. We must make every effort to recapture our past so that we can rediscover yesterday's heroes whose actions live on. We must hold up to the children a reflection of what their lives could be. We ourselves must understand and persuade the media and other image-makers in our community of the dangers inherent in constantly mirroring for our youngsters the images of street life. Between these pages are the stories of many heroes whose lives make up a tradition of heroic action. That is the New Orleans public school tradition.

I have tried to reshape this institution and redirect its resources so that the New Orleans public schools can educate the children of poverty with the same ease they educate the children of privilege. This dual and oftentimes contradictory demand is a wonder when it succeeds and a source of bottomless frustration when it fails. One of the major concerns of my administration has been to direct more money to early childhood education.

I firmly believe that if we can reach the children at a younger age, we can show them that although the promises of street life are short-lived, the promises of education are without limit. That is our job and we must persevere.

I am also proud of the fact that for the first time in more than 30 years, a property tax increase for the public schools was approved while I was superintendent. It proves that it is possible to build support for the schools. But we must not stop there. We must work untiringly to maintain that support.

I conclude with the same message Superintendent William O. Rogers used when he ended his report to the school board in 1878. It is remarkable how little has changed:

> Here, as elsewhere, public education is in a crisis of its history. With the most rigorous economy, large expenditures are needed. Those who are taxed for the education of others are not always cheerful contributors, and their objections sound a note of alarm, the echo of which vibrates through every school-room. Our city schools have had their share of such experience, but, as they have endured in the past, through many vicissitudes of history, so they will doubtless endure in the future, sustained by the confidence and the good will of the great mass of our citizens. . . .[12]

I know that my name has earned a place in the historical records of the New Orleans public schools by virtue of being the city's first black superintendent. However, I hope that I will be remembered for my accomplishments more than for what color I happened to be. I am also aware that, like my predecessors, my tenure in this office will be judged by future historians. I look forward to a bright future—one in which we achieve our goal to educate all of the children. Like my predecessors, I will do everything within my power to make this goal a reality.

Afterword

by
Betty Jefferson, Ed. D., President
Orleans Parish School Board

The book comes to a close; but, the full story is just beginning to emerge. Our historical celebrations this year have made us realize that each day offers more stories to be rediscovered and retold. The stories can give us insight into ourselves. When a record of present events is not preserved and studied, it can all too rapidly fade into forgotten emptiness. Individuals and institutions become obscured or lost.

When we are unable to establish a link to our past, we set sail without an anchor, without a compass, without a map. A sense of history gives us a sense of direction. We learn to chart courses that avoid the dangers that confronted those who came before us. To run aground again and again on the same rocky shoals is the fate of those who do not learn from the mistakes of others. The lessons of the past have much to teach this and succeeding generations.

Teachers as well as educational policymakers need to have available to them historical references and resources to give them the clear vision necessary for leadership. Because the perspective offered by newspapers and television is often without context, events seem to happen suddenly and without connection to previous events. A few voices in the community tend to be magnified while the feelings and attitudes of many others are seldom heard. The images of chaos fill the front pages and dominate the evening news, but they offer neither perspective nor direction--only a fragmented puzzle of disconnected events and actions. It is only through reasoned study and analysis that a more complete picture emerges. When the historians finally piece together the fragments, the whole picture begins to come into focus. The chaos is balanced by stories of dedicated individuals striving to work for the good of the children and the community.

303

What has made this book a credible historical contribution is that the authors, who are respected historians, had the final say on what went into the book. They were never restrained. A serious study of an institution such as a public school system is not served by a selective narrative that conveniently avoids mistakes and paints a false picture. Nostalgia based upon a selective memory hurts more than it helps. We need a complete story, told without rancor and told without restraint. I challenge school board members, school superintendents, and others who will follow to encourage continued scrutiny by historians. I also challenge the historians of today and tomorrow to continue to pursue this line of historical inquiry. The local colleges and universities should encourage their undergraduate and graduate students to investigate public education in New Orleans. In particular I would challenge the colleges of education to require their students to learn about the history of local public education so that future teachers and administrators will better understand the importance of their careers. The New Orleans Public School District's Historical Collection at the University of New Orleans invites research into the political, social, and cultural developments in the schools. The wealth of records from 1841 to the present will provide material for scholars for many years to come. The references in this book also highlight many other local historical collections that possess information about the schools.

The years of research that went into *Crescent City Schools* have produced a solid foundation on which to build a body of historical works. We now need the contributions of disciplined researchers and talented writers to provide additional books, dissertations, theses, articles, term papers, and photographic essays about public education and the individuals who have nurtured it.

305

Orleans Parish School Board, 1991

From left: Dwight L. McKenna (at-large), Gail M. Glapion, Paul N. Sens, Avra O'Dwyer, Harwood "Woody" Koppel (at-large), Betty Jefferson, Carl D. Robinson.

Appendices

APPENDIX I

The Architecture of Education: The Public School Buildings of New Orleans

by
John C. Ferguson

APPENDIX II

New Orleans School Boards, 1862-1991

APPENDIX I

The Architecture of Education:
The Public School Buildings of
New Orleans

by
John C. Ferguson

The history of public education in New Orleans encompasses more than just the desires of its citizens to educate their children and the steps taken by the school board to implement those desires. The history of public education in this city also includes the many fine buildings that housed classrooms, as well as the individuals who were responsible for designing those buildings. Without consideration of those buildings and their architects, the story of public education in New Orleans remains incomplete.

This essay sketches the role which architecture played in the service of public education in New Orleans, particularly between the years 1860 and 1960. Within that hundred-year period, there were three distinct phases of building activity, each of which added to the depth and richness of New Orleans's architectural tradition. This three-part record of the Orleans Parish School Board's building program provides a fine case study for the history of the development of school architecture in the United States, an important subject which has remained relatively unexplored by scholars.

William A. Freret and the Building of the McDonogh Schools

The will of John McDonogh provided the city of New Orleans with an enormous source of capital which, according to the terms of the will, was to be used to further the education of the children of the city through the erection of school buildings. The money was to be used only for buildings and its expenditure was the responsibility of an independent commission. Teachers and other school board personnel were not to be paid out of McDonogh funds, but by the Orleans Parish School Board. But

309

Plate 1   McDonogh Number 7 School, 1111 Milan Street.   The least altered of the surviving schools designed by William A. Freret, McDonogh No. 7 displays the ornamental brickwork that was a major feature of the architect's work.

McDonogh's will did provide funds for the repair and maintenance of other buildings built or purchased by the school board. While the McDonogh Fund was available for school construction by 1860, the advent of the Civil War prevented its full use until the early 1870s.

Much of our knowledge of the activities of the commissioners of the McDonogh Fund is derived from their surviving account books, which detail the dispersal of funds. Unfortunately, the minutes of the commissioners' meetings in the nineteenth century have not survived, which means we have no record of discussions relative to school construction or to the important process of selecting architects. We can only rely on the account books and on the designs of the schools themselves. But taken together, those rich sources yield an abundance of information.

New Orleans in the 1870s was a prosperous city with a number of talented architects. Starting in late 1875, the commissioners established what would become a long-term relationship with one of those architects, William A. Freret, a relationship which would lead to his designing thirteen schools. Between 1875 and 1884, Freret built schools from one end of the city to the other, including the West Bank. Freret was already well known in New Orleans social and political circles. His father had been twice elected mayor of the city, and his family's friends likely included many members of the school board as well as the McDonogh Fund Commission.

Before being employed by the commissioners of the McDonogh Fund, Freret was best known for designing commercial buildings, which were among the more distinctive in the city. The sole remaining example of this aspect of his work is the lofty building at 622 Canal Street. With its elaborate and beautifully designed and proportioned cast-iron facade, it shows Freret to have been nothing if not both original and talented.

The first two schools built from Freret's designs, McDonogh No. 6 and No. 7, still stand at 923 Napoleon Avenue and 1111 Milan Street. Towering two full stories above an open, raised basement, these masonry buildings made excellent use of Gothic details, carried out in brick, and cast-iron ornamental finials atop the roof. (Plate 1 shows McDonogh No. 7 today.) The simple rectangular mass of the structure is skillfully broken up by the series of brick buttresses which rise from the ground, dividing the facade into a series of bays. Begun in 1876 and completed in 1877, this

Plate 2 McDonogh Number 10 School, 2407 Baronne Street. While it removes the building from its actual setting, this rendering does show the dramatic character of its design, with the purely ornamental corner towers.

312

Elevation on Palmyra St.

Commenced 1878.   Completed 1879.

Plate 3 McDonogh Number 11 School, 2009 Palmyra Street. For this school, Freret turned towards a more French image, with the complex roofline and pavilions on either side of the entrance.

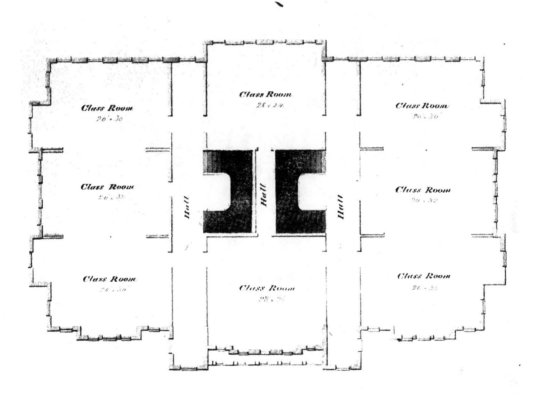

Mᶜ DONOGH Nº 11.

Class Room
20 × 30

Class Room
28 × 24

Class Room
20 × 30

Class Room
20 × 32

Hall

Hall

Hall

Class Room
20 × 32

Class Room
20 × 30

Class Room
28 × 24

Class Room
20 × 32

FIRST STORY.

Plate 4 First floor plan, McDonogh Number 11 School. Note the use of sliding doors to define the classrooms, a favorite nineteenth-century school planning device.

314

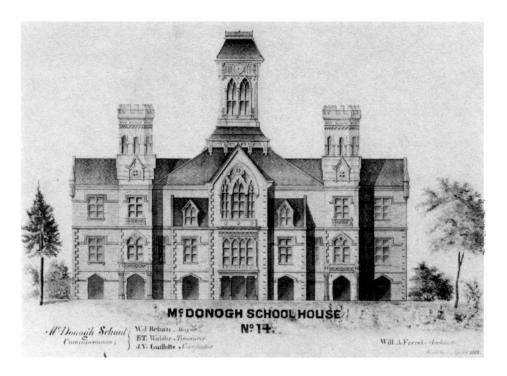

Plate 5 McDonogh Number 14 School. This school, now demolished, was the most outwardly extravagant of the Freret designed buildings, dominated by its central clock tower.

315

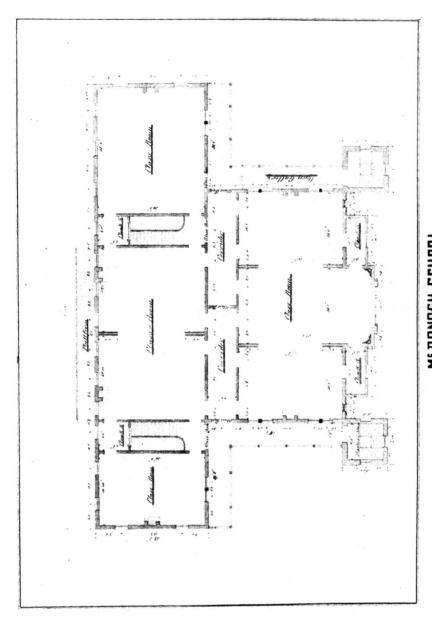

MᶜDONOGH SCHOOL.
Nº 14.

Plate 6   Second floor plan, McDonogh Number 14 School. Note the use of the towers on the front of the building for stairs, one of which was reserved for teachers only.

building was enlarged in 1890, and is today still in use as an elementary school, making it the oldest public school building in New Orleans.

Freret's abilities at brick detailing were to improve with later school designs. In 1878 he designed two of his most extravagant schools, McDonogh No. 10 at 2405 Baronne Street and McDonogh No. 11 at Prieur and Palmyra streets. McDonogh No. 10 represents Freret's first Italianate style school, complete with corner towers. While the circa 1890 rendering (Plate No. 2) makes it appear that the outside walls of this school—as well as the other Freret-designed schools included in this series of watercolor renderings of the first twenty McDonogh Schools—were finished in stone or stucco, in fact, they were all finished in common brick.

McDonogh No. 11 (Plate 3) presents an even more complicated exterior and roofscape than McDonogh No. 10. Here the architect chose to work in the French Second Empire style, complete with a steeply pitched Mansard roof. Following the pattern he set with Numbers 6 and 7, Freret continued to use an open basement as covered play space, with the two upper floors devoted to classrooms. (Plate 4) Freret's penchant for flamboyant design reached its peak in 1884 with the construction of McDonogh No. 14, on Jefferson Avenue between Camp and Chestnut streets. With its soaring clock tower in the center of the main facade and its vaguely English Gothic detailing, it might have been based upon some Elizabethan country house. Plate 5 shows a watercolor rendering of the school's Jefferson Avenue facade. Plate 6 shows one of the schoolroom floor plans, a fascinating piece of design which neatly fits classrooms and hallways into the complex form of the building. This school was demolished in 1913.

In 1885, Freret completed work on McDonogh No. 18 (Plates 7 and 8), located on Rampart between St. Louis and Toulouse streets. Built on a small and cramped site, this school, with its decorative center gable, rose vertically above its residential neighbors. The small site led to an interior plan that had to function without the benefit of hallways, as shown in Plate 8. Leaving out hallways was a common practice in nineteenth-century school building. Rooms were divided by movable partitions which permitted students to go from room to room without halls, and also allowed for the creation of a single large room—by sliding all the partitions to one side—creating a meeting space that could hold the entire student body.

In some of the outlying areas of the city, where population density was light, Freret came up with a type of school building which, for a lack of a

Plate 7 McDonogh Number 18 School. Now demolished, this compact school was located on the edge of the French Quarter on North Rampart Street.

318

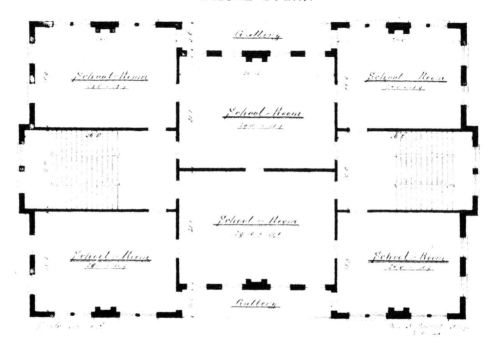

Plate 8   Second floor plan, McDonogh Number 18 School.   As a result of its small site, the interior of this school could not afford the luxury of hallways, with the large staircases serving that purpose.

Plate 9 McDonogh Number 19 School, Tricou and Douglass streets. This photograph, taken before the school was severely altered, shows the cottage-like character of this frame building.

better word, could be called a cottage school. These cottage schools were
frame structures set on high brick piers. In keeping with the tradition he
had established with his larger schools, Freret left the basements open, to
be used as covered play areas. McDonogh Nos. 5 and 19, built in 1882 and
1884, are almost residential in scale, with low pitched roofs forming a
broad, gable-faced main elevation. These two schools were designed to
house approximately three hundred students each. McDonogh No. 5 stood
in Algiers, and McDonogh No. 19 still survives at 500 Tricou Street,
although it has been altered beyond recognition. Its original form is shown
in Plate 9. The cottage schools were popular with the commissioners of
the McDonogh Fund, and they were to have two other schools of this type
built in the 1890s, after Freret had retired from his architectural practice.

The schools that William Freret designed for the McDonogh Fund are
excellent examples of nineteenth-century U. S. school architecture. They
provided for large classrooms, well lit by large and numerous windows, as
well as ample playground space, even when located on small sites. To
modern eyes, there are some aspects of these schools which seem peculiar,
particularly movable partitions between classrooms and numerous
stairways. The multiple staircases had more to do with the then common
practice of segregating the students on the basis of sex than on requirements
of fire codes. In spite of their age, many of these schools from the 1870s
and 1880s remained in active use well into this century. One, McDonogh
No. 7, still serves as a public elementary school. But, the steady growth of
the school-age population would compel the school board to embark on an
even more ambitious building program early in the twentieth century.

E. A. Christy and the Creation of the Modern Public School

At the opening of the twentieth century, the Orleans Parish School
Board was faced with the need to erect a number of new school buildings.
Many of the existing buildings were simply too small for the needs of the
school system. And new needs such as auditoriums and gymnasiums also
required that new schools be built.

With a handful of exceptions, the new schools were all the work of a
remarkable if relatively little-known architect, Edgar Angelo Christy.
Christy, who preferred to use only the initials E. A., held the position of
supervising architect of the Orleans Parish School Board from the creation
of the post in 1911 until his retirement in 1940. Born in 1881, Christy did

not attend an architectural school, but got his training as an apprentice to the local firm of Andry & Bendernagel. He was hired by the city in 1904 to serve as city architect. In that capacity he designed a variety of city buildings, principally fire stations, many of which still stand. When he became architect for the school board in 1911, he was put in charge of a small staff which never exceeded five draftsmen. That small group produced designs for over forty buildings between 1911 and 1940, including a number of very large high schools. With only a small staff, Christy himself had to do most of the actual design work, as well as some of the drawing.

Christy's early work for the school board was influenced by the work of his former employers, Andry & Bendernagel. That firm had designed at least two schools between 1904 and 1910, McDonogh No. 16, at 1831 St. Charles Avenue, and McDonogh No. 31 at 836 North Rendon Street. Both schools were done in what is often called Mediterranean Style, which incorporates various design elements of Spanish and Italian origin. The school featured low-pitched roofs clad in terra cotta tiles and simple classical decoration, including brackets under the roofline.

One of Christy's early works, Live Oak Elementary School, on Constance between Eighth and Ninth streets, built in 1912, provides us with a fine example of this style. Plates 10 and 11 show the original elevation of the school and the plan of its first floor. The exterior of the school was of light colored, tawny brick walls, which contrasted with the dark red of the roof tiles. The interior plan shows a wide hallway designed to allow easy movement from one room to another. It is interesting to note that the kindergarten room was placed on the south side of the school, assuring ample warm sunlight in winter. Comparison of this plan with those developed by William Freret in the nineteenth century clearly shows the advances being made in the design of public school buildings.

Almost as soon as he was appointed supervising architect, Christy was given responsibility for designing the city's first modern high school buildings. The first of these was Sophie Wright High School for girls, at 1400 Napoleon Avenue, completed in 1912. It was followed in 1913 by the even more imposing Warren Easton High School for boys at 3019 Canal Street. (Plates 12 and 13.) Both Wright and Easton were Gothic in style, although ornament was limited to moldings above the large windows, and at Easton, concentrated around the towered main entrance.

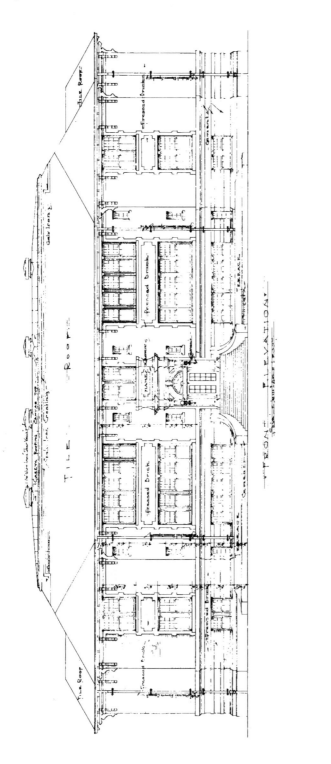

Plate 10   Live Oak School, 3128 Constance Street.   Typical of the early public school designs of E. A. Christy, Live Oak features large window bays and a use of contrasting materials on its exterior.

323

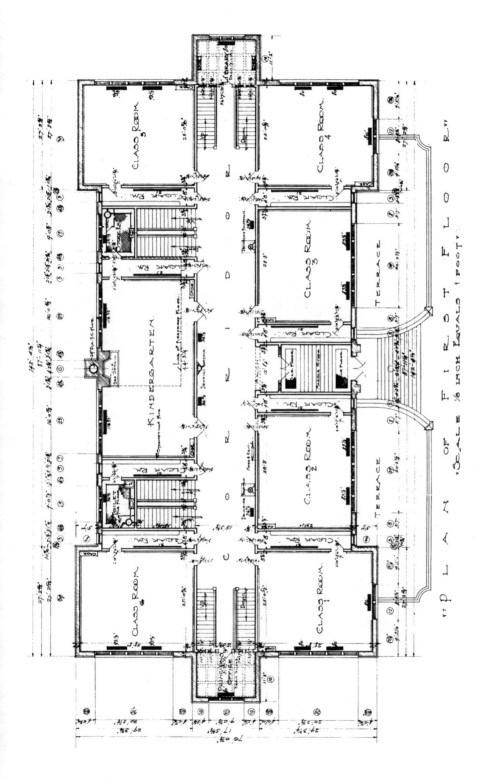

Plate 11   First floor plan, Live Oak School. This simple but highly workable floor plan characterizes Christy's elementary school designs, with each classroom being well separated from its neighbors.

324

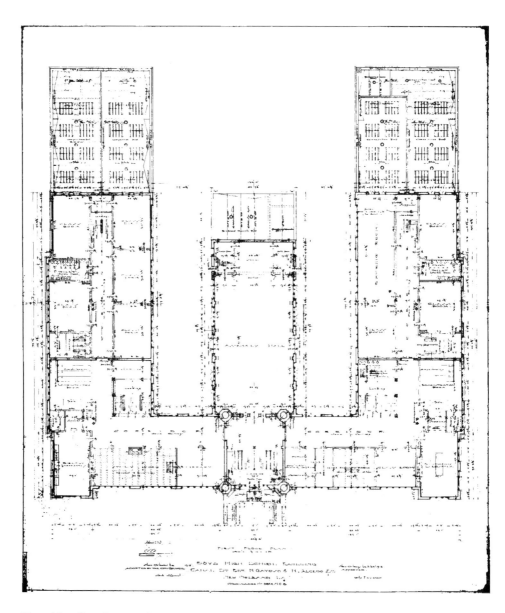

Plate 12   Facade elevations of Warren Easton High School, 3019 Canal Street. For the first true high school building in New Orleans, Christy chose a simplified Gothic style for the exterior.

325

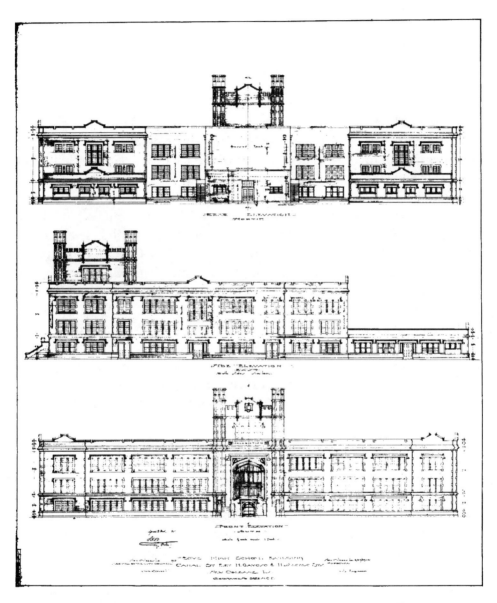

Plate 13   First floor plan, Warren Easton High School. The use of the E-shaped plan of Easton enabled the architect to place the auditorium apart from the noise of the classrooms, and provide it with light and ventilation.

The plan of Easton shows how Christy linked classrooms with the assembly hall by the use of an E-shaped floor plan. This allowed the assembly hall to have windows on both sides, a necessity in the days before air conditioning.

By the 1920s, Christy had adopted many classical elements such as Greek and Roman columns. Plate 14 shows a partial elevation for the Henry Watkins Allen School at 5625 Loyola, which was dominated by a monumental classical portico at the main entrance. The entrance doors themselves were set in a frame which borrowed its details from American colonial architecture of the late 1700s. For the Charles J. Colton School at 2300 St. Claude Avenue, Christy elected to use Italian Renaissance style for the main entrance, shown in Plate 15. Here, he stacked three stories of classical columns one atop another to emphasize the entrance, which projected out from the dark red brick of the building's walls. The plan of this school, built in 1929 (Plate 16), again shows Christy's ability to combine diverse functions within a single structure. The building included indoor recreation areas, an auditorium, and a small gymnasium, as well as an indoor swimming pool.

In some cases, the schools that Christy designed replaced earlier buildings, as in the case of his new McDonogh No. 14, now James Lewis School, located at 1116 Jefferson Avenue. Shown in Plate 17, this building followed the example of its predecessor in providing the neighborhood with a clock tower atop the school. Unfortunately, the tower no longer stands.

In 1929 Christy designed a new school for Algiers Point, which was named in honor of former mayor Martin Behrman, who grew up in that section of the city. Located at 715 Opelousas Avenue, Behrman School (Plates 18 and 19) is notable for its unusual combination of design elements, most prominently the fine Spanish colonial entry and tower (Plate 18) and groupings of window bays were important sources of classroom illumination, for artificial lighting of the period remained limited.

Just before the onset of the Great Depression, Christy's office was assigned the task of designing two new high school buildings, both in the uptown area. The first of these to be completed, in 1930, was Alcée Fortier, located at 5624 Freret Street (Plate 20). Here, Christy borrowed the classical entry portal from the design for Colton School, but in this case, the main doors are set at the head of a grand flight of steps. The plan of Fortier is a simple U shape. The plan drawing (Plate 21) shows how Christy placed multi-purpose rooms across the long Freret Street side of the school and the library at the center of the complex, and linked the latter directly to the study halls.

In 1931, the Eleanor McMain High School for girls was completed. Located at 5712 South Claiborne Avenue, McMain occupied a unique place in terms of Christy's overall work, for with its design he turned towards a new architectural style, Art Moderne. Up until that point, Christy had used only historical styles, as seen in the Behrman, Fortier, and Colton schools. Plate 22 shows the elevation drawings for McMain, with its abstract decoration concentrated on the main entrance. In side elevations, McMain looks almost like a factory building, with large metal-framed windows and no ornamental detail. The auditorium, on the Nashville Avenue side of the building, was given its own entrance onto the street, allowing it to be used without opening the rest of the school. Plate 23 shows the ground floor plan which, in typical Christy fashion, successfully combined a multitude of functions, including indoor recreation space and a school cafeteria. Classrooms were placed on the second and third floors, with access to the upper floors provided by four large staircases, each near a corner of the building.

For the remainder of his career, Christy was hindered by the economic hardships of the depression. The schools built after 1931 tended to be only pale, inexpensive imitations of those that he and his staff had designed earlier. Some of these later schools were built with money from the federal government's Works Progress Administration.

The quality of Christy's work is marked by the fact that, even after seventy-odd years of service, almost all of his schools are still in use. Their utility and solid construction far surpassed many of the schools built later. New Orleans owes a significant debt to the work of E. A. Christy.

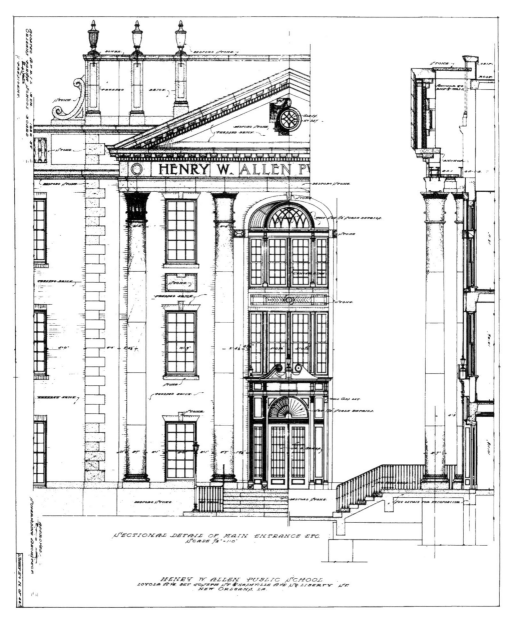

Plate 14 Facade detail, Henry W. Allen School, 5625 Loyola Avenue. This remarkable drawing shows the lengths to which Christy's draftsmen had to go to convey information to the contractor.

329

Plate 15 Charles J. Colton School, 2300 St. Claude Avenue. This view of the central portion of the school's block-long facade shows the use of contrasting materials that were so much a part of Christy's school designs.

330

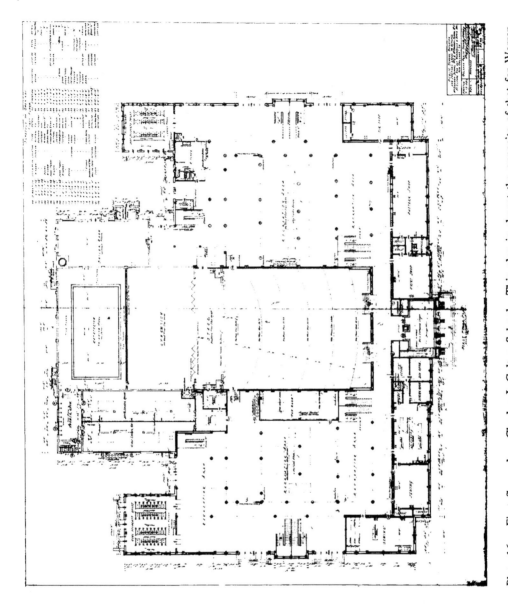

Plate 16   First floor plan, Charles J. Colton School.   This plan is almost the opposite of that for Warren Easton, with the auditorium being surrounded by other rooms, including an indoor swimming pool.

Plate 17   McDonogh Number 14 School, 1116 Jefferson Avenue.   Built to replace the flamboyant school shown in Plate 5, this Christy design perpetuated the clock tower of the earlier school.   Sadly, this tower no longer stands.

332

Plate 18   Martin Behrman School, 715 Opelousas Avenue.   For this school in Algiers,
Christy chose the Spanish Colonial Revival style, complete with a combination bell and
clock tower.

333

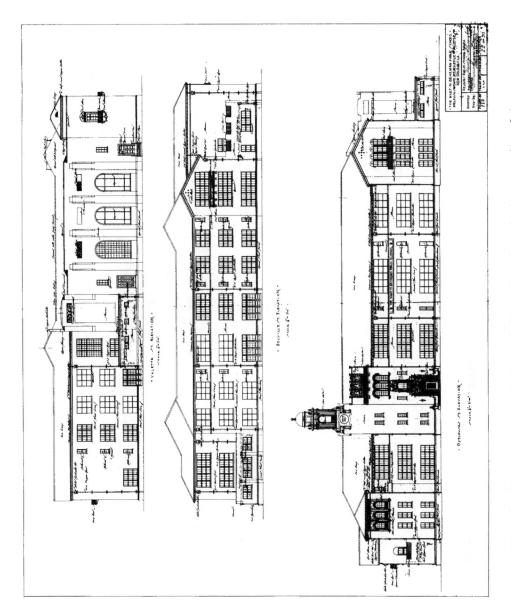

Plate 19   Facade elevations, Behrman School. Note that with the exception of the entry tower, the school is rather barren of ornamentation.

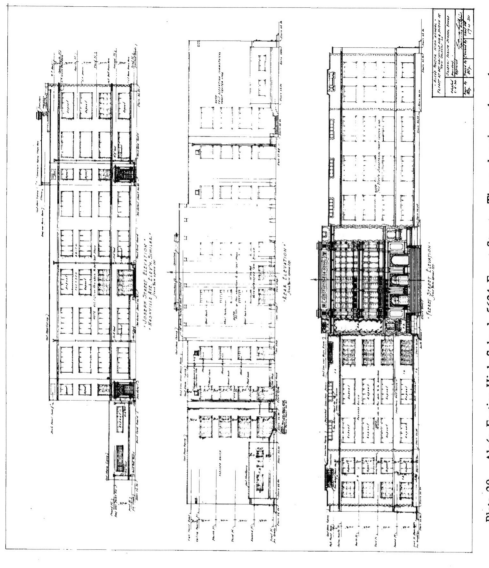

Plate 20 Alcée Fortier High School, 5624 Freret Street. These elevations show that, as was the case with Behrman, the details were focused on the main entry to the school.

335

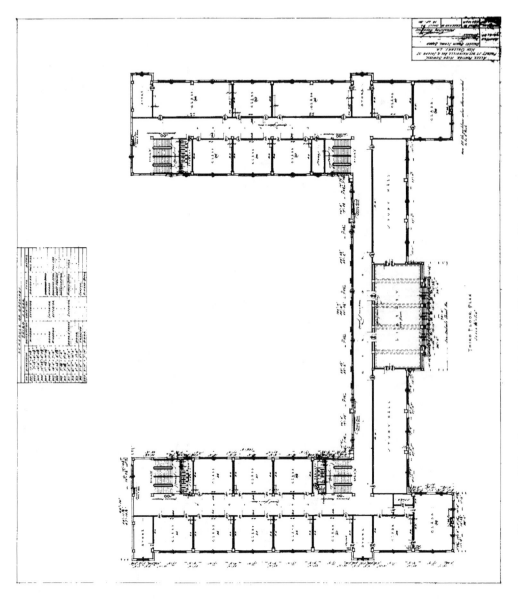

Plate 21   Third floor plan, Alcée Fortier High School. Note the separation of the classrooms from the library, and study halls.

336

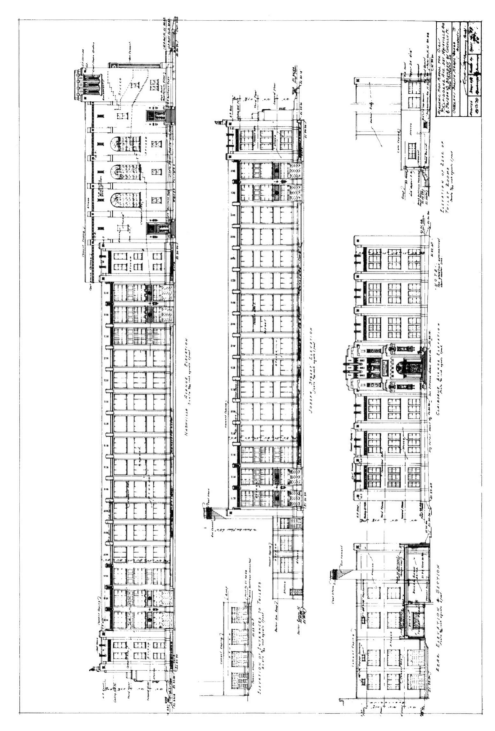

Plate 22   Eleanor McMain High School for Girls, 5712 South Claiborne Avenue.   For this important new high school, Christy left the more traditional styles for the Art Moderne, which was then in fashion.   Again, note the focus on the main entry, shown at the bottom of this sheet of elevation drawings.

337

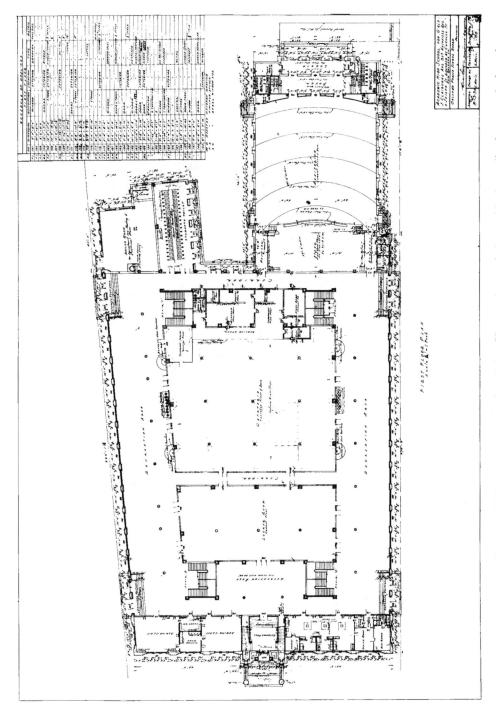

Plate 23   First floor plan, Eleanor McMain High School for Girls. Yet another variation, with the auditorium attached to the mass of the main building, giving it more privacy from the noise of the halls and the recreation areas on the first floor.

The Schools of the 1950s: The International Style in New Orleans

As the decade of the 1950s began, the school board initiated a study of its overall physical plant. Undertaken by the newly created Office of Planning and Construction, this study was published in 1952. Written by Charles R. Colbert, school board architect and planner, the study identified both short- and long-range needs. Colbert concluded that the general condition of the city's public school buildings was deplorable, that many if not most were located in neighborhoods that no longer had large student-age populations, and that a significant imbalance existed between schools that housed white students and those that housed black students.

The recommendations made in this study would lead to construction of thirty new schools between 1952 and 1960, and to additions being added to eighteen existing schools. In contrast to the years when E. A. Christy was supervising architect for the school board, the Office of Planning and Construction was not responsible for the actual design of the new buildings. Designs could be submitted by local architects in a competition similar to that used in awarding construction contracts on bid. In spite of the fact that one person no longer designed all school buildings, considerable stylistic similarity showed up in the schools built during the 1950s. In the years following World War I, architects in Europe, particularly in Germany and France, rebelled against the previously popular "historic styles," and proposed a new style for the twentieth century, one which would avoid the use of historic ornament of any kind. Because architects around the world adopted the new design idiom, it was dubbed the International Style by the organizers of an exhibition at New York's Museum of Modern Art in 1932. But because of the Great Depression and World War II, there was not a great deal of building done in the International Style in the U. S. until after 1945.

The principal characteristics of the International Style were the lack of any sort of decorative architectural ornament, use of new building materials such as aluminum and lightweight concrete, placement of windows in continuous bands, and lifting of the building off the ground by placing them on concrete or steel piers.

The International Style also produced a new design plan for schools. The new design solved the problem of ventilation by creating what were to become known as "finger schools". Plate 24 shows the architectural model

339

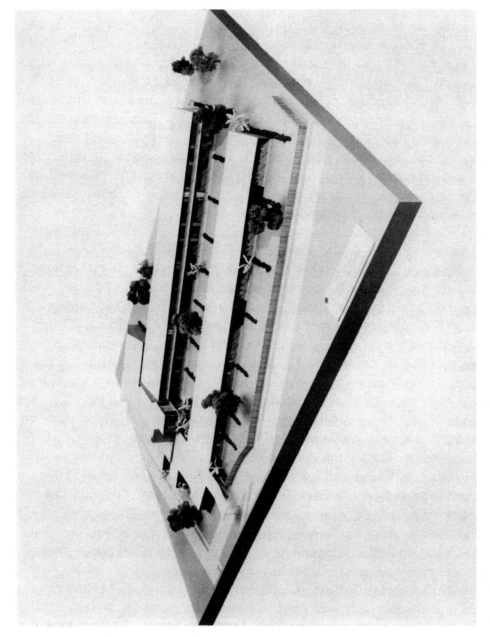

Plate 24 Architectural model of the Stuart R. Bradley School, 2401 Humanity Street. This miniature birds-eye view clearly shows the almost residential character of this school, with the play spaces directly outside the classroom windows.

for the Stuart R. Bradley School, designed by I. William Ricciuti and Herbert A. Benson and constructed in 1953 at 2401 Humanity Street in New Orleans. In the "finger school," long rectangular classroom wings were connected only at one end, and there, not to each other, but to an administration building. The classroom wings also made use of covered outdoor passageways rather than inside hallways. These open passages allowed both sides of "finger" classrooms to be fitted with operable windows for maximum ventilation. At the same time, overhanging rooflines shaded the classrooms' huge glass window walls. Overall, the design was marked by extreme simplicity, with flat or gently sloping, unornamented rooflines set on top of austere walls.

In 1954, one of the more unusual solutions to school design in New Orleans was offered by the architectural firm of Curtis and Davis for the new Thomy Lafon Elementary School at 2601 Seventh Street. Plate 25 shows the original model for this school, which has undergone many alterations and additions since it was built. The building consists of distinct but connected upper and lower parts. At ground level sits a rectangular block which houses a food service area and faculty meeting rooms. Above, in the shape of a boomerang, rises the classroom portion, supported on concrete piers. Access to the classrooms is provided by a series of six staircases. At one end of the classroom building are a pair of playrooms, which are reached by a ramp that rises from the playground. Plate 26 shows the playroom end of the classroom building shortly after it was completed. Lifting the classroom building off the ground recalled one of the important features of Louisiana colonial architecture: raising houses so that they could benefit from prevailing breezes. Plate 27 shows one of the twelve classrooms, with exposed metal framework across the ceiling and alternating clear and opaque glass forming the upper portion of the outer classroom walls. Large pivoting windows in the lower portion of the glass walls were designed to catch any available breezes.

In 1955, Charles Colbert, the author of the 1952 study of the school board's physical plant, was commissioned to design the new Phyllis Wheatley Elementary school at 2300 Dumaine Street. Colbert took the concept of the raised platform school even further than Curtis and Davis. He produced a building that seemed about to take flight. Plate 28 shows the Wheatley School's classrooms cantilevered out from their concrete support piers. This daring scheme was made possible by the use of steel

341

Plate 25   Architectural model, Thomy Lafon School, 2601 Seventh Street.   This model illustrates the separation of the classrooms, contained in the long curved section, from the group-use spaces in the rectangular segment at ground level.

342

Plate 26   Thomy Lafon School. This photo, taken shortly after the school opened, shows the classroom wing elevated above the ground.

Plate 27   Thomy Lafon School. A typical classroom interior, shortly after the school opened. Note the largely glass outer walls and the light metal structure of the ceiling.

344

Plate 28 Phillis Wheatley School, 2300 Dumaine Street. Perhaps the most startling of the 1950s school designs, Wheatley appears to be almost suspended in the air, courtesy of a series of structural trusses.

Plate 29 Architectural model, Francis W. Gregory Junior High School, 1700 Pratt Drive. For a larger and more complex school project, the buildings are here linked via covered walkways.

345

structural trusses to support the outer walls of the building, which, being
entirely of glass, were light in weight. As at Lafon, this raised school
allowed for a covered play space underneath. Wheatley had twenty-two
classrooms, reached via an open, covered walkway in the center of the
structure. The classrooms formed a rectangle, hollow at the center, which
allowed for additional natural ventilation. Unfortunately, the beauty of
Wheatley's splendid design has been marred by the replacement of most of
its original clear glass with cheap opaque plexiglass.

Solving the problem of providing for the greater variety of specific
activities needed by junior and senior high schools was exceptionaly well
handled in the design for the Francis W. Gregory Junior High School, built
in 1958 at 1700 Pratt Drive. Designed by the architectural firm of Burk,
LeBreton & Lamantia, Gregory is illustrated in Plate 29. The model
presents us with an overall view of the school complex of six buildings,
which are linked to one another by covered walkways. The large structure
on the right-hand side of the model is the gymnasium, and the structure
covered with a bowed roof is the auditorium. The other buildings house
classrooms and science labs. The several different roof treatments at
Gregory add character and variety to the overall design.

In 1958, the school board also began construction of what became the
most imposing of all of the 1950s schools. The 1952 planning study
introduced the concept of a "school village" in order to maximize the use of
a large site. A "school village" would contain an elementary, a junior
high, and a senior high school, all on the same site. Thus a student could
go through the entire public school curriculum without transferring to
another school. The site for the "school village" was near the intersection
of Louisa and Higgins Boulevard, near the Industrial Canal. The firm of
Curtis and Davis designed it. The complex was to contain the Helen
Sylvania Edwards elementary school and the George Washington Carver
junior and senior high schools. Plate 30 shows a model of the complex,
and Plate 31, a view from the air. In the model, the section of the complex
to the lower left is Edwards Elementary, and the large structure with the
curved roof, which stands next to the twin classroom blocks, is the
auditorium, which served all three schools. The long structure which
divides the complex into two parts housed the classrooms for the junior and
senior high schools. The junior and senior high school libraries were at the
center of this enormous building, and the science classrooms were in the

347

Plate 30 Architectural model, Helen Sylvania Edwards Elementary School and George Washington Carver Junior and Senior High schools, 3059 Higgins Boulevard. This spectacular model conveys the interconnected nature of this award-winning design, combining three schools on one campus.

348

Plate 31   Helen Sylvania Edwards Elementary School and George Washington Carver Junior and Senior High schools, 3059 Higgins Boulevard.   This aerial photo, taken before the addition of more classroom buildings, shows that the completed school complex exactly matches the form and plan fo the model shown in Plate 30.

two smaller rectangular wings at either end. Behind the junior and senior high school classrooms stood the gymnasium. The aerial photograph shows that the design proposed in the model was translated into reality with almost no alterations.

The design for this "school village" was recognized by the national journal *Progressive Architecture* in its annual awards issue of January, 1957. It was given the First Design Award, the highest prize. The Orleans Parish School Board had erected a school complex considered to be among the most advanced in the nation.

Among American cities, New Orleans possesses an unusually rich legacy in its many historic public school buildings and in its long tradition of school building. The one offers opportunities for important historical research into American school architecture, and the other, opportunities for the preservation of these uniquely important structures. Other cities such as Boston have recognized the value of their old school buildings and converted them, through adaptive use, into viable and valuable office space and senior citizens' centers. If New Orleans is to save, for future generations, any appreciable number of its uniquely fine school buildings, work must begin now.

APPENDIX II

New Orleans School Boards, 1862-1991

1. Bureau of Education, 1862-1864

In 1862, the Union military government which occupied the city during the Civil War consolidated the four antebellum school boards of New Orleans. According to ordinance 6082, passed on September 2, 1862, membership on the first citywide board, the Bureau of Education, was all ex officio and consisted of the military mayor of the city, the chairman of the Bureau of Finance, the chairman of the Bureau of Streets and Landings, the city Treasurer, and the city Comptroller.

Member	Service
Deming, Henry C.	1862
Dewees, D. L.	1863
Durrell, E. H.	1862-63
Estlin, C. F.	1863
Flanders, Benjamin F.	1862
Heald, John H.	1863
Howell, Stoddard	1862-63
Hoyt, Stephen	1863
Miller, James F.	1862
Neville, Julian	1862
Riddell, J. L.	1862
Walton, John S.	1862-63
Weitzel, Godfrey	1862

2. Board of Directors, 1864-1865

On June 30, 1864, city council ordinance no. 6226 set up a sixteen-member Board of Directors composed of the mayor, the chairman of the Committee of Finance, the chairman of the Committee of Streets and Landings, and thirteen members elected by the city council.

Member	Service
Bright, George S.	1864-65
Dewees, D. L.	1864-65
Dostie, A. P.	1864-65
Durell, E. H.	1864-65
Fish, W. R.	1864-65
Goldman, E.	1864-65
Handlin, W. W.	1864-65
Heath, E.	1864-65
Heistand, E.	1864-65
Howell, Stoddard	1864-65
Hoyt, Stephen	1864-65
Kennedy, Hugh	1864-65
Magne, J.	1864-65
Quincy, S. M.	1865
Roberts, John A.	1864-65
Tissot, A. L.	1864-65
Walton, John S.	1864-65
Whitaker, J. S.	1864-65

3. Board of Directors, 1865-1869

During the restoration of civilian control under President Andrew
Johnson, the new city council passed an ordinance on August 25, 1865,
which set up a board of twenty-four men appointed by the mayor. Half
were to serve for two years and half for one year. Members decided the
length of their terms by lot.

Before the school year began in 1866, the city council passed an
ordinance on July 11, 1866 to create a new board. The enactment retained a
board of twenty-four members but required them to be elected by the
council, six from each of the four prewar school districts. Three from each
district were to be appointed for one year and three for two years. The next
spring, when a new city council came into existence following the passage
of the Reconstruction Act of 1867, the existing school board went to court
to maintain its authority in defiance of the new council. The board filled
all of their own vacancies and legally stayed in office until the spring of
1870.

Member	Service
Adams, John J.	1865-66
Aikens, J. S.	1869-70
Ames, E.	1865-66
Augustin, Donation	1865-66
Baker, M. A.	1866-67
Benit, Jules	1866-70
Bermudez, Edward	1866-70
Boyer, P. C.	1865-66
Brewer, James	1866-67
Bruff, Charles	1868-67
Burke, Glendy	1865-66
Chiapella, Achille	1865-66
Collens, Paul W.	1866-68
Correjolles, Gabriel	1869-70
Cronan, George	1866-70
Culbertson, Charles W.	1866-70
Dowler, M. M.	1866-67
Duconge, F. P.	1865-66
Goldman, E.	1865-66
Goldthwaite, W. F.	1868-69
Gubernator, ?	1868-69
Hare, Robert	1866-67
Harper, Sidney P.	1868-70
Holliday, D. C.	1865-66
Hubbard, R. D.	1868-70
Huyghe, Robert	1866-70
Jewell, Edward L.	1865-66
Keep, E. S.	1865-66
Kelly, Edmund C.	1866-69
Ker, Robert J.	1865-66
Lagan, M. D.	1868-69
Leeds, Charles J.	1869-70
Leefe, J. B.	1866-70
Macon, Thomas L.	1866-68
Magne, J.	1865-66
Massicot, J. J. E.	1866-67
McCoard, D.	1865-66

McConnell, James	1866-67
McCulloch, ?	1868-69
Moore, John T.	1865-66
Mount, Williams S.	1866-67
O'Neal, Tim	1866-70
Parham, John G.	1866-70
Pasley, John	1868-69
Philips, Issac N.	1867-70
Pope, John H.	1868-70
Prados, Louis	1866-70
Race, George W.	1866-68
Raymond, W. C.	1865-66, 1867-69
Richards, Newton	1865-66
Rogers, Walter H.	1868-70
Ruleff, George	1865-66
Sambola, Anthony	1866-70
Santini, Joseph	1869-70
Schumacher, F.	1869-70
Shields, Thomas H.	1866-68
Sloo, Thomas	1865-66
Stickney, David W.	1866-68
Thieneman, Theodore F.	1866-70
Tissot, J. L.	1865-66
Turpin, John	1865-66
Tuyes, J.	1865-66
Viavent, Augustine	1865-66
Walsh, William F.	1865-66
Watkins, John A.	1866-70
White, George W.	1865-66
White, James A.	1865-66
Wiltz, Louis A.	1868-69
Zehender, H.	1866-70

4. Reconstruction Boards, 1870-1877

In 1869, after the passage of the state constitution of 1868, the state legislature set up a new board to run the schools of New Orleans. After the board failed to gain legitimacy in the state courts, the legislature reshaped public education throughout the state on March 24, 1870 (Act No. 108). It repealed the state law of 1855 under which the New Orleans board had been organized in 1866, terminated that board, and prohibited the city from maintaining its own separate school system.

Under the new state system, New Orleans was administered as the Sixth District among six districts in the state. The law stipulated that the New Orleans board would have eleven members serving for two-year terms, six appointed by the state board of education and five appointed by the New Orleans city council. If the council refused to act within three months, the state board was permitted to appoint all members. The New Orleans board began its official duties on May 1, 1870. In 1873, the legislature set up a board of twenty members, twelve appointed by the state board of education and six by the city council. Two served ex officio, the superintendent and the city administrator of finance.

Members	Service
Billings, E. C.	1873-75
Boothby, Charles W.	1871-77
Bourges, Alfred	1875-77
Carey, Thomas	1873-75
Casey, James S.	1873-75
Clark, J. S.	1873-75
Clay, John Racquet	1871-74
Cooper, J. B.	1871-74
DeKlyne, T. W.	1873-74
Denis, J. C.	1876-77
Dibble, Henry C.	1871-77
Dumont, A. J.	1874-77
Dunn, Fabius McK.	1870-71
Fayerweather, George H.	1870-71
Flanders, Benjamin F.	1875-76
Gaudet, J. B.	1873-75
Gardner, L. H.	1875-76
Glaudin, C. F.	1874-77
Grant, William	1870-71
Hahn, Michael	1870-73
Hartzell, Joseph C.	1875-76
Heath, Edward	1875-77

Ingraham, James H.	1873-75
Jackson, J. T.	1871-73
Joubert, B. F.	1871-73
Loan, W. F.	1873-74
Longstreet, James	1871-77
Lynch, B. L.	1875-77
Lynne, Thomas	1871-73
Marks, Isaac N.	1875-77
Massicot, J. A.	1875-77
Matlack, L. C.	1871-73
McCarthy, Victor Eugene	1873-75
McConnell, W. G.	1873-75, 1876-77
Mead, W. F.	1870-71
Packard, C. C.	1870-71
Pilsbury, ?	1876-77
Pinchback, P. B. S.	1871-77
Rey, Henry Louis	1873-77
Russell, S. C.	1873-74
Shaw, Alfred	1874-75
Shelley, A.	1870-71
Staes, Eugene	1870-71
Stamps, T. B.	1874-77
Thompson, Charles H.	1873-75
Tissot, J. L.	1870-71
Toy, W. H.	1871-73
Tracy, T. G.	1870-71, 1874-77
Trévigne, Paul	1876-77
Van Norden, Warner	1870-71
Walker, C. L.	1876-77
Waples, Rufus	1875-77

5. Board of Directors, 1877-1908

In 1877, the new Democratic legislature reorganized the New Orleans school board. The new board had twenty members, eight appointed by the state board of education and twelve appointed by the city council. Only a few changes in the board structure took place for the next thirty years. In 1884, after a reorganization of the state department of education, a complete new set of appointments was made for the New Orleans board. In 1888, another law transferred the state appointments to the governor. Except for the aborted appointments in 1884, all terms lasted for four years.

Members	Service
Aikman, J. B.	1888-95
Andry, Charles G.	1889-91
Atkinson, William	1898-1902
Ault, Louis P.	1898-1906
Bartley, Robert H.	1877-88
Behrman, Martin	1895-99
Bercegeay, J.	1891-94
Bertoli, Leon	1881-84
Bienvenu, N.	1891-1900
Bienvenu, W.	1880-81
Bower, E. L.	1880-81
Boyle, Charles F.	1883-88
Brennan, James A.	1902-08
Brosnan, D. M.	1881-84
Brown, R. L.	1884-88
Buck, Charles F.	1888-93, 1899-1901
Buhler, Eugene F.	1903-08
Buhler, John	1878-81
Capdau, J. Ernest	1900-04
Capdevielle, Paul	1877-81
Carlisle, S. S.	1881-84
Cason, Benjamin W.	1890-91
Castellanos, Henry C.	1882
Castleman, Thomas W.	1899-1907
Chaffe, W. H.	1888-90
Chalin, L. F.	1889-93
Chiapella, Henry	1888-90
Chrétien, Frank D.	1891-1901
Cleary, Thomas B.	1905-08
Clegg, John	1907-08
Cohn, Dave	1884-88
Coleman, Lloyd	1877-80
Collins, Joseph	1877-82
Colton, Charles J.	1904-08

Connell, J. D.	1888-89
Craig, Joseph A.	1877-79
Curtis, W. P.	1891-98
Day, Robert S.	1890-95
DeFuentes, C. L.	1883-88, 1891-1908
Deibel, Fred	1893-97
Denis, Jules C.	1877-78
Desdunes, Eugene	1880-82
Duffy, John W.	1904-08
Edwards, J. B.	1883-84
Escoffier, S.	1888-1891
Faust, W. C.	1884-88, 1891-93, 1898-1908
Fayerweather, George H.	1877-81
Ferguson, H. B.	1877-80
Florance, E. T.	1893-1900
Flynn, George W.	1884-88
Flynn, J. Q.	1892-96
Ford, F. Codman	1888-94
Foster, G. W.	1896-99
Frantz, William	1901-08
Grima, Alfred	1888-89
Gutheim, J. K.	1877-82
Hackett, M.	1883-84
Handy, Thomas H.	1877-85
Hassinger, Jacob	1877-78
Hebrard, B. W.	1884-86
Henning, Frank	1903-08
Henry, S. L.	1883-84
Herbert, George, Jr.	1899-1903
Hollingsworth, L. B.	1881-1883
Hoth, Jacob	1883-84
Houston, James D.	1884-88
Howe, G. K.	1884, 1888-90
Howe, Matthew	1884-88
Issacson, A. H.	1878-81
Joyce, P. A.	1889-95
Junker, Adam	1902-04
Kernaghan, W. J.	1888-92

Knickerbocker, Harry H.	1903-08
Kohn, Joseph	1898-1902, 1903-08
Kohnke, E. F.	1890-1906
Kronenberger, George G.	1903-08
Kruttschnitt, Ernest B.	1884-1903
Lanaux, Pierre	1877-88
Leche, A. S.	1888-91
Leppert, William J.	1900-02
Levy, William L.	1906-08
Lochte, Henry	1905-06
Loeber, E. F.	1888-90
Luzenberg, Chandler C.	1901-03
Lyman, W. R.	1888-90
Maginnis, A. A.	1888-90
Mahoney, Martin S.	1903-08
Martinet, Louis A.	1877-81
Mauer, John P.	1881-83
McCann, J.	1895-97
McColl, J.	1880-81
McElroy, Frank	1879-88
McGivney, Eugene	1895-99
McLean, James Lea	1886-88
McLean, John O.	1877-81, 1882-84
McNamara, M.	1881-84
Mellen, W. F.	1881-83
Mercier, C. S.	1884-88
Michel, John T.	1893-95
Mitchell, Archibald	1877-80
Morris, J. C.	1884-1900
Moss, A. Trigg	1894-98, 1905-08
Moss, Alfred	1896-1903
Mulledy, M. T.	1882-83
O'Brien, John J.	1883-84
O'Neil, Timothy	1879-82
O'Reilly, William T.	1903-04
Parham, J. G.	1883-87
Pedarre, Henry R.	1900-08
Penrose, C. B.	1894-95

Perkins, Louis W.	1877-79
Pettis, P. W.	1881-83
Place, Frank L.	1902-05
Prados, Louis	1879-81
Quinn, Edward	1883-84
Read, C. H.	1892-93
Richardson, T. G.	1884-85
Rogers, William O.	1885-1896
Roux, Emile	1885-86
Saxon, Walter L.	1888
Sease, H. L.	1899-1903
Seeman, Charles F.	1877-81, 1884-88
Semmes, Thomas J.	1877-80, 1882-84
Sirjacques, W. L.	1897-1903
Stanton, Thomas J.	1896-1903
Stringer, Frederick	1881-84
Swarbrick, George	1877-79
Swarbrick, James G.	1902-08
Terry, A. T.	1890-99
Theard, Charles J.	1890-91
Tourné, P. M.	1877-78
Turnbull, F. T.	1895-96
Turner, W. G.	1898-1902
Vinet, John B.	1886-88, 1891
Walmsley, R. M.	1884-88
Walshe, B. T.	1881-84
Weber, Emile	1893
Wild, William	1906-08
Williams, E. A.	1893-98
Wilson, Andrew H.	1887-1908
Winship, J. M.	1888-92
Wisdom, M. N.	1895-97
Yenni, Charles H.	1888-89

6. Board of Directors, 1908-1912

A legislative act in 1906 (Act No. 6) enabled New Orleans voters in each of the seventeen wards of the city to elect a representative from their ward to a new board. Three men also served ex officio to make up a twenty-member board: the mayor, the city treasurer, and the city comptroller. The first election was held in November 1908, and the winners of the election organized the new board on December 5, 1908. All vacancies were filled by the governor.

Member	Service
Behrman, Martin	1908-12
Briede, Otto F.	1908-12
Cleary, Thomas B.	1908-12
Colton, Charles J.	1908-12
Cusachs, Gaspar	1908-12
Dorrestein, C. A. M.	1908-12
Doyle, Thomas	1908-12
Duffy, John Watt	1908-12
Frantz, William	1908-12
Henning, Frank	1908-11
Kennedy, Charles R.	1908-12
Knickerbocker, Harry H.	1908
Kostmayer, George H.	1911
Kronenberger, G. G.	1908-11
Leckert, John T.	1908-09
Levy, William M.	1908-12
Loeb, Ernest M.	1908-12
Magruder, M. J.	1912
Owens, Frank J.	1910-12
Parsons, Edward A.	1908-12
Reuther, Joseph	1908-12
Spearing, J. Zach	1908-11
Stern, Edgar	1912
Swarbrick, James G.	1908-12
Wild, William	1908-12

7. Orleans Parish School Board, 1912-1988

In order to reorganize public education in Louisiana the state legislature passed the General School Act of 1912. The bill, popularly known as the Burke Act, set up a five-member board in New Orleans to be elected at large

by the voters of the city for terms of four years. In 1916, another state law
(Act No. 120) changed the terms to six years but limited the initial terms
for three of the members elected in November 1916 so that future terms
would overlap. The highest two vote winners received six year terms, the
next highest two received four year terms, and the fifth highest received a
two year term. The 1916 act also changed the name of the board to the
Orleans Parish School Board.

Member	Service
Baumgartner, Fannie	1920-26
Besse, C. P.	1950-56
Blomberg, Mildred	1969-74
Buckley, Joseph P.	1912-15
Capdau, P. A.	1916-19
Colton, Charles J.	1912-15
Ellis, Daniel	1962-64
Fletcher, William C.	1943-50
Fortier, James J. A.	1922-26
Frantz, William	1914-20
Garland, Edmund J.	1928-34
Glapion, Gail M.	1984-88
Goodman, Harry	1926-28
Haas, Robert M.	1934-52
Heller, Isaac	1928-40
Hess, Victor H., Jr.	1964-70
Hotard, Theodore O.	1932-43
Kabacoff, Pres	1988
Knight, Edward H.	1971-76
Koppel, Harwood "Woody"	1975-88
Loving, Rose	1977-88
Mahoney, R. Emmet	1943-50
McKenna, Dwight L.	1987-88
Moise, Percy H.	1920-26
McCulloch, Jacqueline*	1948-54
Murphy, Daniel L.	1918-24
Pilie, Louis H.	1940-52

* In 1950, she married and thereafter used the name Jacqueline T. Leonhard. She was the first woman to
serve as head of the board, 1950-52.

Rack, Elizabeth	1979-1984
Reeves, William D.	1973-78
Reuter, Joseph	1916-20
Ricks, Phil G.	1926-32
Riecke, Louis G.	1956-68
Rinker, Andrew	1964-70
Rittner, Lloyd J.	1956-68, 1971-83
Robbert, John F.	1983-88
Roccaforte, S.	1942-48
Sarpy, Henry L.	1916
Schabel, August	1926-32
Schaumburg, Henry C.	1919-20, 1924-41
Scheps, Clarence	1950-56
Sharon, A. C.	1916-18
Shephard, Theodore H., Jr.	1952-64
Smith, Robert C.	1966-72
Soniat, Charles T.	1912-13
Spearing, J. Zach	1916-20
Spears, Mack	1969-86
Sutherland, Matthew R.	1954-66
Treadwell, George A.	1932-43
Valloft, Louis Edward	1913
Wagner, Emile A., Jr.	1952-62
Wegmann, John X.	1912-15
Wexler, Sol	1912-15
Zengel, Fred W., Jr.	1922-28

8. Orleans Parish School Board, 1989

In 1988, voters in New Orleans endorsed a constitutional amendment that changed the board by expanding it to seven members, each for four year concurrent terms. Five members run in separate districts and two run at large. Elected in 1988, the new board members began their duties in January 1989. The members are

Jefferson, Betty
Glapion, Gail M.
Koppel, Harwood "Woody" (at large)
McKenna, Dwight L. (at large)

O'Dwyer, Avra
Robinson, Carl D.
Sens, Paul N.

NOTES

Introduction

[1] Richard Wade, "Historical Analogies and Public Policy: The Black and Immigrant Experience in Urban American," in *Essays on Urban America*, ed. M. F. Morris and E. West (Austin, 1975), 138, as quoted in Vincent P. Franklin, "Continuity and Discontinuity in Black and Immigrant Minority Education in Urban America: A Historical Assessment," in *Educating an Urban People: The New York City Experience*, ed. Diane Ravitch and Ronald K. Goodenow (New York, 1981), 49.

Chapter I

[1] J. Baldwin to Horace Mann, April 7, 1841, Horace Mann Papers, Massachusetts Historical Society.

[2] Lawrence A. Cremin, *American Education: The National Experience, 1783-1876* (New York, 1980), pp. 154-156.

[3] Stuart G. Noble, "Education in Colonial Louisiana," *Louisiana Historical Quarterly*, XXXII (1949), 759-776; Cremin, *American Education: The National Experience*, p. 149.

[4] Stuart G. Noble, "Governor Claiborne and the Public School System of the Territorial Government of Louisiana," *Louisiana Historical Quarterly*, XI (1928), 550. Carl F. Kaestle, who studied education in New York, the only other state with substantial non-Anglo European groups, noted that he found no evidence of Anglo-American leaders wishing to use schools for the assimilation of Dutch and other non-English settlers. Carl F. Kaestle, *The Evolution of an Urban School System: New York City, 1750-1850* (Cambridge, Mass., 1973), pp. 18-23.

[5] Edwin Whitefield Fay, *The History of Education in Louisiana* (Washington, D. C., 1898), 43-45; *Gibson's Guide and Directory of the State of Louisiana, and the Cities of Orleans and Lafayette* (New Orleans, 1838), pp. 266-267.

[6] Robert C. Reinders, "New England Influences on the Foundation of Public Schools in New Orleans," *Journal of Southern History*, XXX (1964), 181-195.

[7] In the periodical that Barnard ran both before and after the Civil War, he claimed credit for providing New Orleans officials with a general plan for their schools: *Journal of Education*, XXV (1873), 276.

[8] Minutes, Board of Directors of Public Schools of the Second Municipality of New Orleans, May 15, 1841. Hereafter cited as Minutes, Muni 2 Schools. The original state and municipal ordinances of 1841 were copied into the board's minutes of May 13, 1847.

[9] J. Baldwin to Horace Mann, August 28, 1841, Horace Mann Papers.

[10] Jonathan Messerli, *Horace Mann: A Biography* (New York, 1972), pp. 184, 210, 214, 370-371, 499. Mary Peabody Mann said in her biography of her husband that New Orleans was the only school district in the South where Mann recommended someone to start a school system because he thought that slavery made a true system of public education impossible: *Life of Horace Mann* (Boston, 1865), pp. 108-159. One cannot find such clear objections from Mann in the early 1840s, but he does not seem to have had such a direct role in any other Southern school system. See the two articles by Edgar W. Knight on this general subject: "Some Evidence of Horace Mann's Influence in the South," *School and Society*, LXV (1947), 33-37; and "More Evidence of Horace Mann's Influence in the South," *The Educational Forum*, XII (1948), 167-184.

Society, LXV (1947), pp. 33-37; and "More Evidence of Horace Mann's Influence in the South," *The Educational Forum*, XII (1948), 167-184.

[11]Richard M. Hodges, *A Memorial Address Read at the Funeral of John Angier Shaw . . .* (Cambridge, Mass., 1874), pp. 30, 33, 41.

[12] Messerli, *Horace Mann*, 327-335; Shaw's long report defending Mann appeared in the *Common School Journal*, II (1840), 225-240. See also John A. Shaw to Horace Mann, March 10, 1840 and April 5, 1841, Horace Mann Papers.

[13] John A. Shaw to Horace Mann, April 5, 1841, Horace Mann Papers.

[14] John A. Shaw, *An Address Delivered Before the Bridgewater Society for the Promotion of Temperance, February 22, 1828* (Boston, 1928), pp. 4, 20.

[15] *American Annals of Education*, VIII (1838), 236. This journal noted the impact of the work of Calvin Stowe, Harriet Beecher Stowe's eventual husband: "Almost every newspaper we take up contains extracts of it." It also observed that the Massachusetts legislature of 1838 commissioned a special printing of 2,500 copies "for their exclusive use."

[16] Minutes, Muni 2 Schools, November 13, 1841. Horace Mann's letter of 29 October 1841 recommending Shaw for superintendent is mentioned in the same minutes.

[17] John A. Shaw to Horace Mann, October 25, 1841, Horace Mann Papers.

[18] John A. Shaw to Horace Mann, November 29, 1841, Horace Mann Papers.

[19] Shaw noted at the end of the school term to a fellow reformer: "Our schools have been thus far conducted much on the plan of the Boston schools." His letter also shows that he did not visit the schools of New York, Philadelphia, and Connecticut until the summer of 1842. John A. Shaw to Henry Barnard, 26 September 1842, Henry Barnard papers at New York University. Hereafter cited as the Henry Barnard Papers. For a note on Shaw's 1842 summer tour of other northeastern cities, see Minutes, Muni 2 Schools, December 3, 1842.

[20] The first school arranged for boys was in a "four story brick house . . . belonging to Mr. Edward E. Parker." The girl's school opened in the building next door. *Ibid.*, 6 November 1841. The Third Municipality set up its school program after the Second Municipality but opened a school a few months earlier, on November 15, 1841, by absorbing a private school of George W. Harby, who served as its principal. See Alma Hobbs Peterson, "The Administration of Public Schools in New Orleans, 1841-1861," (Ph. D. dissertation, Louisiana State University, 1964), pp. 98-101.

[21] Minutes, Muni 2 Schools, March 23, 1848. See the long report to the Municipal Council.

[22] Henry Barnard to Horace Mann, March 26, 1843, Horace Mann Papers. *The Common School Journal*, VI (1844), 214.

[23] *Ibid.*, 216; Mann quoted these phrases from the second annual report presented to the Council of the Second Municipality. For similar remarks, see also Minutes, Muni 2 Schools, October 23, 1843.

[24] Thelma Welch, "Salary Policies for Teachers in the New Orleans Public Schools, 1841-1941" (M. A. thesis, Tulane University, New Orleans, 1942), pp. 17, 41.

[25] American Institute of Instruction, *The Lectures . . . Including the Journal of the Proceedings and a List of the Officers* (Boston, 1838-1850).

[26] Henry Barnard, *Memoirs of Teachers, Educators and Promoters and Benefactors of Education, Literature, and Science* (New York, 1861), pp. 400-404.

[27] *Common School Journal*, XIII (1851), 169-172. Fowle, who took over from Mann in 1849, made marginal notes in the file of the journal now at the Gutman Library of Harvard University. He noted along side an earlier flattering report of Shaw's work in volume XII (1850), 148-152, that Boston had tried to start free textbooks in 1847-48 but put off the reform until 1855. Fowle, who wrote the Boston law, was obviously influenced by Shaw's innovation.

[28] In 1845, the school board of the Second Municipality learned that Natchez, "our Sister City," had set up "a System of Public School instruction, upon a basis similar to that now in successful operation in our city." In 1846, Robert H. McNair, a New Orleans principal, went to become superintendent in Galveston, to "assist in the organization of the public schools of that City." Minutes, Muni 2 Schools, April 5, 1845; November 7, 1846. For the influence of New Orleans in Alabama, see the *Alabama Educational Journal*, I (1858), 101; (1859), 232.

[29] Peterson, "The Administration of Public Schools in New Orleans," 71-84. Raleigh A. Suarez, "Chronicle of a Failure: Public Education in Antebellum Louisiana," *Louisiana History*, XII (1971), 109-122. For contemporary observations, see *American Journal of Education*, II (1856), 473; *The New York Teacher*, VIII (1859), 381-82; *The Massachusetts Teacher*, XIII (1860), 152-53.

[30] The Third Municipality set up its school system last with an ordinance on July 19, 1841 but actually open the first school run by G. W. Harby for boys and girls on November 15, 1841 on Victory Street near Marigny Street. This system, for which records have been lost, was the slowest to develop. Peterson, "The Administration of Public Schools in New Orleans," 85-120.

[31] Minutes, Muni 1 Schools, October 3, 1843.

[32] *Ibid.*, November 14, 1843; May 11, 1844; October 21, 1847; January 25; June 1, 1850.

[33] *Ibid.*, October 28, 1843. Randall M. Millier and Jon L. Wakelyn, eds., *Catholics in the Old South* (Macon, Ga., 1983), pp. 34-37.

[34] Minutes, Muni 1 Schools, October 28, November 14, 1843, January 1, 1844. J. Mackin Halsey to Henry Barnard, December 9, 1843, Henry Barnard Papers.

[35] *Ibid.*, September 13, 1844; January 11, April 24, 30, June 4, November 1, 4, 1845; May 13, 1846. Between 1841 and 1852, the First Municipality schools had seven different superintendents: James Murrays (1841-1843); F. A. Sawyer (1843-44); Charles Cuvellier (1845); Thomas Théard (1845-46); G. Bellanger (1846-47); James Butler Carter (1847); Alexander Fabre (1847-52).

[36] *Ibid.*, July 6, 1848; January 25, 1850; March 1, 1851; December 19, 1853.

[37] Joseph Logsdon, "Immigration through the Port of New Orleans," in *Forgotten Doors: The Other Ports of Entry to the United States*, edited by M. Mark Stolarik (Philadelphia, 1988), pp. 105-124.

[38] Minutes, Muni 2 Schools, June 13, 1850. For earlier debates over funding, see January 30, 1847; March 23, 1848.

[39] Mandatory scripture reading and a proscribed daily prayer was adopted in 1843. It took until 1845, however, for the board to agree on a prayer. Minutes, Muni 2 Schools, May 6, 1843; February 8, 1845. During the height of the potato famine migration from Ireland in 1848, Shaw found it necessary to defend his religious policies. In the fall of 1850, however, a new board tried to abolish the objectionable rules and created a furious division until the City Countil finally intervened, on February 18, 1851, to end the religious practices. The dispute fueled nativism in the city and accelerated a movement to build parochial schools especially for the Irish in uptown New Orleans. *Ibid.*, November 7, 1850; February 14, 20, 1851.

[40] *Ibid.*, February 20, 1851.

[41] James A. Shaw, *An Address to the Teachers of the Public Schools in Municipality Number Two, City of New Orleans on Resigning His Office May 31, 1851* (New Orleans, 1851), [typescript copy at Tulane University], pp. 8-9.

[42] J. A. Shaw to H. Barnard, May 17, 1851, in the Henry Barnard Papers. In the same collection, see also the letters of the board member in charge of the recruitment campaign: J. S. Copes to Henry Barnard, April 15, June 16, July 26, 1851.

[43] *Ibid.* The quote of Copes comes from his letter of 15 April.

[44] New Orleans *Weekly Picayune*, 14 July 14, 1851; New Orleans *Weekly Delta*, August 7, 1853. *De Bow's Review*, XXVII (September, 1859), 278. For a quite different view by De Bow before the Wilmot Proviso crisis, see I (January, 1846), 83, when he claimed that "the true system of common schools in New Orleans gave it "proud pre-eminence . . . among southern cities." Regarding the normal school, a *Picayune* editorial declared: "It aims to establish a professional pride and to create a corps of young instructors who understand Southern mind, sympathise with Southern opinion, and are imbued with pride in the success of Southern schools. . . . It contains in it the genius of Southern intellectual independence." From an undated clipping about 1858, in the "Scrapbooks," vol. 1, of the William O. Rogers Papers, Tulane University.

[45] In each case, the allotment covered only about a third of the cost of building these schools. The custom of naming all schools built with McDonogh funds after the benefactor and assigning them numbers—McDonogh No. 1 or McDonogh No. 2—began after the Civil War when larger amounts of money began to flow into the public school system. Only three of the four schools funded in 1861 were completed before the war disrupted any further construction. The First District never started its proposed school; the Second built the St. Philip School (now the site of McDonogh 15); the Third built the McCarty School; and the Fourth built the McDonogh School, the only one named in honor of the benefactor. The McDonogh School, on Laurel between Philip and First Streets, eventually became McDonogh No. 1. Robert Meyer, Jr., *Names Over New Orleans Public Schools* (New Orleans, 1975), pp. 145-149. See also Minutes of the McDonogh Fund, March 11, 1861, and the city ordinance 5008 of March 14, 1860, pasted into the minute book on page 38, in the Orleans Parish Public School Collection.

[46] Minutes, District 2, December 29, 1859.

[47] Minutes, Dist. 2, May 17, 1852. The quotations of Gayarré and Dimitry are taken from Reinders, "New England Influences," 193.

[48] "Memorial," attached to the Minutes, Dist. 2, February 2, 1856. See also the meetings of January 31 and February 8, for further information on this protest.

[49] *Common School Journal*, X (1848), 384. The information that "The Second Municipality has for many years furnished a copy of our Journal to each of the public teachers" appeared in a signed article of the magazine's meticulous publisher, W. B. Fowle. *Ibid.*, XIII (1851), 169.

Chapter II

[1] John W. Blassingame, *Black New Orleans, 1860-1880* (Chicago, 1973), p. 107. See also H. E. Sterx, *The Free Negro in Ante-Bellum Louisiana* (Cranbury, N. J., 1972), pp. 268-274.

[2] Charles E. Nolan, *Bayou Carmel: The Sisters of Mount Carmel of Louisiana, 1833-1903* (Kenner, La., 1977), pp. 17-20. *Golden Jubilee of the Sisters of the Holy Family* (New Orleans, 1892), pp. 3-7. A copy of this rare pamphlet is in the Marcus Christian Collection at the University of New Orleans.

[3] *Prospectus de l'institution catholique des ophelins indigents* (New Orleans, 1847), pp. 1-2.

[4] Board of Directors, *History of the Catholic Indigent Orphan Institute* (New Orleans, c. 1916). For an account by a former student of the school, see Rodolphe Desdunes, *Our People and Our History* (Baton Rouge, La., 1973), pp. 13-24, 101-108. For some issues left out of his published accounts, see the correspondence between Rodolphe Desdunes and Rene Grandjean in the Rene Grandjean Collection at the University of New Orleans.

[5] *Common School Journal*, XI (1849), 30-31.

[6] Nathan Willey, "Education of the Colored Population of Louisiana," *Harpers New Monthly Magazine*, XXXIII (July, 1866), 249-250. Desdunes, *Our People and Our History*, pp. 25-108.

[7] Nathan Willey, "Education of the Colored Population of Louisiana," 250.

[8] Minutes, Board of Vicitors of District 2; September 22, October 29, November 4, December 1, 20, 1862. Benjamin Flanders, a former principal in the district, appears to have helped worked out this compromise. Minutes, Bureau of Education, September 30, 1862. Flanders, considered by some to an abolitionist, had been forced to flee New Orleans during Confederate control. See Peyton McCrary, *Abraham Lincoln and Reconstruction: The Louisiana Experiment* (Princeton, 1978), pp. 96-98.

[9] Minutes, Bureau of Education, September 25, October 4, November 22, 1862.

[10] *Ibid.*, March 18, April 4, 1863; for discontent in the visitors' boards, see the minutes for Board of Visitors of District 4; November 10, 1863 and minutes of the Bureau of Education, March 2, April 4, 1863.

[11] *Ibid.*, April 4, May 2, June 3, 6, 1863. On prayer, see March 18, 1863.

[12] *Ibid.*, June 30, 1863.

[13] On singing patriotic songs, see *ibid.*, March 18, May 16, 1863. For problems of enforcement among students and teachers, see the minutes of the Board of Visitors of District 2; June 1, 1863, and for District 4, April 28, 1863.

[14] Minutes, Bureau of Education, June 24, 1864. A printed copy of the new ordinance was pasted on a page following the minutes of the last meeting of the Bureau of Education.

[15] Minutes, School Board, July 7, August 19, 26, September 13, 1864.

[16] *Ibid.*, September 23, 1864.

[17] *Anglo-African*, June 13, 1863. Isabelle's letter was dated May 16, 1863. He claimed to have started the schools on August 4, 1862. He was aided by Mrs. Carla Hyde, the black wife of white radical in New Orleans.

[18] John W. Blassingame, "The Union Army as an Educational Institution for Negroes, 1862-1865," *Journal of Negro Education*, XXXIV (1965), 152-59.

[19] Minutes, Board of Visitors for District 2; September 13, 18, 29, 1862.

[20] *Boston Daily Advertiser*, April 13, 1864, as quoted in the *Liberator*, April 15, 1864. For more on the activity of this delegation, see Joseph Logsdon, "Americans and Creoles in New Orleans: The Origins of Black Citizenship in the United States," *Amerikastudien/American Studies*, 34 (1989), 189-96.

[21] William F. Messner, *Freedmen and the Ideology of Free Labor: Louisiana 1862-1865* (Lafayette, La., 1978), pp. 166-169. Charles Vincent, *Black Legislators in Louisiana During Reconstruction* (Baton Rouge, La., 1976), pp. 11-12.

[22] Department of the Gulf, *Report of the Board of Education for Freedmen for the Year 1864* (New Orleans, 1865), pp. 6, 12.

[23] Banks to Lincoln, July 25, 1864, R. T. Lincoln Coll., as quoted in LaWanda Cox, *Lincoln and Black Freedman* (Columbia, S. C., 1981), p. 179.

[24] School Board Minutes, September 23, 28, October 3, November 7, 1864.

[25] *Ibid.*, February 6, November 7, 1864.

[26] *Ibid.*, September 18, 25, 1865.

[27] William O. Rogers to George Clark, April 30, 1866, Letterbook, Superintendent's Office, Orleans Parish School Board Collection.

[28] *Ibid.*

[29] *Ibid.*, William O. Rogers to W. A. B. Chandler, June 1, 1866.

[30] Ted Tunnell, *Crucible of Reconstruction: War, Radicalism and Race in Louisiana, 1862-1877* (Baton Rouge, La., 1984), pp. 103-107.

[31] Joe Gray Taylor, *Louisiana Reconstructed 1863-1877* (Baton Rouge, La., 1974), pp. 103-13.

[32] School Board Minutes, September 5, November 7, 1866.

[33] William O. Rogers to principals [circular], December 13, 1867; February 7, 1868, Letterbook, Superintendent's Office. The resulting French policy was very similar to what Rogers had carried over from the unionist system in the 1865-66 school year. See School Board Minutes, October 17, December 5, 1865; January 2, 1866.

[34] *Ibid.*, August 15, 1866.

[35] Roger A. Fischer, *The Segregation Struggle in Louisiana, 1862-77* (Urbana, Ill., 1974), pp. 35-41. *New Orleans Tribune*, July 9, 1867.

[36] New Orleans *Daily Picayune*, July 31, August 7, 1867.

[37] Howard A. White, *The Freedmen's Bureau in Louisiana* (Baton Rouge, La., 1970), pp. 17-22, 166-200.

[38] School Board Minutes, September 16, 1867. The rather candid report of the committee was related in detail. It was released to the New Orleans *Daily Crescent*, which printed it on September 15, 1867. New Orleans *Tribune*, July 31, 1867. For a detailed report black leaders' views on accepting the school board's offer of segregated schools, see New Orleans *Republican*, September 21, 1867. P. M. Williams, who had graduated from Dartmouth and taught in a segregated black school in New York City, favored integrated schools and insisted that the school board's report misrepresented his views.

[39] School Board Minutes, November 6, December 4, 1867. For self-admission of the gross inferiority of the black schools, see the report of Asst. Superintendent Dimitry, *ibid.*, May 21, 1868.

[40] *Ibid.*, May 7, 1868.

[41] *Ibid.*, May 21, September 2, 1868; earlier, a white father also made a formal complaint to the board about their barring his son, whom he acknowledged as racially mixed. See *ibid.*, February 5, 1868.

[42] *Ibid.*, January 13, February 2, 1869.

[43] *Ibid.*, October 7, 1868; Fischer, *The Segregation Struggle*, pp. 115-19. See also Mary DiMartini, "Education in New Orleans during Reconstruction" (M. A. these, Tulane University, 1935), particularly her appendices showing the annual openings of private and parochial schools, pp. 159-181.

[44] *Weekly Louisianian*, December 12, 1874. On Dunn's leadership, see Fischer, *The Segregation Struggle in Louisiana*, p. 114.

[45] *Daily Picayune*, October 19, 1872.

[46] Harlan, "Desegregation in New Orleans Public Schools," 668-69. Already in early 1872, Superintendent Carter reported the return of students because of "the superiority of the public schools." Journal, State Board of Education, January 2, 1872.

[47] Harlan, "Desegregation in New Orleans Public Schools," 670.

[48] T. Harry Williams, "The Louisiana Unification Movement of 1873," *Journal of Southern History*, XI (1945), 349-69. For a profile of the Republican board in 1871, see the *Weekly Louisianian*, April 27, 1872. That paper reflected black leaders' admiration for the bold departure of Longstreet: "The moral courage displayed in his manly acceptance of the results of the war has given him an influence. . . ." Longstreet stayed on the board until 1877.

[49] *Weekly Louisianian*, September 18, 1875.

[50] George Washington Cable, "My Politics," republished in *The Negro Question*, edited by Arlin Turner (New York, 1958), p. 8. See also Arlin Turner, *George W. Cable* (Baton Rouge, La., 1966), pp. 74-75, 196-197.

[51] *Weekly Louisiana*, 6 March 1875. Journal, State Board of Education, April 10, 1875. For a lengthy report of the McDonogh report, see State of Louisiana, Superintendent of Public Education, *Annual Report* (1875), pp. 53-73.

[52] *Weekly Louisiana*, July 18, 1873.

[53] *Daily Picayune*, December 18, 1874.

[54] *Weekly Louisianian*, December 19, 26, 1874.

[55] *Ibid.*, September 18, 1875. The black community probably helped to quiet renewed trouble by threatening to release a list of White Leaguers whom they claimed to know to have some black ancestry. For the last two years of relative quiet, see Fischer, *The Segregation Struggle*, pp. 127-129.

[56] Harlan, "Desegregation in New Orleans Public Schools," 675.

Chapter III

[1] Orleans Parish School Board Meeting Minutes, April 4, 1877. Hereafter cited as OPSB Minutes.

[2] OPSB Minutes, June 22, 1877.

[3] *Ibid.*, July 3, 1877.

[4] For a full review of this debate, see the classic work, August Meier, *Negro Thought in America, 1880-1915: Racial Ideologies in the Age of Booker T. Washington* (Ann Arbor, 1963).

[5] Louisiana Constitution, 1868. See also article 136 which clearly spelled out the duty of the school board in New Orleans: "No municipal corporation shall make any rules or regulations contrary to the spirit and intention of article 135."

[6] *Daily Picayune*, February 20, 1879.

[7] William Preston Vaughn, *Schools for All, The Blacks and Public Education in the South, 1865-1877* (Lexington, Ky., 1874), p. 101.

[8] William O. Rogers to J. T. Leath, July 23, 1877, a copy in the correspondence of the Superintendent found in the rear of the OPSB Minutes, Book 5A.

[9] William O. Rogers to D. B. Hagan, December 26, 1869, *ibid.*

[10] Mary DiMartino, "Education in New Orleans during Reconstruction" (M. A. thesis, Tulane University, 1935), pp. 172-181. For the an account of the dozen or so Lutheran and other German parochial and private schools, see J. Hanno Deiler, "Germany's Contribution to the Present Population of New Orleans, with a Census of the German Schools," *Louisiana Journal of Education* VIII (1886), 89-93.

[11] OPSB Minutes, June 22, 1877.

[12] In response to the recommendation to close the high schools, the board decided to preserve them but to reduce expenses "within reasonable limits." OPSB Minutes, July 3, 1877.

[13] *Louisiana Journal of Education*, I (1879), 15; I (1879), 179; I (1880), 264; V (1882), 189.

[14] *Southwestern Christian Advocate*, February 12, 1880.

[15] Charles Vincent, *A Centennial History of Southern University and A & M College, 1880-1980* (Baton Rouge, 1981), pp. 7-62.

[16] William O. Rogers to Administrators of the John F. Slater Fund, May 31, 1882, a copy in the correspondence of the Superintendent's Office, vol. 13A of the OPSB Minutes. For his 1883 directive, see Circular 89, March 7, 1883, *ibid.*

[17] OPSB Minutes, January 4, 1879, March 3, 1880, May 28, 1880, February 7, 1883.

[18] OPSB Minutes, June 6, 1867, June 3, 1868, June 12, 1878.

[19] William O. Rogers to J. S. M. Curry, October 4, 1883, vol. 13A, OPSB Minutes. See also a similar letter by Rogers on the same date to the Rev. A. G. Haygood, the General Agent of the Slater Fund, in which he beseeched on behalf of black students: "Can you aid them . . .?"

[20] *Report of the Chief Superintendent of the Public Schools of the City of New Orleans, 1884* (New Orleans, 1884), p. 7.

[21] A copy of the printed appeal to the city council, December 27, 1883, can be found in the correspondence of the superintendent, OPSB Minutes, Book 13A. See also *Report of the Chief Superintendent of the Public Schools of New Orleans* (1884), pp. 16, 42-44.

[22] William O. Rogers to Major E. A. Burke, October 31, 1883, in OPSB Minutes, Book 13A.

[23] William O. Rogers to E. A. Burke, March 26, 1884; Rogers to LeRoy D. Brown, August 21, 1884, in OPSB Minutes, Book 13A. *Annual Report of the Louisiana Educational Society* (New Orleans, 1885).

[24] William O. Rogers to Warren Easton, August 21, 1884, in OPSB Minutes, Book 13A.

[25] OPSB Minutes, November 26, 1884.

[26] *Louisiana Journal of Education*, II (1880), 137-38; OPSB Minutes, December 3, 1884.

[27] *Journal of Proceedings and Addresses of the National Education Association* (1885), pp. 532, 541, 544.

[28] *Report of the Chief Superintendent of the Public Schools of New Orleans* (1886), pp. 16, 31-32, 43.

[29] *Report of the Chief Superintendent of the Public Schools of New Orleans* (1888), pp. 6-7.

[30] *Ibid.*, p. 39.

[31] OPSB Minutes, April 13, 1894; see also *Report of the Chief Superintendent* (1879), p. 15.

[32] New Orleans *Daily Picayune*, December 27, 1898.

[33] *Louisiana Journal of Education*, II (1883), 317-18; Esther M. Lacarse, "The Normal School in New Orleans, (M. A. thesis, Tulane University, 1942), pp. 42-48.

[34] Gustave Pierre Devron, "Warren Easton—The Educator," (M. A. thesis, Tulane University, 1937), pp. 49-56.

[35] William Ivy Hair, *Bourbonism and Agrarian Protest, Louisiana Politics 1877-1900* (Baton Rouge, 1969), pp. 170-171.

[36] Henry C. Dethloff and Robert F. Jones, "Race Relations in Louisiana, 1877-98," *Louisiana History*, IX (1968), 315-16.

[37] *Official Journal of the Proceedings of the Constitutional Convention of the State of Louisiana* (New Orleans, 1898), pp. 9-10.

[38] *Proceedings of First and Second Annual Reunions of the Members of the Constitutional Convention of 1898*. (n.p.), p. 24.

[39] OPSB Minutes, February 9, June 8, 1900.

[40] OPSB Minutes, June 29, 1900.

[41] *Southwestern Christian Advocate*, July 5, 26,1900.

[42] *Ibid.*, September 27, 1900.

[43] Booker T. Washington to the Editor of the New Orleans *Times-Democrat*, August 29, 1900, *The Booker T. Washington Papers*, edited by Louis R. Harlan and others, V (Urbana, Ill., 1976), pp. 610-12. New Orleans Daily *Picayune*, September 21, 1890.

[44] William Ivy Hair, *Carnival of Fury* (Baton Rouge, 1976), pp. 177-178.

[45] James D. Anderson, *The Education of Blacks in the South, 1860-1935* (Chapel Hill, N. C., 1988), pp. 188, 192-93.

[46] For the outlook of the Augusta superintendent, see Lawton B. Evans, "The South and Its Problems," *Educational Review*, VIII (1894), 333-42. The quotation can be found on page 339.

[47] OPSB Minutes, July 12, 1901.

Chapter IV

[1] OPSB Minutes, January 10, 1902. Other Southern educators also took part in the N.E.A., but Easton noted that he encountered few Louisiana educators at the N.E.A. meetings until the group met in Atlanta in 1904. See OPSB Minutes, March 11, 1904. On the virtual autonomy of the New Orleans schools in Louisiana, see Minns S. Robertson, *Publication Education in Louisiana After 1898* (Baton Rouge, 1952), pp. 146-148.

[2] *Teachers Outlook*, II (1901), 5.

[3] "Outline of the Organization and Work of the Public School Alliance, 1905-1909," p. 1, a pamphlet which can be found in the Orleans Parish School Board Collection at the University of New Orleans, Box 121. In the earlier Louisiana Educational Society formed by William O. Rogers, women were admitted but not permitted to vote for officers. A pioneer feminist in New Orleans, Caroline E. Merrick, resigned in protest when the group's leaders refused to change the policy. See Carmen Lindig, *The Path from the Parlor, Louisiana Women 1879-1920* (Lafayette, La., 1986), pp. 41, 43.

[4] A record of the meetings of the High School Alumnae can be found in the Special Collections of the library at Tulane University. It demonstrates the group's shift from a social gathering to a reform organization.

[5] For studies of the Behrman machine, see John R. Kemp, ed., *Martin Behrman of New Orleans: Memoirs of a City Boss* (Baton Rouge, 1977), pp. xi-xxv; George M. Reynolds, *Machine Politics in New Orleans, 1897-1926* (New York, 1936).

[6] Edward F. Hass, *Political Leadership in a Southern City: New Orleans in the Progressive Era, 1896-1902* (Ruston, La., 1988).

[7] New Orleans *Daily Picayune*, April 10, 1906; hereafter cited as *Picayune*.

[8] Kemp, *Behrman Memoirs*, pp. 27, 41, 109.

[9] *Annual Report of the Board of Education and of the Superintendent of Schools of the City of New Orleans* (1901-1902), p. 12; (1907-08), p. 16. Hereafter cited as *Annual Report*.

[10] *Annual Report* (1907-08), pp. 18, 22-23, 32.

[11] OPSB Minutes, June 26, December 5, 1908; February 15, April 9, June 11, November 15, 1909; April 8, May 13, November 11, 1910; July 14, 1911. Behrman interjected himself in matters ranging from student and faculty discipline to building and educational programs.

[12] OPSB Minutes, January 9, 1903. See Kemp, *Behrman Memoirs*, p. 168.

[13] Steven J. Ozenovich, "The Development of Public Secondary Education in New Orleans, 1877-1914," (M. A. thesis, Tulane University, 1940).

[14] OPSB Minutes, March 8, 1907.

[15] *Annual Report* (1908-09), pp. 10-11.

[16] *Teachers' Outlook*, II (April 1901), 1; *Picayune*, December 25, 1898; Malcolm Rosenberg, Jr., "The New Orleans Parish Public Schools Under the Superintendency of Nicholas Bauer," (Ph. D. diss., Louisiana State University, 1963), pp. 60-74. Hereafter cited as Rosenberg, "Bauer."

[17] OPSB Minutes, October 26, 1910.

[18] *Picayune*, October 29, 1910.

[19] *Picayune*, October 28, 1910.

[20] *Picayune*, November 8, 1910.

[21] OPSB Minutes, November 11, 1910.

[22] *Picayune*, November 11, 1910. The paper reported: "League leaders think the mayor's school board policy is going to help their cause both in the city and state."

[23] *Picayune*, October 27, 1910.

[24] OPSB Minutes,November 11, 1910; *Picayune*, November 16, 1910.

[25] *Picayune*, November 17, 18, 1910.

[26] *Picayune*, November 24, 1910.

[27] *Picayune*, December 6, 1910.

[28] *Picayune*, December 3, 1910. For the paper's earlier criticism of Behrman's actions, see editorials of October 29 and November 12, 1910. For a lineup of the Civic Parade, see November 27, 1910.

[29] *Picayune*, December 6, 1910, September 2, 1912.

[30] *Picayune*, September 3, October 2, November 5, 1912. Elections were held separately on the school board (September), the commission council (October), and the amendments (November).

[31] *Picayune*, October 15, 1912. Behrman was not always so modest. After he had the city council purchase the former gymnasium and pool of the Southern Athletic Club in the Garden District for the use of the public schools, he did not object to its being named the Behrman Gymnasium. OPSB Minutes, May 13, 1910.

[32] Leonard P. Ayres, *Laggards in Our Schools: A Study of Retardation and Elimination in City School Systems* (New York, 1909), pp. 57, 97, 110, 138, 162, 181.

[33] *Annual Report* (1908-09), pp. 81-82.

[34] Acts of Louisiana, Act 222 (1910). The law provided free text books for anyone forced to attend.

[35] *Picayune*, November 12, 1910. For a similar vow, see also November 16. The mayor delivered and the board complied: see OPSB Minutes, January 13, 1911.

[36] *Annual Report* (1910-11), pp. 24-25.

[37] David Spence Hill, *Vocational Survey for the Issac Delgado Central Trades School*, 2 vols (New Orleans, 1914). A few board members and the superintendent of the Orleans Parish Public Schools sat on the Delgado board, but they refused to divert any of their funds to Delgado. See OPSB Minutes of the Committee of the Whole, August 5, 1924. For a brief history of the slow growth of Delgado, see The Issac Delgado Central Trades School, "Annual Report of Activities," [typescript] (1946), 1-12, a copy may be found in the Louisiana Collection at Tulane University.

[38] Acts of Louisiana, Act 231 (1912). The act extended enforcement from the ages of fourteen to sixteen if the child was not employed.

[39] OPSB Minutes, September 8, 1911.

[40] OPSB Minutes, March 14, 1913.

[41] OPSB Minutes, August 24, 1916.

[42] OPSB Minutes, July 9, 1914.

[43] *The Teachers Forum*, I (February 1914), 39-31.

[44] OPSB Minutes, December 11, 1913; April 1, 6, 1914. *The Teachers Forum*, I (April 1914), 44. The New Orleans *Times-Democrat*, on October 15, 1913, gave a vivid depiction of the teachers' reaction to the pay cut. "It was like a subdued and feminized edition of a mob's roar in revolution a la Carlyle . . . time after time the room resounded with stamping of feet, clapping of hands and cries at some particularly daring and plain spoken words, voiced by an indignant teacher."

[45] *The Teachers Forum*, I (April 1914), 44; I (December 1914), 5.

[46] *The Teachers' Forum*, I (April 1914), 44.

[47] *Ibid.*, II (November 1915), 37.

[48] For evidence of Gwinn's success, see OPSB Minutes, January 14, 1912; *Annual Report* (1913-14), p. 64. An outside report by the Russel Sage Foundation confirmed these results, see *Annual Report* (1919-20), pp. 10-11.

[49] OPSB Minutes, October 15, 1913.

[50] OPSB Minutes, October 4, 9, 14, 22, November 11, 1915; May 24, June 1, 1916.

[51] OPSB Minutes, May 3, 12, 25, June 9, 1916. These records show that the mayor and powerful financiers who sat on the self-perpetuating Board of Liquidation drew up the new arrangement without consulting the school board. See also New Orleans *Times-Picayune*, October 22, 23, 24, November 1, 8, 9, 1916. Acts of Louisiana, Act 120 (1916). Hereafter cited as *Times-Picayune*.

[52] *Annual Report* (1915-16), Park I, 21; for the last of the extensive studies by the Division of Educational Research, see Parts II and III.

[53] *Times-Picayune*, December 5, 1918. Gwinn claimed almost a hundred departures from the regular staff aand a much larger number from the former eligibility list, OPSB Minutes, September 26, 1919.

[54] OPSB Minutes, June 27, September 26, 1919.

[55] OPSB Minutes, June 27, 1919.

[56] *Times-Picayune*, January 22, 1920.

[57] *Times-Picayune*, June 25, 26, 28, 1919.

[58] OPSB Minutes, January 27, 1920; *Times-Picayune*, January 22, 23, 28 1920; *Annual Report* (1919-20), pp. 7-9.

[59] OPSB Minutes, March 12, April 13, 1917; February 22, April 8, 9, 26, June 14, September 27, 1918; February 21, 1919. See also *Times-Picayune*, March 10, 11, 13, 14, 15, 16, 1917. As a result of these bans, German was not reintroduced to the high schools until 1926.

[60] Matthew J. Schott, "John M. Parker of Louisiana and the Varieties of American Progressivism," (Ph.D. diss., Vanderbilt University, 1969), pp. 337-349.

[61] OPSB Minutes, May 8, 1923.

[62] All three of the reform candidates elected in 1920 and 1922 left the board in 1926. Baumgartner and Percy Moise lost their reelection bids to Old Regular candidates, and just a few months earlier, James Fortier resigned to take an appointment on a newly created state insurance commission. *Times-Picayune*, October 28, November 3, 1926. For Fortier's resignation, see OPSB Minutes, September 10, 1926.

[63] OPSB Minutes, May 8, 1923.

[64] *Times-Picayune*, May 10, 1923.

[65] Rosenberg, "Nicholas Bauer," pp. 108, 112, 247, 250.

[66] See the General File of the Orleans Parish School board for the folder entitled, "New Orleans Clearing House," which contains the correspondence between the local banks and the school board. The transcription of a long conference between several board members and officers of the banks on March 16, 1932, reveals the decisions that forced the salary cuts.

[67] Rosenberg, "Bauer," pp. 160-165, 173-179. For the schedule of cuts, see OPSB Minutes, August 12, 1932. For the outlook of teachers, see a teachers' journal that came into existence n the early states of the depression, *Quartee*, I (October 1931), 11, 26, 43; II (March 1932), 41-43.

[68] See the untitled history of the League of Women Voters, particularly the 1974 letter of reminiscences in its introduction by Emily Blanchard. Mrs. Blanchard was a remarkable radical who joined the Southern Conference for Human Welfare in 1938 and championed integration and the rights of blacks. When the League of Women Voters reorganized in New Orleans with her help in 1942, they shortly afterwards asked her to resign because of her demands for integration of the League. The New Orleans chapter did not open its doors to black women until the late 1950s. See League of Women Voters Collection, Tulane University, Box 1, Folder 2.

[69] Louisiana State Department of Education, "Report of the State Equalization Committee to Superintendent John E. Coxe," [typescript] (Baton Rouge, 1946), pp. 1-2.

[70] Acts of Louisiana, Act 79 (1936); OPSB Minutes, September 12, 1936; Rosenberg, "Bauer," pp. 302-4; Citizens Planning Committee for Public Education in New Orleans, *Financial Background of the Schools*, Monograph VI of *Tomorrow's Citizens* (New Orleans, 1939), pp. 448, 451. As a proportion of the total budget of the New Orleans public schools, state funding rose from 15 percent in 1932 to 33.7 percent in 1938. By 1946, the percentage had grown to 47 percent. See Louisiana Committee on Educational Survey, *Education in Louisiana, A Study and Recommendations for Improvement* (Baton Rouge, 1948), pp. 54-55.

[71] *Quartee* IV (November 1933), 13, 15. Orleans Parish School Board, Office of the Superintendent, "Proposed Program for the Improvement of the Public Schools of New Orleans," [typescript] (1948), pp. 35-36. A copy of this report can be found in the Louisiana Collection of the Tulane University library. Hereafter cited as OPSB, "Program for Improvement," (1948).

[72] The Grace report came in two forms. The initial publication in 1939 contained seven different monographs, under the title: Citizens' Planning Committee for Public Education in New Orleans, *Tomorrow's Citizens, A Study and Program for the Improvement of the New Orleans Public Schools*. A synopsis of the larger work, *Summary Report on the New Orleans Study and Program of Public Education*, appeared several months later in 1940. Hereafter cited as *Tomorrow's Citizens*, along with the monograph title and date of publication. The citation came from the *Summary Report* (1940), pp. 74-77.

[73] *Tomorrow's Citizens, Summary Report* (1940), p. 94.

[74] *Ibid.*

[75] In 1921, the school board turned down a citizen's call for coeducation of the high schools as "impracticable." Earlier, teachers criticized the practice in the grammar schools, but they too thought that "convenience and expediency . . . may make it necessary to segregate boys and girls during the latter part of their school work." See OPSB Minutes, January 14, 1921; *The Teachers' Forum*, I (May 1914), 23. During the 1930s, some teachers began to criticize the practice. And editorial in the *Quartee* noted that "tradition and private school practice in this city are strong influences for segregation. The mid-Victorian 'womanly woman' and 'manly man' are still phases that pass current in New Orleans, though the conditions that called forth such banalities have as completely passed in New Orleans as everywhere else." *Quartee*, IV (January 1934), 18.

[76] *Tomorrow's Citizens, Summary Report* (1940), p. 94.

[77] *Ibid.*, pp. 87, 95.

[78] *Ibid.*, p. 113.

[79] In 1948, a new superintendent, Lionel Bourgeois, said of the Grace survey: "It cannot be said that any realistic attempt has been made to give effect to the recommendations contained in the report." OPSB, "Program for Improvement," (1948), p. 2.

[80] New Orleans *Item*, January 8, 9, 10, 30, 1942; New Orleans *States*, January 9, 1942.

Chapter V

[1] Annual Report of the Superintendent of the Public Schools of the Parish of Orleans, 1915-1916. Orleans Parish School Board Collection, Archives and Manuscripts/Special Collection Department, University of New Orleans, hereinafter cited as N. O. Annual Report.

[2] N. O. Annual Report, 1910-1911 and 1920-1921; *Louisiana Weekly*, October 3,1925.

[3] *Louisiana Weekly*, October 3, 1925, May 8, 1926.

[4] OPSB Minutes, January 13, 1928.

[5] *Louisiana Weekly*, November 2, 1929; OPSB Minutes, August 7, 1928.

[6] N. O. Annual Report, 1912-1913.

[7] N. O. Annual Report(s), 1900-1920 - Statistical Report of the New Orleans Public Schools of the Parish of Orleans, 1924-1940. Orleans Parish School Board Collection, Archives and Manuscripts/Special Collections Department, University of New Orleans, hereinafter cited as N. O. Statistical Report.

[8] OPSB Minutes, April 19, 1907, November 11, 1910, November 14, 1913, September 20, 1923, October 9, 1931, October 14, 1938; *Louisiana Weekly*, October 20, 1933.

[9] OPSB Minutes, March 11, 1915, October 27, 1922, January 13, 1928, October 9, 1931.

[10] *Ibid.*, October 9, 1936, September 15, 1940.

[11] Vincent, *A Centennial History of Southern University*, pp. 63-72.

[12] OPSB Minutes, July 2, 1913, August 8, 1913, January 26, 1915.

[13] Thomas Sowell, *Education: Assumption Versus History* (Stanford, California, 1986), pp. 9, 18-21; OPSB Minutes, August 13, 1914, August 24, 1917, September 14, 1917.

[14] OPSB Minutes, September 28, 1917.

[15] N. O. Annual Report, 1917-1918.

[16] N. O. Annual Report, 1920-1921; Louisiana *Weekly*, March 19, 1927.

[17] N. O. Annual Report, 1917-1918.

[18] N. O. Annual Report, 1920-1921; N. O. Statistical Report(s), 1924-1940.

[19] U. S. Department of Commerce, Bureau of the Census, *Abstract of the Fourteenth Census of the United States, 1920* (Washington, 1923); OPSB Minutes, July 10, 1903, November 3, 1903, May 13, 1904, November 10, 1905, August 14, 1908, October 13, 1911; N. O. Annual Report, 1903-1904, 1905-1906, 1911-1912.

[20] *Southwestern Christian Advocate*, November 9, 1911.

[21] Lawrence A. Cremin, *American Education: The Metropolitan Experience, 1876-1980* (New York, 1988), p. 231.

[22] N. O. Annual Report(s), 1918-1919, 1920-1921; N. O. Statistical Report(s), 1924-1940.

[23] *Louisiana Weekly*, March 19, 1927, April 16, 1927; OPSB Minutes, January 12, 1900, April 13, 1916, June 19, 1916, November 1, 1918, December 27, 1918.

[24] OPSB Minutes, January 26, 1923, February 12, 1930; *Louisiana Weekly*, February 22, 1930.

[25] *Louisiana Weekly*, February 22, 1931.

[26] *Times-Picayune*, February 1, 1931.

[27] *Louisiana Weekly*, September 26, 1931.

[28] *Ibid.*, September 26, 1931, November 3, 1934, December 15, 22, 1934.

[29] OPSB Minutes, November 16, 1934, March 12, 1937, May 12, 1939, September 13, 1940; Louisiana *Weekly*, August 13, 1938.

[30] OPSB Minutes, July 22, 1922.

[31] *Ibid.*, January 12, 1923.

[32] *Ibid.*

[33] *Ibid.*

[34] OPSB Minutes, January 18, 1923.

[35] *Times-Picayune*, January 9, 1923.

[36] *Ibid.*, January 27, 1923, February 9, 1923.

[37] OPSB Minutes, February 9, 1923.

[38] *Ibid.*

[39] *Times-Picayune*, February 10, 1923; OPSB Minutes, February 9, 1923.

[40] OPSB Minutes, February 9, 1923.

[41] *Times-Picayune*, February 10, 1923; OPSB Minutes, February 9, 1923; *Louisiana Weekly*, January 1, 1927.

[42] Anderson, *Education of Blacks in the South*, pp. 110-114; Horace M. Bond, *The Education of the Negro in the American Social Order* (New York, 1934), pp. 264-268; Henry A. Bullock, *A History of Negro Education in the South, From 1619 to the Present* (Cambridge, 1967), pp. 183-184.

[43] Southwest Christian *Advocate*, February 9, 1911; N. O. Annual Report, 1903-1904; OPSB Minutes, December 14, 1900, March 11, 1904, August 12, 1904, June 29, 1906, August 9, 1907, October 11, 1907, July 8, 1910, September 19, 1910.

[44] OPSB Minutes, January 11, 1907, August 8, 1913, August 2, 1915, September 14, 1916.

[45] *Ibid.*, April 8, 1915, May 13, 1915, January 13, 1916, June 25, 1919.

[46] *The Voice* (A newsletter published by New Orleans League of Classroom Teachers), November, 1938, Alexander P. Tureaud Collection, Amistad Research Center, New Orleans, Louisiana, hereinafter cited as Tureaud Collection.

[47] Raphael Cassimere, Jr., "Equalizing Teachers' Pay in Louisiana," *Integrateducation* (1977), 5.

[48] OPSB Minutes, May 31, 1923.

[49] *Louisiana Weekly*, August 28, 1937; OPSB Minutes, May 9, 1941.

[50] Tureaud to Henry Schaumburg, May 22, 1941; August Tete to Tureaud, May 23, 1941, Tureaud Collection.

[51] Tureaud to Thurgood Marshall, September 4, 1941; Marshall to Tureaud, 8eptember 8, 1941, Tureaud Collection.

[52] Marshall to Tureaud, January 12, 1942; Tureaud to Marshall, February 3, 1942, Tureaud Collection.

[53] Tureaud to Marshall, June 14, 1942; Marshall to Tureaud, June 19, 1942, Tureaud Collection.

[54] Tureaud to Marshall, July 22, 1942; Marshall to Tureaud, July 27, 1942, Tureaud Collection.

[55] Cassimere, "Equalizing Teachers' Pay," 6; *Times-Picayune*, September 3, 1942; *Louisiana Weekly*, September 5, 1942.

[56] Alonzo G. Grace, *Tomorrow's Citizens: A Study and Program for the Improvement of the New Orleans Public Schools (New Orleans, 1939)*, pp. 28, 32.

[57] *Tomorrow's Citizens*, pp. 30-31.

[58] *Ibid.*, pp. 337-341.

[59] *Ibid.*, pp. 253, 348-349.

[60] *Ibid.*, p. 138.

[61] *Ibid.*, pp. 132-136.

Chapter VI

[1] Samson P. Bordelon, "The New Orleans Public Schools Under the Superintendency of Lionel John Bourgeois," (Ph. D. dissertation, University of Southern Mississippi, 1965), p. 7; OPSB Minutes, July 29, 1946.

[2] Bordelon, "Superintendency of Lionel John Bourgeois," pp. 51-54.

[3] *Ibid.*, pp. 7-13.

[4] *Times-Picayune*, November 2, 3, 1948.

[5] *Times-Picayune*, November 5, 1948.

[6] OPSB Minutes, October 17, 1949.

[7] OPSB Minutes, March 12, 1948.

[8] Bordelon, "Superintendency of Lionel John Bourgeois," pp. 94-95, 156-157; OPSB Minutes, March 12, 1948, March 18, 1948.

[9] Mary Lee Muller, "The Orleans Parish School Board and Negro Education, 1940-1960," (M. A. thesis, University of New Orleans, 1975), p. 20.

[10] Muller, "OPSB and Negro Education," pp. 21-22; OPSB Minutes, November 30, 1948.

[11] OPSB Minutes, May 21, 1948, August 12, 1949.

[12] Lionel J. Bourgeois to Alexander P. Tureaud, September 30, 1947, Tureaud Collection.

[13] OPSB Minutes, June 11, 1948.

[14] OPSB Minutes, August 12, 1949.

[15] OPSB Minutes, July 6, 1948.

[16] Bordelon, "Superintendency of Lionel J. Bourgeois," p. 61.

[17] *Ibid.*, p. 208.

[18] *Ibid.*, p. 211.

[19] *New Orleans Item*, April 26, 1950, April 28, 1950.

[20] OPSB Minutes, April 28, 1950.

[21] Bordelon, "Superintendency of Lionel J. Bourgeois," pp. 217-219.

[22] The Independent Women's Organization, one of the leading groups in the city advocating school reform, supported Scheps and Besse in the 1950 election. See, Edward F. Haas, *DeLesseps S. Morrison and the Image of Reform: New Orleans Politics, 1946-1961* (Baton Rouge, 1974), p. 170.

[23] Robert Haas case the lone dissenting vote, OPSB Minutes, December 21, 1950.

[24] OPSB Minutes, December 21, 1950.

[25] *Ibid.*

[26] OPSB Minutes, January 9, 1951.

[27] OPSB Minutes, January 10, 1951.

[28] Bordelon, "Superintendency of Lionel J. Bourgeois," pp. 229-236; *Times Picayune*, May 31, 1951.

[29] OPSB Minutes, November 12, 1951.

[30] Board resolution, dated November 26, 1951 in Box 43, Tureaud Collection.

[31] OPSB Minutes, September 12, 1952.

[32] Mark V. Tushnet, *The NAACP's Legal Strategy Against Segregated Education, 1925-1950* (Chapel Hill, 1987), pp. 138-143.

[33] Black enrollment during the 1952-1953 school year was 31,031 compared to 34,760 for whites. New Orleans Public School Facts and Figures, Orleans Parish School Board Collection, University of New Orleans, Archives and Manuscripts/Special Collection Department.

[34] Daniel E. Byrd to Robert Richmond, December 16, 1953, Daniel E. Byrd Collection, Amistad Research Center, New Orleans, Louisiana.

[35] Richard Kluger, *Simple Justice: The History of Brown v. Board of Education and Black America's Struggle for Equality* (New York, 1975), p. 782; Louisiana *Weekly*, May 22, 1954.

[36] Numan V. Bartley, *The Rise of Massive Resistance: Race and Politics in the South During the 1950s* (Baton Rouge, 1969), pp. 97-103; Earleen Mary McCarrick, "Louisiana's Official Resistance To Desegregation" (Ph. D. dissertation, Vanderbilt University, 1964), pp. 26-44, 105-131; *Times Picayune*, May 20, 25, 1954.

[37] Louisiana, Acts of the State Legislature, Regular Session, 1954, Acts 555, 556.

[38] Nashville, *Southern School News*, December 1954; OPSB Minutes, May 31, 1954.,

[39] *Southern School News*, June 1955.

[40] *Ibid.*, November 1954.

[41] *Ibid.*, July 1955.

[42] *Ibid.*, July, August, September 1955.

[43] *Ibid.*, January 1956.

[44] *Earl Benjamin Bush et. al.* v. *Orleans Parish School Board et. al.*, 138 Federal Supplement, pp. 336, 341-342.

[45] *Southern School News*, March, June 1956.

[46] *Ibid.*

[47] Neil McMillen, *The Citizens' Council: Organized Resistance to the Second Reconstruction, 1954-1964* (Urbana, 1971), pp. 59-67.

[48] *Southern School News*, April, June 1956; McMillen, *Citizens' Council*, p. 66.

[49] *Southern School News*, November 1954, May, June, December 1956; Roy Wilkens to Doretha A. Combre, February 15, 1960, NAACP, New Orleans Branch Collection, Archives and Manuscripts/Special Collections Department, University of New Orleans.

[50] *Southern School News*, April 1956; OPSB Minutes, September 12, 26, 1955.

[51] *Southern School News*, July 1959.

[52] *Ibid.*, September 1959.

[53] *Louisiana Weekly*, May 7, 14, 1960; *Southern School News*, May 1960.

[54] OPSB Minutes, May 24, 1960.

[55] *Ibid.*, June 20, 1960.

[56] NAACP Papers, Box 70.

[57] Morton Inger, *Politics and Reality in an American City: The New Orleans School Crisis of 1960* (New York, 1969), pp. 22-30; McCarrick, "Official Resistance To Desegregation," pp. 125-126.

[58] *The New Orleans School Crisis*, Report of the Louisiana State Advisory Committee to the United States Commission on Civil Rights (Washington, D.C., 1961), p. 6; Inger, *Politics and Reality*, pp. 29-30; *Times-Picayune*, August 5, 1960.

[59] *Times-Picayune*, August 18, 21, 26, 1960.

[60] *Ibid.*, August 29, 1960.

[61] OPSB Minutes, August 29, 1960; *Times-Picayune*, August 29, 1960.

[62] *Times-Picayune*, August 29, 1960.

[63] OPSB Minutes, October 24, November 10, 1960; *Southern School News*, August 1960.

[64] Alan Wieder, "The New Orleans School Crisis of 1960: Causes and Consequences," *Phylon* 48 (1987): 129; Louisiana *Weekly*, November 5, 10, 1960; OPSB Minutes, November 10, 1960.

[65] *Times Picayune*, November 15, 1960; Louisiana *Weekly*, November 19, 1960.

[66] Louisiana *Weekly*, November 19, 26; *Times-Picayune*, November 16, 18, 19, 1960.

[67] Responses are filed in Box 71, NAACP Papers.

Chapter VII

[1] Byrd to Erma Landix, March 5, 1953, Byrd Collection.

[2] New Orleans Public Schools, Facts and Finances, 1961-1962, OPSB Collection; *Times-Picayune*, September 7, 1961.

[3] *Times-Picayune*, April 4, 1962.

[4] *Ibid.*

[5] OPSB Minutes, April 9, 1962; *Times-Picayune*, April 4, 1962.

[6] *Times-Picayune*, April 4, 1962.

[7] *Times-Picayune*, May 4, 1962.

[8] *New Orleans States-Item*, May 9, 1962.

[9] *Times-Picayune*, May 9, 1962.

[10] OPSB Minutes, May 14, 1962.

[11] *Times-Picayune*, May 24, 1962.

[12] Facts and Finances, 1962-1963, 1963-1964, 1964-1965.

[13] See, transcript of trial proceedings of April 22 and 23, 1965, in box 46, OPSB Collection.

[14] *Ibid.*

[15] *Ibid.*

[16] *Ibid.*

[17] *Ibid.*

[18] By January 1962 only twenty students attended McDonogh 19, and the board voted on January 8 to convert the school to black use. That decision, if implemented, would have caused the transfer of the remaining fifteen white students in attendance but would have also relieved overcrowding at several neighboring black schools. Nonetheless, Tureaud, unwilling to concede at such an early date to resegregation, requested and received a restraining order preventing the board from making the change.

[19] Transcript of trial of April 22 and 23, 1965.

[20] *Ibid.*

[21] *Ibid.*

[22] *Times-Picayune*, April 24, 1965.

[23] Facts and Finances, 1961-1962, 1964-1965.

[24] Facts and Finances, 1966-1967.

[26] Facts and Finances, 1960-1961 to 1980-1981.

[25] Facts and Finances, 1969-1970 to 1979-1980.

[27] Samuel Scarnato files, box 16, OPSB Collection.

[28] *Ibid.*

[29] "Informational Report on Staff Desegregation in the School," Scarnato files, box, 16, OPSB Collection.

[30] *Ibid.*

[31] OPSB Minutes, July 10, 1972.

[32] *Times-Picayune*, August 18, 1972.

[33] *Harry G. Caire v. OPSB*, copy of trial transcript in OPSB Collection.

[34] *Ibid.*

[35] William W. Orr to Samuel Rosenberg, November 15, 1972 and December 5, 1972, Alfred Hebeisen to Rosenberg, December 11, 1972, Rosenberg to Lawrence Smith, November 20, 1972, Scarnato files, box 108.

[36] Scarnato files, box 16.

[37] Williams to school principals, January 25, 1973, Scarnato files, box 16.

[38] OPSB Minutes, 20 August 1962, January 14, 1963; Facts and Finances, 1962-1963 to 1968-1969.

[39] Alonzo Hamby, *Liberalism and Its Challengers: FDR to Reagan* (New York, 1985), p. 259; Allen J. Matusow, *The Unraveling of America: A History of Liberalism in the 1960s* (New York, 1984), pp. 221-226; Facts and Finances, 1964-1965 to 1974-1975.

[40] N. O. Annual Report, 1963-1964.

[41] *Ibid.*

[42] Scarnato files, box 53.

[43] New Orleans *Figaro*, September 6, 1978.

[44] *States-Item*, September 15, 1978.

[45] *Ibid.*

[46] Mack Spears to school board employees, August 28, 1978, Scarnato files, box 53.

[47] *Times-Picayune*, September 7, 1978.

[48] *Ibid.*, September 2, 1978.

[49] *States-Item*, September 15, 1978.

[50] Superintendent's announcement to teachers, September 5, 1978, Scarnato files, box 53; *States-Item*, September 5, 1978; *Times Picayune*, September 6, 7, 1978.

[51] *Times-Picayune*, September 6, 7, 1978.

[52] *Ibid.*, September 12, 13, 1978.

[53] *Ibid.*, September 13, 21, 1978.

[54] *Figaro*, September 20, 1978.

[55] *States-Item*, September 12, 1978.

Illustration Attributions

Chapter I

1. From an engraving in University of Alabama Library copy of Henry Barnard, *American Educational Biography* . . . (Syracuse, N.Y., c. 1874).

2. Courtesy The Historic New Orleans Collection, Museum/Research Center (hereafter HNOC), Acc. No. 1946.2 (detail).

3. Courtesy HNOC, Acc. No. 1974.25.27.72.

4. Courtesy HNOC, Acc. No. 1949.7.

5. Orleans Parish School Board Collection at the University of New Orleans (hereafter OPSB Coll.).

6. Reproduced from original photographic print in Library of Congress copy of *A Memorial Address Read at the Funeral of John Angier Shaw . . . October 8, 1873*, edited by Richard M. Hodges (Cambridge, Mass., 1874).

7. OPSB Coll.

8. From an engraving in University of Alabama Library copy of Henry Barnard, *American Educational Biography* . . . (Syracuse, N.Y., c. 1874).

9. OPSB Coll.

10. Courtesy HNOC, Acc. No. 1982.167.7.

11. Louisiana Collection, Tulane University.

12. Courtesy HNOC, Acc. No. 57-38-L.

13. Courtesy HNOC, Acc. No. 1970.11.119.

14. (Left) courtesy of McDonogh School, McDonogh Maryland; (Right) courtesy of the University of New Orleans.

15. Courtesy HNOC, Acc. No. 1974.25.3.383.

Chapter II

16. Courtesy The Historic New Orleans Collection, Museum/Research Center (hereafter HNOC), Acc. No. 87-632-RL.

17. Amistad Research Center, Tulane University.

18. Courtesy HNOC, Acc. No. 1974.25.13.198. The original plaque remains at the Louisiana Museum.

19. University of New Orleans.

20. From the library files of the New Orleans *Times-Picayune*, copyright, The Times-Picayune Publishing Corp. (hereafter New Orleans *Times-Picayune*).

21. Courtesy HNOC, Acc. No. 1974.25.27.18.

22. Courtesy HNOC, Acc. No. 1953.82.

23. New Orleans *Times-Picayune*.

24. Courtesy HNOC, Acc. No. 1979.183i-xxx.

25. Courtesy HNOC, Acc. No. 1974.25.27.451.

26. University of New Orleans.

27. Courtesy HNOC, Acc. No. 1979.302v.

28. Courtesy HNOC, Acc. No. 1974.25.27.56.

29. Photographs of the first six McDonogh Schools are from the OPSB Coll.

30. From the Marcus B. Christian Collection at the University of New Orleans.

Chapter III

31. Courtesy The Historic New Orleans Collection, Museum/Research Center (hereafter HNOC), Acc. No. 1974.25.27.353.

32. Coutesy HNOC, Acc. No. 1974.25.27.8.

33. Courtesy HNOC, Acc. No. 1959.34.

34. Louisiana Collection, Tulane University.

35. Louisiana Collection, Tulane University.

36. University Archives, Tulane University.

37. Courtesy HNOC, Acc. No. 1979.325.1950.

38. Courtesy HNOC, Acc. No. 1974.25.2.91i.

39. University Archives, Tulane University.

40. University of New Orleans.

41. Orleans Parish School Board Collection at the University of New Orleans (OPSB Coll.).

42. University of New Orleans. From the New Orleans *Daily Picayune*, December 27, 1898, p. 10.

43. Louisiana State Museum.

44. OPSB Coll.

45. Louisiana State Museum.

46. Louisiana State Museum.

47. OPSB Coll..

48. Louisiana State Museum.

49. William O. Rogers Collection, Tulane University.

50. Louisiana State Museum.

51. Courtesy HNOC, Acc. No. 81-1082-RL.

Chapter IV

52. Frank B. Moore Collection, University of New Orleans.

53. Portrait in Board Room at Dillard University, painted by Sidney E. Dickinson, 1933. Courtesy Dillard University.

54. Louisiana Collection, Tulane University.

55. Orleans Parish School Board Collection (OPSB Coll.) at the University of New Orleans.

56. Courtesy The Historic New Orleans Collection, Museum/Research Center (hereafter HNOC), Acc. No. 1979.325.1823.

57. Courtesy HNOC, Acc. No. 1979.325.1920.

58. OPSB Coll.

59. OPSB Coll. (Upper and Lower photos)

60. John R. Conniff Papers, Tulane University.

61. Courtesy HNOC, Acc. No. 77-868-RL.

62. Courtesy HNOC, Acc. No. 77-868-RL.

63. University Archives, Tulane University.

64. OPSB Coll.

65. OPSB Coll.

66. Courtesy HNOC, Acc. No. 1980.145.53.

67. Courtesy HNOC, Acc. No. 69-203-LP.

68. Courtesy HNOC, Acc. No. 1974.25.25.159.

69. OPSB Coll. (Upper and Lower Photos).

70. OPSB Coll.

71. OPSB Coll.

72. OPSB Coll.

73. OPSB Coll.

74. OPSB Coll.

75. OPSB Coll.

76. OPSB Coll.

77. Upper, Louisiana Collection, Tulane University; lower, OPSB Coll.

78. OPSB Coll.

79. OPSB Coll.

80. OPSB Coll.

81. OPSB Coll.

82. Courtesy HNOC, Acc. No. 1979.325.4244.

83. OPSB Coll.

84. Sarah Towles Reed Collection, University of New Orleans.

85. Courtesy HNOC, Acc. No. 1979.325.1872.

86. Courtesy HNOC, Acc. No. 1979.325.1875.

87. Courtesy HNOC, Acc. No. 1979.325.1876.

88. Courtesy HNOC, Acc. No. 1979.325.1824.

89. Courtesy HNOC, Acc. No. 1979.325.4184.

90. Courtesy HNOC, Acc. No. 1979.325.1848.

91. University of New Orleans.

Chapter V

92. Xavier University Archives and Special Collections.

93. Courtesy The Historic New Orleans Collection, Museum/Research Center (hereafter HNOC), Acc. No. 1974.25.23.112.

94. Courtesy HNOC, Acc. No. 1979/325.1846.

95. Louisiana State Museum.

96. Courtesy HNOC, Acc. No. 1979.325.1852.

97. Louisiana State Museum.

98. HNOC

99. HNOC

100. Louisiana State Museum.

101. Louisiana State Museum.

102. Louisian State Museum.

103. Courtesy HNOC, Acc. No. 1979.325.1870

104. Xavier University Archives and Special Collections.

105. Courtesy HNOC, Acc. No. 1979.325.1915.

106. Courtesy HNOC, Acc. No. 1979.325.1813.

107. Xavier University Archives and Special Collections.

108. Xavier University Archives and Special Collections.

109. Xavier University Archives and Special Collections.

110. OPSB Coll.

111. George Longe Collection, Amistad Research Center.

Chapter VI

112. OPSB Coll.

113. OPSB Coll.

114. *Times-Picayune*, copyright, The Times-Picayune Publishing Corp.

115. *Times-Picayune*, copyright, The Times-Picayune Publishing Corp.

116. OPSB Coll.

117. OPSB Coll.

118. OPSB Coll.

119. OPSB Coll.

120. OPSB Coll.

121. OPSB Coll.

122. OPSB Coll.

123. United Press International (hereafter UPI).

124. UPI

125. UPI

126. UPI

127. UPI

128. UPI

Chapter VII

Appendix I

Plate 2. City Archives Collection, Louisiana Division, New Orleans Public Library. New Orleans, LA, Commissioners of the McDonogh School Fund, McDonogh School Plans. (Hereafter, City Archives Collection).

Plate 3. City Archives Collection.

Plate 4. City Archives Collection.

Plate 5. City Archives Collection.

Plate 6. City Archives Collection.

Plate 7. City Archives Collection.

Plate 8. City Archives Collection.

Plate 9. OPSB Coll.

Plate 10. Facility Planning Department, Orleans Parish School Board (Hereafter, Facility Planning Department).

Plate 11. Facility Planning Department.

Plate 12. Facility Planning Department.

Plate 13. Facility Planning Department.

Plate 14. Facility Planning Department.

Plate 15. Robert Brantley Photography, Copyright 1990.

Plate 16. Facility Planning Department.

Plate 17. OPSB Coll.

Plate 18. Robert Brantley Photography, Copyright 1990.

Plate 19. Facility Planning Department.

Plate 20. Facility Planning Department.

Plate 21. Facility Planning Department.

Plate 22. Facility Planning Department.

Plate 23. Facility Planning Department.

Plate 24. OPSB Coll.

Plate 25. Frank Lotz Miller, Photographer, Courtesy Nathaniel Curtis, F.A.I.A., Architect.

Plate 26. Frank Lotz Miller, Photographer, Courtesy Nathaniel Curtis, F.A.I.A., Architect.

Plate 27. Frank Lotz Miller, Photographer, Courtesy Nathaniel Courtis, F.A.I.A., Architect.

Plate 28. Frank Lotz Miller, Photographer. Courtesy , Frank Lotz Miller.

Plate 29. OPSB Coll.

Plate 30. Frank Lotz Miller, Photographer, Courtesy Nanthaniel Curtis, F.A.I.A., Architect.

Plate 31. Frank Lotz Miller, Photographer, Courtesy Nathaniel Curtis, F.A.I.A., Architect.

Index